# marxism

## *1844-1990*

*origins,*

*betrayal,*

*rebirth*

*roger*

*s. gottlieb*

*routledge*

*new york • london*

First published in 1992 by

Routledge
an imprint of
Routledge, Chapman & Hall, Inc.
29 West 35 Street
New York, NY 10001

Published in Great Britain by

Routledge
11 New Fetter Lane
London EC4P 4EE

**Library of Congress Cataloging in Publication Data**

Gottlieb, Roger S.
    Marxism 1844–1990 : origins, betrayal, rebirth / Roger S. Gottlieb.
        p.   cm. — (Revolutionary thought/radical movements)
    Includes bibliographical references and index.
    ISBN 0-415-90653-9 (HB). — ISBN 0-415-90654-7 (PB)
    1. Marx, Karl, 1816–1883—Influence. 2. Communism—History.
    3. Socialism—History. I. Title. II. Series.
HX39.5.G675   1992
335.4—dc20
                                                        92-18624
                                                              CIP

**British Library Cataloguing in Publication Data also available.**

# marxism

## *1844-1990*

# Revolutionary Thought/
# Radical Movements

A book series edited by Roger S. Gottlieb

## Other books in the series:

The Gay and Lesbian Liberation Movement
*Margaret Cruikshank*

Radical Ecology: The Search for a Livable World
*Carolyn Merchant*

Women in Movement: Feminism and Social Action
*Sheila Rowbotham*

*For all those*
*who continue to struggle for justice*
*in dark times*

# CONTENTS

SERIES EDITOR'S PREFACE                                    ix

PREFACE                                                   xv

ACKNOWLEDGMENTS                                          xvii

### I  ORIGINS

1  MARXISM: THE ORIGINAL THEORY                            3

2  MARXISM: BASIC FLAWS                                   39

### II  BETRAYAL

3  SOCIAL-DEMOCRACY: THE PLAGUE                           59
   OF POSITIVISM

4  SOVIET COMMUNISM: THE DEATH OF                         77
   MARXISM

### III  REBIRTH

5  WESTERN MARXISM: THE ROLE OF                          109
   CONSCIOUSNESS

CONTENTS

6  SOCIALIST-FEMINISM AND THE          130
   POLITICS OF DIFFERENCE

           *IV  PRESENT AND FUTURE*

7  MARXISM AND CONTEMPORARY            149
   CAPITALISM

8  MARXISM AND SOME RADICAL            170
   CRITICS

9  MARXISM AND SPIRITUALITY            197


   NOTES                                223
   BIBLIOGRAPHY                         235
   INDEX                                245

# SERIES EDITOR'S PREFACE

This book, like its companions in the *Revolutionary Thought/Radical Movements* series, challenges contemporary society and civilization.

Perhaps the heart of this challenge is a deeply felt anguish and outrage over the sheer magnitude of human suffering—along with the terrible frustration of knowing that much of this suffering could be avoided. Radicals refuse to blame homelessness and starvation, the rape of women and abuse of children, the theft of labor and land, hope and self-respect on divine Providence or unchangeable human nature. Rather, they believe that much of it comes from injustice, exploitation, violence, and organized cruelty that can be eradicated. If we drastically alter our social arrangements in the direction of equality, justice, and human fulfillment, the brutal realities of the present can give way to vastly increased material security, social harmony, and self-realization.

Philanthropists and political reformers share radicals' concern for human suffering. But unlike reformers and philanthropists, radicals and revolutionaries address whole *systems* of injustice. In these systems, particular groups are humiliated, denied rights, subject to unjust control. The few become rich while the many suffer from poverty or economic insecurity. The select get privileges while millions learn submission or humiliation. We are conditioned to false needs for endless consumption while nature is poisoned. The powers-that-be profit from these systems, "common sense" enshrines them as necessary, and ideological mystification obscures their origin and nature by blaming the victims. Responses to people's pain, if they are to be truly and lastingly effective, must be aimed *at the system:* at capitalism, sexism, racism, imperialism, homophobia, the bureaucratic state, and the domination of nature.

Governments and economies, families and culture, science and individual psychology—all are shaped by these systems of domination and exclusion. That is why the radical ideal goes beyond piecemeal improvements to a Utopian vision; and tries to realize that vision in everyday struggles for a fair distribution of power, human dignity, and a livable environment. Revolutionaries have argued that a modern economy can be democratically controlled and oriented to human needs rather than profit; can do without vast differences of wealth and power; and can preserve rather than destroy the earth. Radicals claim that in a true 'democracy' ordinary men and women would help shape the basic conditions which affect their lives: not just by an occasional trip to the ballot box, but by active involvement in decisions about political and economic life.

How will these sweeping changes take place? Revolutionaries have offered many answers—from large political parties to angry uprisings, from decentralized groups based in consciousness-raising to international organizations. In any case, however, the conception of radicalism which informs the series stipulates that authentic revolutionary change requires the self-action of sizable groups of people, not the self-promotion of a self-proclaimed revolutionary "elite." The only way to prevent the betrayal of the revolution by a privileged bureaucracy is to base radical politics on free discussion, mutual respect, and collective empowerment *from the beginning.* This is one of the clearest and most painful lessons from the history of communism.

Of course much of this sounds good on paper. Yet it may be—as many have claimed—that radical visions are really unrealistic fantasies. However, if we abandon these visions we also abandon human life to its current misery, with little to hope for but token reforms. Radicals reject this essentially cynical "realism," opting for a continuing faith in the human capacity for a fundamentally different and profoundly liberating form of life.

In fact, people have always dreamed of a better world. Yet it is only since the late eighteenth century that organized groups developed a systematic theoretical critique of social life; and tried to embody that critique in mass political movements designed to overthrow the existing order of economic ownership and political control. American revolutionaries claimed that "All men are endowed with certain inalienable rights." The French revolution demanded "liberty, equality, fraternity."

Since then Marxist, socialist, feminist, national liberation, civil rights, gay and lesbian liberation, and ecology movements have been born. Each movement utilized some of the accomplishments of its predecessors, criticized the past for its limitations, and broke new ground. *Revolutionary Thought/Radical Movements* will focus on the theory and practice, successes and failures, of these movements.

While the series' authors are part of the radical tradition, we are painfully aware that this tradition has committed grave errors and at times failed completely. The communism of the Eastern bloc, while maintaining certain valuable social welfare programs, combined economic inefficiency, brutal tyranny, and ecological devastation. Many of us who took to the streets in the 1960s joined arrogance with idealism, self-indulgence with utopian hopes. Much of contemporary radical or socialist feminism fails to reach beyond a circle of the already converted.

These and other failures of radicalism are certainly apparent today. Daily headlines trumpet the collapse of the Eastern bloc, the US victory in the Cold War, the eternal superiority of capitalism and free markets, and the transformation of yesterday's radicals into today's yuppies. Governments of countries that had called themselves "socialist" or "communist" (however much they were distorting the meaning of these terms) trip over each other rushing west for foreign corporate investment and economic advice.

But there are also *successes,* ways in which radicals have changed social life for the better. Though these achievements have been partial reforms rather than sweeping revolutions, many of the basic freedoms, rights, and material advantages of modern life were fought for by people called radicals, dangerous revolutionaries, or anti-American:

- restrictions on the exploitation of workers, from the eight-hour day to the right to unionize;
- resistance to cultural imperialism and racial discrimination;
- a host of government programs, from unemployment insurance to social security, from the Environmental Protection Agency to fair housing laws;
- restrictions on opportunistic and destructive American foreign policy in Vietnam, El Salvador, Nicaragua, and other nations.

While radicals have not been alone in seeking these goals, they have often led the fight. Perhaps more important, they have offered a theoretical analysis which shows the *connections* between problems which may appear to be separate. They have argued that the sexist treatment of women and ecological devastation may have the same root. They have shown the links between the private control of wealth and an expansionist foreign policy. They have analyzed the family, the factory, the army, and the government as parts of the same system of domination.

Along with both the concrete successes and the global vision, radicals have—sadly—too often reproduced the ideas and relationships they sought to destroy. Marxists demanded an end to unjust society— yet formed authoritarian organizations where dissent was repressed. Radical feminists proclaimed "sisterhood is powerful," but often ignored Black women or poor women. At times ecologists, in trying to save nature, have been disrespectful of human beings.

Some of the worst failures came, in short, not from being radical, but from *not being radical enough:* not inclusive enough, not honest enough, not willing to examine how radical political programs and group behavior reproduced an oppressive, unjust society. Awareness of these failures reminds us that revolutionary thought cannot limit itself to critique of the larger society, but also requires self-criticism. While this process can degenerate into petty sectarian hostilities, it also shows that authentic radicalism is not a dead graven image, but a living quest to learn from the past and change the future. In the attempt to create solidarity and community among the oppressed, for instance, radicals have recently spent much effort trying to address and appreciate fundamental differences in social experience—between black and white workers, men and women, temporarily able-bodied and disabled, gay/lesbian and straight. In this effort, radicals have wrestled with the paradox that persons may simultaneously be victims of one system of domination and agents of another one.

The books in this series are part of this radical quest for revolutionary change and continued self-examination. In an era of the sudden fall of totalitarian communism and the frightening rise in the federal deficit, of the possibility of a peace dividend and the specter of the death of nature—these discussions of revolutionary thought and radical movements are needed more than ever before.*

*Roger S. Gottlieb*

*Thanks for editorial suggestions to Bland Addison, Mario Moussa, Miriam Greenspan, Tom Shannon and John Trimbur.

# PREFACE

As I write this Preface in January 1991, the U.S.-Iraq war highlights the murderous militarism of modern nations and temporarily eclipses the long-term, chronic problems faced by our country, the West, and the world community as a whole. These problems include first and foremost a mushrooming environmental crisis followed by crippling inequalities of wealth and power, fundamental antagonisms among races, ethnic groups, and religions, and a modern culture which celebrates endless violence and self-destructive consumption.

Can Marxism be of any help in our struggles against these ills?

I believe that it can, but only if we honestly examine its history, failures, and limits. Such an examination reveals a continuing theoretical power and a series of practical lessons that can be of real service to an attempt to make our country and our world more just, peaceful, and fulfilling.

This book aims to be that examination. I hope that as the Eastern bloc continues to divest itself of the horrors of communist dictatorship, a thoughtful dialogue on the possible uses of Marxist theory and socialist practice can be undertaken in the U.S. Of course, many claim that the failures of communism prove the bankruptcy of Marxism. This is only as true as the statement that the Spanish Inquisition, in which church authorities routinely tortured and murdered any they disliked, "proves" the bankruptcy of Christianity.

I will begin with an outline of Marx's theory (Chapter 1) and of its most general philosophical and political limitations (Chapter 2). In Part II (Chapters 3 and 4) I describe how Marxism was expressed in the theory and practice of the socialist and communist movements between (roughly) 1880 and 1935. These movements were the "betrayal" of the original vision of Marxism, although they *also* point up some crucial weaknesses in the theory itself.

Part III presents what for me are the two essential elements of the "rebirth" of Marxism: Western Marxism and socialist-feminism. These perspectives retain the original Marxist vision of a classless, rational, and emancipating society. They combine that vision with a much more sophisticated and inclusive understanding of what blocks the fulfillment of that vision and what we must do to realize it.

Part IV examines some contemporary concerns. Chapter 7 updates Marxist analysis of present-day capitalist economic and political life. Chapter 8, in somewhat more demanding and detailed ways than the rest of the book, contains examples of ongoing debates concerning the relation between Marxism and other radical perspectives. Finally, in Chapter 9, I argue that there are limitations that Marxism, no matter how "born again," cannot overcome.

There are important areas—especially the role of self-proclaimed Marxists in Third World revolutionary struggles—which are unexplored here. I believe that my analysis of the Bolshevik revolution can be extended to most of those movements. It also seems to me that the social contexts of the Third World are so different from ours that revolutionary movements there can provide neither positive nor negative models for people in this country.

The book as a whole is aimed at general readers rather than specialists. I have therefore tried to keep the academic baggage to a minimum, using notes to direct readers to further sources. I have also aimed to write in a straightforward way that—with the exception of parts of Chapter 8—tends to bypass some technical debates. Readers interested in more detailed treatment of the issues will find resources in the References and in an earlier book of mine: *History and Subjectivity: The Transformation of Marxist Theory* (Temple University Press: 1987).

# ACKNOWLEDGMENTS

I am grateful to several people who were kind enough to take time out of their own busy lives to make tremendously helpful comments on earlier drafts: Bland Addison, Sandra Bartky, Miriam Greenspan, Bill Martin, Mario Moussa, Bob Ross, Doug Allen, Richard Schmitt, Susan Thorne, and Virginia Warren.

Prior versions of some portions of the book appeared in the following places:

Parts of Chapters 3 and 4 in the "Introduction" to *An Anthology of Western Marxism: From Lukács and Gramsci to Socialist-Feminism*, New York: Oxford University Press, 1989.

Part of Chapter 8 in "Three Contemporary Critiques of Historical Materialism," *Philosophy and Social Criticism* 11, no. 2, Fall 1985.

Part of Chapter 8 in "Forces of Production and Social Primacy," *Social Theory and Practice* 11, no. 1, Spring 1985.

# I

## ORIGINS

# 1

## MARXISM: THE ORIGINAL THEORY

Marx's writings, as well as those of more than a century of followers, interpreters, and critics, form an enormously tangled thicket of theory, historical analyses, political strategies, and polemics. I will chart a path through this thicket by first focusing on Marx's own writings[1] and then exploring the most important political and theoretical developments to which they gave rise. The overall task is motivated by my belief that Marxism remains essential to an adequate understanding of contemporary social life. However, I also find basic flaws both present in Marx *and* imported into Marxism by later theorists. These flaws have at times shaped Marxist political practice in disastrous ways, causing injustice and misery. Since human happiness and full self-development were Marx's goals, it is in his spirit that I am presenting and criticizing his ideas and those of his followers.

The discussion begins with a focus on Marx's concept of human nature. In an analysis of "historical materialism," I will then examine Marx's general theory of social structure and his detailed analysis of economic life, ideology, and alienation in capitalism. Finally, I will describe Marx's vision of human freedom and fulfillment.

## HUMAN NATURE

Our knowledge of human nature tells us, we think, what is fundamental and unchangeable about the way people live. We appeal to human nature to explain why society must be divided into classes, why men and women cannot be equal, or what people need in order to be happy. To understand Marx's impact on our conception of human nature, we must briefly examine how other philosophers thought about this question. This is an important issue not just for historical reasons, but because the points of view that Marx reacted against still exist. Marx's approach to human nature, then, is not only the starting point of *his* philosophy, but distinguishes a contemporary Marxist perspective from other philosophical positions.

To understand the traditional concept of human nature, we must first ask about the traditional concept of "nature." This idea first emerged in the writings of Greek and Italian spiritual and naturalist thinkers, roughly between 600 and 500 B.C.E. While their particular claims seem a little bizarre today ("Everything is water," said Thales, the first of them), their perspective foreshadowed what we now think of as science. Like contemporary scientists, they sought to find *basic regularities* amid the ceaseless change in the natural world, and they speculated that these regularities were the product of unifying and simplifying *structures* which underlay the world's seeming diversity. The pre-Socratics' fledgling theories generalized about patterns in the cycle of the seasons, biological growth and death, and planetary motion. As proto-scientists, they did not explain these patterns narratively—that is, by appealing to the actions of gods—but structurally, as the outcome of a few basic elements or principles. The fundamental truth of nature, on this view, is that its complex and bewildering change and variety are appearances produced by fixed principles and basic elements.

The fifth-century B.C.E. Greek philosopher Socrates tried to apply the pre-Socratic notion of nature to human beings. He wanted to find out *who he was* as a person, what forces determined his behavior, structured his needs, and—above all—allowed him rationally to justify his actions and his statements. If he could understand his own *human nature*, he could explain what was most important about him and move beyond tradition or personal taste in showing that his beliefs and actions were right. Thus the idea of human nature was born.

Following Socrates, first Plato and then Aristotle took up this idea of a human nature and generated detailed theories to answer Socrates' questions. While the details of their conceptions are not significant here, it is important to know that for both of them (as for the next two thousand years of Western thought), human nature was fixed, universal, and "internal" to each person. It was the same everywhere, "given" to us rather than chosen, and it was something that was true about us *as individuals.* Just as each lump of coal or tree or star had its nature in and of itself, so every person had a human nature determining their fundamental behavior and what they needed to fulfill themselves. The basic characteristics of human nature were as independent of our control as was the fact that plants needed water and sunlight or that it got colder in the winter.

Subsequent philosophers held a wide variety of opinions about human nature, but they typically shared the early Greek estimation that it was universal, given, and individual. For our purposes, we can see this position start to change with the work of Immanuel Kant (1724–1804) and G. W. F. Hegel (1770–1831).

Kant began with questions. How do we know, he asked, that the physical objects which we see or feel only intermittently actually endure in time? How can we discover that one event *causes* another, since all we directly experience is a succession of events in time? How do we get the notion of a unique, personal self, since our mental and emotional experience is a varying series of perceptions and thoughts? Kant's answer is that such basic ideas as the continuity of physical objects, causality, and a permanent self are built into our minds, not learned from experience. These concepts are imposed on the flux and confusion of brute experience to construct concrete ideas of both physical objects and persons. In this way, Kant saw both physical nature and our own selves as mental products.

This position, usually called Idealism, claimed that many basic and universal features of the world and self were "constituted," or put together, by mental operations of which we are not aware but which could be deduced by philosophical analysis. Where the pre-Socratics saw a nature of regularities and fixed structures, Kant saw phenomena which in some sense were fashioned by the mind. The "human nature" of Plato and Aristotle rested, thought Kant, on our capacity to generate for ourselves a sense of our own personal identity.

What is crucial for us is Kant's stress on the essentially *active and creating* capacity of the human mind. While he believed that the ways in which we were active and creating were fixed and universal, the idea that both the physical world and a sense of self were in some way human products was a revolutionary contribution.

Hegel developed this notion further by adding two critical ingredients: *history* and *society*. For Hegel, the fundamental categories in terms of which people organize society, understand themselves, and conceptualize nature *change over time* and *differ from one culture to another*. Therefore, to understand "human nature" we must understand human history. This history shows that each past epoch was governed by certain fundamental ideas and values which determined how people expressed themselves in the various realms of life: politics, art, philosophy, religion, morality, and the family. Since each expression of ideas and values was limited in some way, past forms of human life were all subject to "contradictions." That is, to redress the limitations of the way they lived, people had to change social life in fundamental ways. In this continuing pattern, expectations are raised that cannot be satisfied unless basic practices are changed, or values give rise to experiences which lead us to new values, or intellectual problems posed by one philosophical system can only be resolved by a fundamentally new system.

The whole process, it must be stressed, is collective. Kant had focused on mental operations reproduced identically but individually in each person's mind. For Hegel, human identity is bound up with activities and ways of thinking that are essentially and necessarily social. Just as one cannot play football or have a love affair alone, so religion, art, science, morality, and political life are not things individuals could ever do by themselves.

We can see a concept of human nature emerging—historically changing, collective, and creative—which is very different from what Socrates began with. Yet Hegel did hold to a vestige of the traditional belief. He understood the entire process of successive contradictions and resolutions of contradictions (which he termed a "dialectic") as an expression of a universal, unchanging, and pre-given force: God. While *we* can only see human groups endlessly changing, Hegel argued, the ultimate pattern is that of God coming to know Himself in time. This self-knowledge is dependent on the development of *human* self-understanding. Human history, then, is essentially the history of the successive ways in which we understand ourselves: how we interpret ourselves and the world, the norms which govern social life, the values we embody in religion, politics, and art. The real source of the contradictions which drive history is the human need to eventually recognize that humanity is an agent—and in some sense a part—of a Divine Development. The dialectic necessarily moves away from a sense of isolation and separateness among people, or between people and their social creations and nature itself. God's self-knowledge in time, developed through human history, is the knowledge of the essential identity of everything which exists. This identity is based in a shared an underlying divine nature.

And this brings us to Marx, who in a sense accepted a Hegelian view of human nature but rejected the idea that a divine force shapes historical appearances. Like Hegel, Marx believed that what is most crucial about us is our social relations.[2] Like Kant, he believed our reality was in some sense produced by us. Marx seeks to understand people in terms of the shared activities, ideas, and institutions in which they participate; and in terms of the way these social realities are human creations and creatively change over time. Ultimately, he believed, we are not constrained by a fixed human nature to any particular form of social life or to any pre-given set of needs.

Marx begins to seriously distinguish himself philosophically when he pushes this theory of the social identity of human beings two steps further, both of which can be understood as rejections of Hegel.

First, he separates the process of human self-becoming from any religious or spiritual source. The emphasis on spirituality, Marx claims, arises because of problems in social life. Spiritual striving expresses and seeks to assuage the pains of a flawed society.

> Religion is . . . man's self-consciousness and self-awareness so long as he has not found himself or has lost himself again. . . . Religion is the sigh of the oppressed creature, the sentiment of a heartless world, and the soul of soulless conditions. It is the *opium* of the people. (Marx, "Contribution to a Critique of Hegel's *Philosophy of Right*: Introduction," in Tucker 1972: 12)

Marx also denies that human history is most fundamentally shaped by the way we think about ourselves or what we think is right or good. We begin not with abstract theories or philosophical values, but as biological creatures, driven by basic biological needs. Any thinking, valuing, or understanding we do follows on the satisfaction of those needs. We are rooted in nature, not thought. (Rader: 1978)

Seeing human identity as active, social, physical, and without spiritual origins does not really advance Marx over other philosophers immediately after Hegel.[3] What is original is the way he organized those insights into a comprehensive theory of human existence.


## HISTORICAL MATERIALISM

The distinctive features of Marx's theory emerge from a group of writings completed between 1843 and 1848. In "Contribution to a Critique of Hegel's *Philosophy of Right*," *The German Ideology*, *Economic and Philosophical Manuscripts of 1844*, *The Poverty of Philosophy*, and the *Communist Manifesto*, Marx created a fundamentally new understanding of social, political, and intellectual life. "Historical materialism," the defining core of Marxism, is his most important doctrine from this period.

Historical materialism is a particular conception of the relative importance and mutual effects of social relations. It answers the question: even if all individuals exist as social beings, are some parts of social life more important than others? For example, is my nationality as important as what I do for a living? Is my society's art as important as the level of its technological development?

Marx answers this question by synthesizing the three essential human characteristics—rooted in biology, fundamentally social, and creative—into the concept of a "mode of production." For Marx, it is the mode of production—and not a fixed human nature, a divine plan, individual choices, or philosophical beliefs—that determines human history and social life.

Two distinguishable but highly interrelated elements make up a mode of production. *Forces of production* include the productive tools and techniques used in material production. At different times these might include wooden plows drawn by oxen or turbine-powered combines, simple rowboats for fishing or mechanized trawlers, hand tools for working leather into shoes or automated factories turning out three thousand pair of Reeboks a day. The knowledge used to guide production might come from science or tradition, be handed down from parent to child, or studied in universities. Despite these differences, human biology demands that we always have some way of transacting with nature to meet our needs. Thus, every society utilizes forces of production. *Relations of production* are the forms of *human* organization which shape our interaction with nature. The essential aspects of the relations of production can be identified by asking a series of basic questions: Who owns or controls the forces of production? How are the products distributed? Who controls the labor process? In certain South Sea island villages the fishing boats were made communally and used by all healthy adult males. The fish brought back were distributed to all families of the community. No one would have understood the question, "Who owns the boats?" because the concept of private ownership—including sole right to use and to sell—simply did not exist. In the feudal mode of production, a small group of immensely wealthy aristocrats controlled enormous tracts of land, while a vast majority of agricultural laborers gave them work or goods. In slavery, workers can be owned. In capitalism, workers without land or capital are employed by the private owners of forces of production.

In short, the mode of production is the way productive forces are used to meet our material needs, the labor process is organized, and the products of labor are distributed.[4] In Marx's theory, it plays the role traditionally played by the concept of human nature for earlier thinkers. As he says:

> This sum of productive forces, forms of capital and social forms of intercourse, which every individual and generation finds in existence as something given, is the real basis of what the philosophers have conceived as "substance" and "essence of man." (Marx and Engels 1947: 29)

Marx believed that the mode of production is more important than other parts of social life in two very critical ways. It explains, more than it is explained by, other aspects of a society at any given time; and its dynamic shapes the flow of historical change over time. Because it has these effects on social life, we may say that the mode of production is "socially primary."

> Our conception of history depends on our ability to expound the real process of production, starting out from the simple material production of life, and to comprehend the form of intercourse connected with this and created by this . . . as the basis of all history. . . . (Marx and Engels 1947: 28)

> In the social production of their existence, men inevitably enter into definite relations, which are independent of their will, namely relations of production appropriate to a given stage in the development of their material forces of production. The totality of these relations of production constitutes the economic structure of society, the real foundation, on which arises a legal and political superstructure and to which correspond definite forms of social consciousness. (Marx 1970: 20)

The concept of a mode of production is both universal and concrete: universal, because every form of human community must have

having a material existence

one; concrete, because in any given society historically specific social structures, technological resources, and social norms, roles, and practices constitute the *actual* mode of production. This concept thus allows us to analyze social life in a way that is both comprehensive and also adequately specific. That is why Marx could reasonably claim to have decisively moved rational understanding of human beings beyond the idealism of Hegel.

He also went beyond the individualism of eighteenth-century philosophy and economic theory, which held that human nature is determined not by social relations but by individual choices, experiences, or desires. For Marx, each individual is necessarily born into some particular mode of production and a corresponding social system structured in a defined way. The choice to live in a feudal world of lords and serfs or a capitalist one of owners and workers is not up to us. The broad features of our life experiences are thus not set by our individual preferences. While the individual may "subjectively raise himself above" his social relations, he remains their "creature" nevertheless. In his understanding of social life, Marx freely admitted, individuals are "personifications of economic categories, embodiments of particular class-relations and class-interests." (Marx 1967 I: 10)

Exactly *how* does the mode of production affect the rest of social life? In what does the social primacy of the mode of production consist? Marx offered many—not entirely consistent—theoretical and historical answers to these questions.[5] Two stand out as central: the mode of production is socially primary because it shapes class struggle and encompasses the development of the productive forces.

While other thinkers focus on how people understand themselves in terms of religion, nationality, or personal life, Marx believed that the mode of production naturally divides social life into antagonistic classes, groups determined by relations to the mode of production.[6] In all but the most primitive societies, an exploited class performs the bulk of the productive labor; and a ruling class controls or owns the forces of production, decides how much of the economic surplus will be distributed, and/or controls the process of production. In one society, the producing class is composed of agricultural laborers who perform unpaid labor for the local lord. In another, a "proletariat" of factory laborers creates profits for capitalist owners of the means of production. In a third, vast landed estates are worked by slaves. In all social forms beyond the most primitive, a fundamental division of labor and social position gives rise to essentially antagonistic interests. The first aspect of the social primacy of the mode of production is thus simply that human beings are divided into groups which differ in terms of income, wealth, power, prestige, control over daily living conditions, and resources to accomplish ends. Our class position— structured by the mode of production—sets a multitude of conditions of our lives. Because of our class we have particular resources, choices, friends, expectations, and problems.

Class divisions also create class *interests*. Members of the ruling class have an interest in protecting and enhancing their superior power and their unearned wealth. The producing classes have an interest in lessening exploitation, increasing their power, and eventually over- turning the system. Capitalists want to pay less wages and get more labor from their employees. Workers want the opposite. Slave owners want docile laborers and slaves want freedom.

Marx believed that people are motivated to act on their material interests, which are structured in the most general way by their class position. Though those interests will be obscured by popular or intel- lectual justifications of existing social arrangements, they will eventu- ally determine how classes will act. Class actions, in turn, shape the overall development of social life. "The history of hitherto existing society is the history of class struggles" (Marx and Engels 1954: 13) is one of Marx's most famous claims. He found frequent examples— peasant revolts studied by Engels, armed insurrections of the 1840s in Europe, the French revolution of 1789—of social conflict centering around class issues: Who will own or control land? Who will pay taxes or tribute? What wages will be paid? He further believed that class struggle, in the context of particular economic and technological devel- opments, would eventually undermine capitalism and create socialism. (See the discussion following.)

The mode of production is a central determiner of social life in a second way: it sets the limits to and provides the resources for all other human activities. The level of technological, scientific, and productive development determines how much time and energy we have for activities other than simply meeting our survival needs. The mode of production provides the resources to support non-laboring intellectuals, artists, and researchers. Thus the possibilities of philosophy, art, and theoretical science exist within bounds determined by how developed the forces of production are. This development not only makes certain activities possible, it rules out others, making old ways of life impossible and demanding new forms of human interaction. The more technology is developed, for instance, the less people need to trust in superstition. The more production is socialized and geographically interdependent, the less meaningful small political boundaries can be. From small dukedoms we forge nations. Out of nations we forge a united Europe.

Perhaps most importantly, people manifest a widespread desire to continually develop the forces of production. If social relations of production interfere with that development, they will be altered. Political revolutions and social change serve to expand our technical, scientific, and productive powers.

To show how central the mode of production is, we may consider the following example. It is not one given by Marx himself, but it helps explain what he had in mind.

Given the long history of women's social inequality, why have feminist movements arisen with such power only in the last three decades? Two fundamental facts, both effects or aspects of the capitalist mode of production, provide an explanation. First, there is the underlying, long-term development of philosophical and political justifications of political equality. In the early years of capitalism, property owners, merchants, and producers who were not landed nobility sought a new social freedom to buy and sell, invest and make profits. They needed economic equality to counteract the inherited privilege and power of the aristocracy. They justified their struggle with the notion of universal human rights. Yet while they intended these rights only for white, male property holders, the notion has naturally been adapted by other groups, including women. There is thus a permanent conceptual base for any oppressed group to demand political equality, a conceptual base which originates in economic class struggle.

Second, the capitalist economy has a systematic, unavoidable tendency to replace labor for immediate use with labor for wages. Five hundred years ago, almost everyone made their own clothes, grew most of their own food, and built their own homes. Now all those things are bought and sold for money. In the advanced capitalism of the late twentieth century, the transition to a full money economy means that women are economically forced to work for wages outside the home. Yet once women work for wages as men do, they have greater access to education and social power. They can demand freedom and equality. The structure of homebound women and wage earning men—which supports notions of women's basic difference from men, inferiority, dependence, etc.—is shattered. The result is feminism.

Thus, to explain the explosive changes in the position of women since the mid 1950s, we turn to forces centered in the mode of production. While women were oppressed for thousands of years, developments in the mode of production—not in the family or in ideas about women—allowed them to fight their oppression in a collective way.

Do the sweeping historical and social changes brought about by class struggle and technological development have an overall direction? Like Hegel, Marx believed that human history has a general meaning or goal. On the one hand, technological progress improves control over nature, lessens the labor time necessary to meet biological needs, and continually expands our sense of what a normal standard of living is. On the other, political developments move towards personal freedom and the rational and just organization of social life. While local class struggle does not seek this overall goal, the cumulative effect of class conflicts does lead towards human liberation. The exploitation built into class society tends to make those societies unstable, for exploitation gives rise to resistance. The fulfillment of material needs leads to the development of new needs: that which is sought, once achieved, becomes the presupposition for new seeking. Human beings will not rest until they have reached a social form which supports unfettered, creative self-transformation.

The realm of freedom actually begins only where labour which is determined by necessity and mundane considerations ceases. . . . Freedom in this field can only consist in socialized man, the associated producers, rationally regulating their interchange with Nature, bringing it under their common control, instead of being ruled by it. . . . Beyond [this rational activity of production] begins that development of human energy which is an end in itself, the true realm of freedom. . . . (Marx 1967 III: 820)

## IDEOLOGY

Marx (and many later Marxists) believed that in many ways historical materialism provides a distinctive and decisively superior way to analyze human existence. To begin with, historical materialism is superior because it focuses on the "study of real men in real conditions." As opposed to Hegel, history is not seen as the product of abstractions such as Humanity, Truth, or God. Instead we study, without philosophical speculation or religious faith, the forces and relations of production, class conflict, and technological development.

Second, historical materialism avoids another prevalent form of distorting abstraction: that of "individualism." Here Marx opposes thinkers who understood various aspects of social life as built up out of characteristics which adhere to persons in isolation. For instance, John Locke believed that social norms and governmental power are created because they help separate individuals preserve their property. Property comes first, then laws and the state. Marx's reply is that this view "abstracts" (that is, separates in an unrealistic and distorting way) the individual from the social arrangements which make property possible at all. The growing class of agricultural capitalists which Locke championed against inherited feudal privilege is not, in fact, a universal phenomenon. Their property rights do not pre-date society but could only be conceived of and enforced within a particular set of social relations.

The individualistic stress on "personal choice" so common in contemporary America is also challenged by Marxism. Personal choices, after all, are only possible in a particular social setting. Our social context gives us a field of possibilities from which to choose and also socializes people into certain choices and wants rather than others.

Private interest is itself already a socially determined interest, which can be achieved only within the conditions laid down by society and with the means provided by society; hence it is bound to the reproduction of these conditions and means. It is the interest of private persons; but its content, as well as the form and means of its realization, is given by social conditions independent of all. (Marx 1973: 156)

Similarly, Existentialist philosophers of the last century and a half (e.g., Kierkegaard, Nietzsche, Sartre) have claimed that human beings are essentially isolated individuals, creating themselves through choices which lack any meaningful justification. Marx never confronted Existentialism directly. However, a response in line with his theory would run as follows: Existentialism accurately describes the kind of personal experience engendered by a capitalist society which uproots people from communities, accelerates historical change, destroys traditions, and disrupts family relations. In this social context, we feel like and to some extent are isolated selves. However, Existentialism is false to the extent that it confuses a particular set of social conditions with the essence of human existence. The isolation and meaninglessness of capitalist society can give way to new forms of community under socialism.

Historical materialism is further distinguished by emphasizing the importance of human biological needs and socially determined interests. As Marx remarked, while certain eras may take religion more seriously than his own, even the Middle Ages lives on bread and not Catholicism. Therefore, when people talk about Truth, Rights, and Goodness, we must make sure their claims do not actually reflect, mask, or reinforce class power. Philosophical ethics, religious values, or definitions of what constitutes scientific as opposed to non-scientific ways of thinking—all these purport to either absolute truth or at least disinterested rationality and objectivity. Yet without awareness of class experience and class interests, they are likely to be not only wrong but to have pernicious effects. The results will not be accurate accounts of history or human nature, but *rationalizations* of the existing distribution of power. These rationalizations may not be self-conscious. They may result from a spontaneous sympathy for the interests of the powerful, or from the limited experience of one who imagines that the social life he knows is the only possible form of social life, or from the not consciously planned selection of those who think in ways congenial to the powerful to be the dominant intellectual and cultural voices. But conscious or not, class biases are clearly evident when the Declaration of Independence proclaims the "rights of man" but restricts them to white men, when religious leaders teach acceptance of hierarchy and wealth, when state support of corporations is presented as sound economic policy while welfare programs are rejected as "creeping socialism" for the idle poor.

Marx's approach also stresses the essentially *historical* nature of human beings. *The mode of production changes over time, giving rise to new forces and relations of production.* Therefore, all forms of human self-understanding and interaction will also change, typically in ways congenial to changes in the mode of production. We should not understand human beings in general on the basis of our experience of human beings in one particular society. If we do, we will then mistakenly see in all previous epochs the purely temporary conditions of our own time. This mistake occurs when people see the "individual"—a social and economic category developed by capitalism over the last three centuries—as present in every historical period. A related mistake occurs when we try to understand the history of some aspect of social life—for instance religion, art, or the family—without seeing how that history reflects changes in the mode of production.

Finally, the notion of the mode of production, like all purportedly scientific concepts, identifies a deep structure which conditions the basic traits of a particular domain. For physics, invisible particles constitute everyday physical objects like baseballs and toasters; for psychoanalysis, unseen needs and feelings shape human behavior. Similarly, Marx believed that the mode of production typically masked by ideas that distort what is really essential in social life or what really guides individual behavior, shapes public institutions and norms and determines private experience. The resulting effects of the mode of production create patterns of social life and, under certain social conditions, establish quasi-laws of societal change and development. The "natural laws of capitalist production" work "with iron necessity towards inevitable results. The country that is more developed industri-

ally only shows, to the less developed, the image of its own future."
(Marx 1967 I: 8–9)

A shorthand way to sum up Marxism's intellectual superiority
over its opponents is to call them "ideological." To say that a theory
is ideological is to say first that it is inadequate or mistaken, and that
it is so because it has *ignored* or *misrepresented* the historical or social
nature of its object. Ideas are also ideological to the extent that they
are put forward or accepted because they *serve the interests* of the economic or political ruling class. Finally, a theory's social role may be
criticized as ideological; i.e., it may *support oppression* or *exploitation*.
Here are examples of Marx's account of ideology:

> We set out from real, active men, and on the basis of their real life-
> processes we demonstrate the development of the ideological reflexes
> and echoes of this life process. . . . Morality, religion, metaphysics, all the
> rest of ideology . . . thus no longer retain the semblance of independence.
> (Marx and Engels 1947: 14)

> But don't wrangle with us so long as you apply to our intended abolition
> of bourgeois property, the standard of your bourgeois notions of freedom,
> culture, law, etc. Your very ideas are but the outgrowth of the conditions
> of your bourgeois production and bourgeois property. [you have] a selfish
> misconception that induces [you] to transform into eternal laws of nature
> and reason, the social forms springing from your present mode of produc-
> tion and form of property.[7] (Marx and Engels 1954: 47)

> Upon the different forms of property, upon the social conditions of
> existence, rises an entire superstructure of distinct and peculiarly formed
> sentiments, illusions, modes of thought and views of life. The entire class
> creates it out of its material foundations and out of the corresponding
> social relations. (Marx 1968: 47)

Critics have asked: what keeps Marx's own theory from being
a self-interested distortion, itself an ideological "reflex" of material
conditions? Marx has a decisive reply. First, he believes that his theory
does serve interests: initially, those of the working class; ultimately,
those of humanity as a whole. His ideas promote a social order in
which nature is mastered, and collective self-creation is manifest with
the least hindrance and the greatest freedom. Second, he agreed that

the theory of historical materialism is a social product. "Even the most abstract categories . . . are by the very definiteness of the abstraction a product of historical conditions." (Marx 1971: 39) Only under modern social conditions in which economic activity is detached from tradition, religious control, custom, etc., and in which technological development moves at an increasingly breakneck pace can the importance of economic life emerge to the mind's eye. While it possessed this importance at other times, it was then obscured by religious justifications of social inequality, systematic lack of development of productive forces tied to the owning of slaves, and the preponderance of comparatively static social forms based in mass subsistence agriculture.

Thus, it is Marx's historical position, combined with his commitment to ending capitalist domination and exploitation, that allows him to "see through" the smokescreens of ideology.

## ALIENATION AND FREEDOM

Although he rejected the idea of an unchanging, universal human nature, Marx did believe that a certain social context would be conducive to human fulfillment. Since human realization centers around self-creation, a fulfilling society must allow people to make maximum use of their capacity for creative activity. When that process—in culture, politics, industry, science—can proceed with as little unnecessary hindrance as possible, then human freedom is being realized.

Historically, the progressive realization of human freedom has two dimensions. First, since human beings must before all else satisfy their physical needs, and since the activity of production is so central to human life, it is necessary to bring our relations with nature under rational control. For most of human history, the materially necessary drudgery of everyday life has precluded very much individual self-awareness or creative activity. People's orientation towards life activity remains rooted in the struggle to survive, and people's self-understanding is determined by a taken-for-granted traditional culture, usually founded in religion.

These constraints of nature had been more or less successfully overcome by Marx's day. Or, at least, it was clear that the technological developments brought about by the rise of capitalism could soon make it possible to have a life of freedom, beyond scarcity and toil.

> The transformation of the process of production from the simple labour process into a scientific process . . . subjects the forces of nature and converts them to the service of human needs. . . . What appears as the mainstay of production and wealth is neither the immediate labour performed by the worker, nor the time that he works—but the appropriation by man of his own general productive force, his understanding of nature, and the mastery of it; in a word, the development of the social individual . . . Individuals are then in a position to develop freely. (Marx 1971: 136, 142)

Thus, Marx saw the problem of human freedom as now centered on the second dimension necessary for human self-realization: social relations. For Marx, capitalist society made this a problem of *alienation*. This term—and the related *fetishism*—refers to the way specifically human abilities and products come to limit or oppress the human beings who are their source. In Marx's classic account of alienation (Marx 1964), he observes that the people who perform the productive labor in capitalist society are contributing to the wealth and power of those who are exploiting them: as the factory owners accumulate profits, the factory laborers become increasingly impoverished.[8] Moreover, the essentially human act of productive labor is degraded into boring, damaging, exhausting tedium. People lose themselves in work, that most potentially human of activities, and find themselves only when work is done. It might be objected that this is not different from pre-capitalist societies; building the pyramids in ancient Egypt or harvesting wheat in twelfth-century France can hardly have been pleasurable or creative. Marx's response is that actually the modern industrial division of labor *does* reduce the creative involvement of the laborer in many ways. Pre-capitalist production typically involved laborers in the creation of a whole artifact, not endless repetition on an assembly line. Much more important, however, is Marx's belief that alienation is a central feature of capitalism *just because* of the possibilities capitalism itself creates. Now that we *can* live beyond toil, there is no longer any reason for the workers' poverty and drudgery. That their own labor is used against them, producing the opposite of human fulfillment, is a measure of the workers' alienation. This condition, it should be stressed, is for Marx an objective state. Workers under capitalism are alienated whether they realize it or not. However, Marx was confident (perhaps mistakenly so) that objective alienation would inevitably lead to subjective dissatisfaction and, eventually, to class struggle.

Alienation takes another form in the distortion of perception and understanding which Marx called *fetishism*, or the *fetishism of commodities*. Fetishism occurs when social relationships which derive from human activity are perceived to be the product of inhuman, unchangeable forces. Marx saw this happening when the economic workings of capitalist society, which were in fact a specific organization of human labor, were perceived as relations between objects being exchanged. Marx had criticized Hegel for treating abstractions as more real than living human beings, considering actual reality to be a quality or product of the evolution of God or the realization of Absolute Knowledge. Similarly, when workers who actually produce the wealth of capitalist society starve in hovels, and this situation is described as an unfortunate but inevitable consequence of impersonal "market forces," then dead commodities are being invested with autonomous powers (fetishized) at the expense of the real subjects of history.

> A commodity is therefore a mysterious thing, simply because in it the social character of men's labour appears to them as an objective character stamped upon the product of that labour; because the relation of the producers to the sum total of their own labour is presented to them as a social relation, existing not between themselves, but between the products of their labour. (Marx 1967 I: 72)

Hegelian idealism and the fetishism of commodities not only populate the world with fictitious entities (Reason, The Market), but they also require a passive acceptance of things as they are. (Colletti 1975) Unless we understand social reality as a product of human activity, that reality will be seen as an uncontrollable expression of the Hegelian

Absolute, the "market," or human nature. Social life becomes idealized as beyond our control—*when in fact it is a product of human relationships, conditioned by human self-understanding, and potentially subject to conscious human control.*

## CAPITALISM

Marx's discussion of capitalism is very complex. I will limit my account to two aspects: the theory of exploitation and the theory of capitalist development and crisis.[9]

We can begin by noting that it is with the concrete analysis of specific societies that Marx's philosophy—especially historical materialism—succeeds or fails. Marx's claim that humans are essentially social, material, and self-creating is an interesting philosophical position. But it begins to convince only when it leads to fruitful analyses of social structure and historical change. Furthermore, while Marx did give accounts of historical development and social change from periods pre-dating capitalism, only capitalism received a detailed and systematic treatment, and only capitalism is the subject of both economic and political predictions and of the political action that Marx engaged in during his entire life.

Marx describes capitalism first and foremost as a mode of production in which the producers and expropriators found in all class societies take the form of proletariat and capitalists. As a class, the proletariat is initially composed of peasants who are forcibly driven off their land and thus economically compelled to join in capitalist production. Members of the proletariat own only their labor power and must work for wages to survive. The capitalist ruling class owns concentrations of the means of production. These concentrations originated in pre-capitalist wealth or from profit on trade, colonial exploitation, or war.[10]

Unlike all pre-capitalist economies, capitalism centers on the production of *commodities*—objects produced in order to be bought and sold rather than consumed by the people who make them. Owning neither land, natural resources, nor machines to produce with, wage laborers must buy the necessities of life. The capitalist class, in turn, uses its accumulated wealth to produce not to satisfy people's needs but to generate profit.

For Marx, the key to understanding any mode of production lies in the way the ruling class exploits the laboring class. In different social settings, the surplus labor—the amount of labor beyond what is used to produce what the worker consumes—of slaves, serfs, or wage laborers is appropriated by an economically dominant class.

> The specific economic form, in which unpaid surplus-labour is pumped out of direct producers, determines the relationship of rulers and ruled, as it grows directly out of production itself and, in turn, reacts upon it as a determining element. (Marx 1967 III: 791)

In pre-capitalist societies, exploitation—or at least unequal exchange—was obvious: peasants paid tribute to lords or to a central authority; slaves were owned outright by masters and had to labor for them. These relationships were justified by tradition or religion and enforced by physical coercion. In capitalism, however, there is typically a fair amount of political freedom: unlike serfs or slaves, workers are generally free to work for whomever they choose, live in one city or another, quit if they do not accept their pay, etc. What, then, is the "specific economic form" of capitalist exploitation?

Marx's answer begins with an analysis of the commodity. All commodities, he claims, possess *exchange value*; i.e., a particular rate at which they exchange against each other. Though commonly measured in money amount, corn or shoes, walkmans or cars, can be compared in value to each other. This comparison—e.g., so many pounds of corn = so many Reeboks = so many Toyotas—is the measure of the exchange value of each commodity. How much exchange value a commodity has, in turn, depends *in the long run* on how much *socially necessary labor time* is embodied in the commodity. By "socially necessary labor time," Marx means the amount of time expended by laborers at a reasonable, socially prevailing rate of efficiency; *plus* the amount of time necessary to produce the raw materials used up; *plus* the amount of time necessary to produce that percentage of the productive forces (tools, machinery, etc.) used up in producing the commodity. We add "in the long run" because Marx is well aware that there may be temporary fluctuations in the exchange value of commodities due to fashion, scarcity, novelty, etc. However, as the demand for an item increases, so does the interest in producing it. High demand and inflated prices necessarily stimulate increased production and an inevitable deflation of the price.[11] The value of a commodity—the amount of social labor worked into it—thus forms the natural center of price fluctuations.

This "labor theory of value" leaves us with a very perplexing question: if commodities typically exchange at a value determined by the labor they contain, and if capitalists are paying for this embodied labor (by paying wages and buying raw material and machinery), *how do capitalists make a profit?* It would seem that by selling the commodity they simply get back what they put in; i.e., the cost of the "living" labor (wages) and the "dead" labor (raw materials and machines). Marx's answer is that there is a source of profit in what he called "surplus value." This surplus is the difference between the value of labor power as a commodity and the value of what that labor power can produce.

How does this work? If the labor theory of value is true, then the only source of exchange value is labor. Objects which can be had without effort (e.g., air) have no exchange value. Even though air is the most immediately desirable "object" for human beings, it is not a commodity just because no labor is necessary to get it. Thus, it is not how much we want or need an item which determines its exchange value. Similarly, natural scarcity—e.g., of diamonds—is simply a measure of how much labor must be expended in order get the item in question.[12]

When the capitalist hires a laborer, he is purchasing the unique commodity—labor power—which creates value. But labor power has *its* value like any other commodity. That value, once again, is determined by how much socially necessary labor time it takes to produce it; i.e., the labor required to produce the food, shelter, clothes, amusements, etc., that the worker needs in order to be sustained for the day's toil. Yet there is a difference—and in this difference, says Marx, is the source of capitalist wealth—between how much a worker *needs* in order to be sustained for a day's work and how much a worker can *produce* in that same amount of time. In one day's work the laborer will produce more than the socially accepted level of consumption. In (for instance) an eight-hour labor day, it might well be that four hours of work corresponds to the amount of exchange value necessary to reproduce the worker. The commodities produced contain eight hours of labor from the worker's input, but the worker receives four hours of value as wages. That leaves another four hours as surplus. This surplus is the source of profit. The difference is expropriated by the capitalist when commodities are sold at their value. Everything— labor, raw materials, machines, finished commodities—can be exchanged at its value. The worker is (politically, though not practically) free to work or not as she chooses and gets paid for her work. *But the wage is less than the value of what the worker produces.* What looks like a fair exchange is exploitation.

> In wage-labour . . . even surplus-labour, or unpaid labor, appears as paid. [In slavery] the property-relation conceals the labour of the slave for himself; [in capitalism] the money-relation conceals the unrequited labour of the wage-labourer. (Marx 1967 I: 540)

There are many theoretical difficulties with Marx's labor theory of value and theory of exploitation. How is one to "prove," after all, that actual prices are determined by value measured in labor time? How is one to determine the precise amount of "socially necessary" labor time? Is all labor really homogeneous, so that highly-trained labor can be calculated simply as untrained labor plus the cost of training? Can natural differences in skill or creativity be ignored? Is the market really so free that natural scarcity or monopoly don't determine exchange rates more than the value of socially necessary labor? These and related questions have received a great deal of attention.[13]

Putting these debates aside, we can find two crucial implications of Marx's position. First, with the theory of exploitation Marx has identified the key source of class conflict in capitalism. The economic analysis serves as the framework for Marx's political perspective: that the interests of the capitalists and of workers are fundamentally and unalterably opposed. The capitalist strategy is to speed up the production line, demand greater output, and lengthen the working day relative to wages paid. Workers seek to raise the socially necessary labor time required in order to produce labor power; i.e., they try to raise the socially accepted value of labor.

This theoretical model matches the historical realities of the early years of capitalist development in Western Europe (as well as the realities of the newly developing capitalisms of today). In the initial years, before an organized working class could resist, the working day was continually lengthened, wages frequently lowered, and the labor process intensified. This led to conditions of such poverty and physical deterioration that there was some question raised by the government of England as to whether the working class could continue to reproduce itself at all.

Second, the theory of exploitation implies that capitalists have another basic strategy to raise the rate of surplus value: to decrease the amount of labor time necessary to reproduce the worker through the development of ever more efficient and sophisticated forces of production. The number of hours the worker can work has a *maximum* set by her physical limits. However, the amount of time needed to repay the worker's wages has only a technical and thus a nearly limitless *minimum*—one which depends on how much the forces of production are developed. The more sophisticated the production techniques, the less time it takes for the worker to produce commodities equal in value to his wages, and the more of the working day is left for surplus value.

The social changes encouraged by the dynamic of exploitation are relevant to the other main area of Marx's economic theory: the theory of capitalist development. Under this heading, we will now examine his conception of the law-governed dynamic of capitalist expansion and the inevitable tendency of capitalism to recurring economic crises.

For Marx, capitalist development involves "expanded reproduction." In this process capitalists invest in labor, raw materials, and machines to produce commodities and sell the products for more money than they invested. Capitalism is thus not simply production for sale on a free market. Self-employed artisans who simply make enough money to support themselves and replace their tools and raw

26

materials are not capitalists. There is no large-scale hiring of labor, and there is no expanded reproduction. In capitalism there is concentrated wealth and "free labor"; i.e., laborers who must work for wages in order to survive. Capitalists demand not simply the replacement of the capital they invest but *profit* on that capital. They are driven to expand the quantity of expropriated surplus value by lengthening the working day relative to wages, intensifying labor, and making labor more productive by employing labor-saving technology. Increasing investment in technology, however, demands that production occur on a progressively greater scale. More profit must be made to compensate for the greater amount of capital invested. For these reasons, there is a natural tendency for capitalist enterprises to increase in size and to develop new technologies. With expansion of production, capitalism must seek new markets. It does so by replacing production for use with commodity production at home and by penetrating non-capitalist societies abroad.

The drive constantly to develop means of production has another motivation: competition among capitalists. Each capitalist is competing with all others who produce the same commodity, as well as with all others who seek investment. The key to competition is producing goods more cheaply. While this is partly accomplished by lowering wages, the major drive is to introduce increasingly sophisticated production techniques.

In short, capitalism is the only mode of production in which the drive to develop the forces of production is built into the relations of production. All pre-capitalist ruling classes expanded wealth through war or squeezing the slaves or serfs a little harder. Capitalists do this to their workers as well, but without developing the forces of production, they will be destroyed by the competition.

It is this constant development—Marx uses the term "revolutionizing"—of the forces of production that gives capitalism its power as a form of social life and its crucial role in human history. Through its development of productive forces, capitalism offers human beings the capacity to meet their material needs with less labor and to produce new objects—and thus create new needs—on a previously unknown scale. This is why capitalism so easily brushes aside pre-capitalist social relations at home and abroad. Marx was of course bitterly critical of the human costs of the triumph of capitalism: the raging poverty suffered by the creators of wealth, alienation at work, the destruction of the physical environment, and the suffering imposed by the capitalist cycles of booms and busts (see below). Yet by forcing the continual expansion of human productive powers, capitalism paves the way for human victory over material want and scarcity. Capitalism, that is, provides the resources that can be used to create a truly free and fulfilling society.

Paradoxically, the process of capitalist development unfolds in a way which seems singularly *out* of human control. Capitalists who do not compete are eliminated. Workers have to contribute to accumulation by producing surplus value if they are not to starve to death. The system has a logic of its own which transcends contrary desires of any of its participants. The system also shapes those desires, since people naturally tend to conform to the system which determines their material situation.

Why can't this system simply expand forever? Marx's general answer is that the capitalism is structured around a "contradiction": a feature that is both essential to it and which will compel it to change. That feature is the tension between socialized production and private ownership. As capitalism develops, it creates ever larger productive enterprises, ever more national and international economic interdependence, and ever greater sharing of technical resources. Yet control of the production process and of the surplus continues to be held in private hands. The economy is oriented to profits rather than human needs, the production process is unnecessarily alienating, workers are used up and disposed of. From a point of view of the needs and interests of society as a whole, these conditions give rise to too much needless suffering. As in Hegel, a form of life creates resources which can be utilized and problems which can be solved only after sweeping social change.

More concretely, the general contradiction between socialized production and private control gives rise to a series of economic crises. It was these crises, Marx believed, that would eventually tip the scales towards the creation of a new social order.

Capitalist accumulation, Marx argues, occurs when capitalists in-

Hasn't created a new social order.

28

vest to make a profit. If that profit does not appear, capitalists simply withdraw capital and production drastically slows. The succession of favorable and unfavorable conditions for profit making has since been termed the "business cycle." The business cycle begins with favorable conditions for investment. Wages are comparatively low, there is an abundance of labor, raw materials are available, there is widespread demand for products, and profits are high. Since profits are high, more and more money is invested to produce more and more commodities; more workers are hired, more machinery is used. The search for profits fuels competition among capitalists; they compete by trying to produce more efficiently, by driving down wages, by intensifying the labor process, and by lengthening the working day.

Two things then happen.

*First*, there is a pattern of *underconsumption*. Capitalists compete with each other and seek to replace expensive labor by continuously developing the means of production. They do so by investing a significant percentage of the total social surplus in forces of production and using those forces to produce commodities. The end result is an increase in the production of consumer goods. But the percentage of social surplus used to develop the means of production leaves an insufficient amount of wealth in the hands of those—especially workers—who are supposed to consume what is produced. Given the additional attempt to keep wages down, there is not enough "demand"—ability to pay—for what is produced. The working class cannot consume all that it produces and capitalists (and other classes) cannot consume it in other ways. The stores are full of goods which cannot be bought. Profits fall, unemployment rises, there is a depression. The "ultimate reason for all real crises always remains the poverty and restricted consumption of the masses as opposed to the drive of capitalist production to develop the productive forces." (Marx 1967 III: 484)[14]

*Second*, there is a general tendency for the *rate of profit to fall*. In order to compete with other capitalists and lower wages relative to the length of the working day, capitalists increase their investment in productive machinery and techniques ("constant capital"). The ratio of constant capital to "variable capital" (wages) grows. A shrinking percentage of the total investment goes to pay for labor. But since labor is the source of profit, the rate (not the quantity) of profit tends to fall. The profit on investment declines. With this decline there is less and less reason to invest. So investment dries up, unemployment rises, there is less demand, the rate of profit declines, there is less demand—and, again, the result is a depression.[15]

Both underconsumptionist and falling rate of profit explanations of the business cycle can be found in Marx's writings. It is not hard to see how they are linked. The falling rate of profit results from the same structural flaw as the problem of underconsumption: the imbalance between private control of the means of production and the interests of the rest of society.

Both of these crises are "solved" (temporarily) by depressions. In a depression, the price of productive machinery lessens, since the falling rate of profit diminishes the desire to invest. The cost of labor drops, since a high rate of unemployment leads workers to accept lower wages. Many businesses fail, so the normal drive to competition by cutting prices is abated. The result is a renewal of the factors which make for a "healthy" business climate: cheaper constant capital and wages and less competition. The times become ripe for renewed invest-ment. The cycle begins again.

As Marx described it, this circular process was also part of a spiral-like pattern of capitalist development. After every depression, capital gets more concentrated, the productive forces more developed, and both the local and the international economy more dominated by capitalist social relations. Small producers are constantly supplanted by the vastly more efficient and technologically developed capitalist firms. People must earn a living by investing or laboring. And the entire system is subject to greater and greater fluctuations of the busi-ness cycle, since more and more of the world is part of the capitalist system. Expansion leads to crisis and then to more expansion.

In these crises a great part not only of the existing products, but also of the previously created productive forces, are periodically destroyed. . . . There breaks out an epidemic that, in all earlier epochs, would have seemed an absurdity—the epidemic of overproduction. . . . And how does the bourgeoisie get over these crises? on the one hand by enforced destruction of a mass of productive forces; on the other, by the conquest of new markets, and by the more thorough exploitation of the old ones. That is to say, *by paving the way for more extensive and more destructive crises* and by diminishing the means whereby crises are prevented. (Marx and Engels 1954: 25–26, my emphasis)

This spiral of capitalist development leads *inevitably*, Marx claims, to concentration and monopolization, periods of high unemployment and poverty, technological development, and the attrition of small businesses and farms.

Besides these more narrowly economic patterns, Marx diagnosed brilliantly the social effects of capitalist development:

The need of a constantly expanding market for its products chases the bourgeoisie over the whole surface of the globe. . . . In place of old wants, satisfied by the productions of the country, we find new wants, requiring for their satisfaction the products of distant lands and climes. . . . National one-sidedness and narrow-mindedness become more and more impossible. . . . It compels all nations . . . to adopt the bourgeois mode of production. . . . It has created enormous cities . . . as it has made the country dependent on the towns, so it has made barbarian and semi-barbarian countries dependent on the civilized ones. . . . It has agglomerated population, centralized the means of production, and has concentrated property in a few hands. The necessary consequence of this was political centralization. Independent . . . provinces, with separate interests, laws, government, and systems of taxation, become lumped together into one nation, with one government, one code of laws, one national class-interest, one frontier and one customs-tariff. . . . Differences of age and sex have no longer any distinctive social validity. (Marx and Engels 1954: 22–27)

This compelling analysis of the dynamic and effects of capitalism was far ahead of its time. Further, there is the vindication—*at least for this particular period of competitive capitalism*—of Marx's claims about the social primacy of the mode of production. The interests generated by the economic structure did give rise to predictable actions and social changes. As in the example of the condition of women and the family, the entire social fabric became subject to the logic of capitalism. Human relations in general took on the form of commodities, historical change was accelerated by rapid development of technology, education and socialization were adapted to producing workers, owners, and consumers. Competition, the drive for "success," and the freedom to buy, sell, and consume were enshrined as the highest social values. Religion, family life, the physical structure of cities, political institutions—all were re-formed to meet the needs of a society dominated by commodity production.

This system, however, not only forms a world in its own image; it also creates its own undoing.

## POLITICS, REVOLUTION, SOCIALISM

Marx's theory of ideology, we may remember, argues that our understanding of social life, morality, and human relationships is broadly determined by the mode of production. It is on this basis that he can predict the end of capitalism and the advent of socialism. His views on socialist revolution also come from his direct experience of the various European uprisings of 1848, of the First "International" of workers' organizations and radical political parties, and of the revolutionary Paris Commune of 1871. From these events and movements, Marx had immediate knowledge of mass struggles against aristocratic privilege and capitalist power.

Marx's theory of revolution states that capitalist expansion, increasingly severe business cycles, and extensive commodification of social life will have certain predictable effects on the proletariat. As highly developed capitalist enterprises replace independent producers and political strategies undermine peasant communities, the working class will become the majority of the population. As capitalism spreads, people's work experience in particular and social experience in general will become increasingly homogeneous. People will work in similar kinds of jobs, in similar kinds of modernized or modernizing societies. Differences of age, sex, nationality, region, religion or culture will be increasingly unimportant. Class identity will determine self-understanding and values. The increasing severity of the capitalist business cycle will have increasingly bitter effects on workers' lives. The proletariat will experience recurrent bouts of unemployment, dire poverty, constant attempts by capitalists to run speedups or lower wages, and physical/cultural dislocation. Even if workers' absolute standard of living improves, the gap between them and the ruling class will increase. These experiences will create a growing class consciousness among workers, an awareness of shared interests and common situation.

> The highest development of productive power together with the greatest expansion of existing wealth will coincide with the depreciation of capital, degradation of the labourer, and a most straitened exhaustion of his vital powers. These contradictions lead to explosions, cataclysms, crises. . . . These regularly recurring catastrophes lead to their repetition on a higher scale, and finally to [capitalism's] violent overthrow. (Marx 1973: 750)

Since it is their labor which is the source of social wealth, the working class has the potential social power to overthrow capitalism. Other groups may dislike capitalism, but none are central to the social structure. As the class that suffers most from the business cycle, it has clear and immediate interests in establishing socialism. As the potential inheritor of immense technological development, it has resources for the realization of human freedom. Once productive powers are unchained from the logic of profit, they can be directed to human fulfillment. As the enemy of the ruling class, the proletariat has an interest in eliminating all forms of oppression that politically divide workers. Racism, ethnic hatred, male chauvinism, etc., only distract attention from the "real" enemy. After capitalism is eliminated, they will disappear. For these reasons, the proletariat is the "universal" class in the sense that the redress of its wrongs will signal the liberation of all of humanity. While other classes—e.g., the bourgeoisie in its appeal to "human" rights—claim to represent all of society, only the working class will in fact do so.

> The condition for the emancipation of the working class is the abolition of every class. . . . The working class . . . will substitute for the old civil society an association which will exclude classes and their antagonism. . . . (Marx 1963: 174)

While the workers' objective condition is radicalizing them, "communists" will organize, agitate, and teach. Their specific message should always to be twofold. First, they will help people facing *local* conditions of exploitation become aware of their common cause with the *national* and *global* interests of the working class as a whole. Second, they will teach that these conditions of oppression cannot be overcome in any final or adequate way by *reforms*. Only with the complete removal of the structural opposition between capitalists and workers will the full potential of social life be reached.

What kind of social life did Marx expect "after the revolution"? Most generally, he envisaged a set of social relations which would end systematic class antagonisms and harmonize personal fulfillment and social justice. The technological development of capitalism would drastically shrink the amount of time necessary to meet material needs, even needs which had grown with the increase of the productive forces. The means of production would be subject to democratic, egalitarian relations of production. They could then serve human needs rather than private profit. Also, the systematic ideological distortions of capitalist society would be eliminated. Social relations would no longer hide exploitation under the mask of the wage contract; the fetishism of commodities would no longer obscure the fact that human activities determine social life. In short, social life would be characterized by freedom, equality of power, a just exchange of labor for money, and rational organization. In the first stage, which he called "socialism," exploitation would be eliminated and workers would receive fair recompense for their work. As society fully adjusted to the revolutionary changes, the forces of production further matured, and people's values and understanding of social solidarity came to match the evolving relations of production, society could move towards "communism." Here people no longer work for wages, even "fair" wages. Creative activity comes to be the dominant mode of self-expression, and people function under the maxim: "From each according to his ability, to each according to his needs." (Marx, *Critique of the Gotha Program*, in Tucker 1972: 388)

Marx's ideas about the concrete political structures of socialism derive from his general theory of political life. He believed that political institutions generally are a reflection of the interests and balance of forces of economic classes. Typically, political power is wielded by the ruling class or its representatives and is used to maintain and advance its rule. While claiming to represent everyone (the "nation," "God's will," etc.), the state under capitalism is often simply "a committee for managing the *common* affairs of the *whole* bourgeoisie." (Marx and Engels 1954: 18, my emphasis) At other times, conflicts within the ruling class or between the ruling and the exploited class may make it necessary to give some independence to the government/ state or to have some intermediary group take power.[16] When class struggle rises, we see corresponding political (and ideological) struggle: uprisings, radical political parties, revolutions. In any case, understanding the state ultimately requires understanding how it reflects or serves the interests of economic classes. Like the realm of ideology, politics has no real autonomy of its own. That is why turning to political reform—e.g., laws protecting workers or regulating capitalists—is at best a temporary measure producing limited improvement in workers' lives. Since politics expresses interests derived from the class structure, political action must ultimately be aimed at defending or overthrowing that structure.

What are the politics of a classless, post-capitalist society? Marx never provided a detailed answer to this question, believing (consistently) that such an answer could only be forthcoming during and after a major revolutionary upheaval. But from comments he made during the entire course of his life, we know that his model of socialist politics had the following three features. First, it was *democratic*, giving ordinary citizens some direct control over social life. Yet Marx was careful to distinguish socialist from liberal or bourgeois democracy. The political life of capitalism used political equality (voting) to mask economic inequality (private control of the means of production). Socialist democracy extends popular power to *all* critical dimensions of social life, especially key economic decisions. This should not involve collective control over personal matters. But it should extend to those economic issues which have major implications for the community. Modern economic life is simply too complex and interdependent to be left to private interests. Socialist politics would also be *representative*. Representatives should be recallable by popular vote at any time, have a salary equal to no more than that of the average factory worker, and conduct governmental deliberations in an open and accessible way. Consequently, the socialist state should function *in the interests of the vast majority of the population*. With the eventual end of class domination, political life would simply become a matter of rational, non-conflictual administration.

These three characteristics, drawn directly and without interpretation from Marx's explicit statements, refute any claims that he would have supported political tyranny of any kind. When he spoke of a "dictatorship of the proletariat," he had in mind the coercive force necessary to end capitalist power and represent the interests of the vast mass of the population. Any government which is undemocratic, outlaws labor unions, uses physical intimidation on ordinary citizens to get them to support the power of a particular clique of leaders, or restricts freedom of expression or association is simply not functioning in accord with Marx's ideas. While Marx's theory had many errors and limitations, an attraction to dictatorships is not one of them.

## IS SOCIALISM POSSIBLE?

In subsequent chapters I will criticize Marx's overall philosophical framework, analysis of capitalism, and political strategy. I will conclude here by defending his conception of socialism against two frequently made criticisms.

It is often argued[17] that however attractive some people might find it, socialism is simply incompatible with human nature. People are too aggressive, competitive, and selfish to live in a cooperative, non-hierarchical society. They will always want to be better off or more powerful than others. Expecting us to live for the social good rather than our own betterment is simply unrealistic.

A Marxist reply cautions against reading into all of human life the specific psychology generated by capitalism. Of course a mode of production structured by economic competition will produce competitive people, and our educational system and culture foster this mentality. But a non-ideological examination of the record will show countless societies in which people simply did not think in terms of getting ahead, progress, or doing better than their neighbor. In those societies people were rooted in tradition and community. Their sense of themselves was not defined by separation from others, but by connection to them. This kind of selfhood will, Marx believes, reappear under socialism.

The argument from a competitive human nature also ignores the countless instances of cooperation and support which occur even in capitalism. Within family life, on athletic teams, in times of war or national emergency, self-interested strategizing can give way to empathy, cooperation, and caring in which the good of the self and the good of the group unite.

Further, the notion of a human nature constraining social life is itself an ideological illusion. At best, Marx claims, we can say that it is our "human nature" to be social, rooted in nature, and creative. But such a human nature neither determines the form which social life must take nor provides a universal basis for limiting human fulfillment.

Second, it has been argued against Marx that without competition and hierarchy, an economy just cannot function effectively. Where is the motivation to do well or to create? Where is the reward for talent or hard work? In the enforced equality of socialism, we will have a bland and safe economic world of mediocrity. The competitive, progress-creating drive of capitalism will be lost.

Marx would again suggest that we take a closer look at the actualities of capitalist society. While capitalism has been spectacularly successful at technological development, such development is now hardly the work of isolated individuals. At this point in time, the complicated structure of technology makes innovation a matter of the cooperation of large numbers of researchers, scientists, engineers, product developers, etc. When we consign most of the population to alienated labor and social subservience, we lose a tremendous measure of creativity that could contribute to this process. In a socialist society, in which the labor process would not be organized to make workers powerless and unskilled, that creativity could be tapped.[18] Additionally, structuring the economy towards profit rather than need has resulted in ecological devastation and distorted technology. One need only think how different a rational, socially-oriented transportation system might be.

It is also not essential to Marx's vision of socialism that all wages be equal or all workers have the same responsibilities. He wanted an end to exploitation, not a mechanical uniformity. People might well receive higher wages for harder, more dangerous, or more demanding jobs. And complex production would clearly demand some delegation of tasks and some managerial structure. What is outlawed under social-ism, however, is allowing wealth or management to provide unjust social power and the right to exploit others. A particularly hardwork-ing or creative worker might make much more money that someone else, but he would not therefore get the power to organize society for his benefit at others' expense.

The critic of socialism may well pause at this point in the argument. However, there probably will remain the unspoken thought: "But look at the endless oppression, violence, and exploitation in human history. Is it really possible that this can be changed?"

Marx's answer is, as we have seen, that it can. And he believed his confidence in this outcome was justified by a rational assessment of history and social life. We shall now see to what extent that confidence was justified.

# 2

# MARXISM: BASIC FLAWS

In a sense, we are all Marxists. Whatever our opinions of the Soviet Union or Cuba, it is generally acknowledged that economic structure and class conflict are central to social life, and that human identity is decisively shaped by historical change. These broad insights of Marxism permeate virtually all social theories. Yet Marx's theory also has some very basic weaknesses which will be sketched here and described in greater detail in subsequent chapters.

Consider, for instance, that while Marx's immediate predictions for the future of capitalist society were confirmed, his more long-term expectations about economic crises and political revolution have been disappointed. Advanced capitalism has become more, not less, stable. At present there is no international socialist movement of any kind, and working-class struggles have generally aimed at immediately beneficial reforms rather than revolutionary change. Also, many oppressed groups have not looked to workers for political leadership, and there have been sources of radical political consciousness other than economic exploitation.

Equally perplexing to traditional Marxism are dramatic social developments—the threat to world ecology, the advent of mass consumer culture, the enormous role of the state in capitalist economies, the continuing relevance of racial, ethnic, and national antagonisms—which Marxism (at least in its original form) seems to comprehend but poorly. We also find, contrary to Marx's expectations, that spiritual values and religious identity continue to motivate people in powerful ways.

Perhaps most threateningly, self-proclaimed Marxists, communists, and socialists have taken power in a number of relatively backward countries and created tyrannical and exploitative regimes. The end of capitalism (such as it was) or colonialism in these countries at times led to increases in the standard of living but all too often came with a denial of human rights. With the recent collapse of most of these regimes, the very language of Marxism is for many people synonymous with political brutality and economic failure.

As we examine the basic flaws of Marxism, we will ask what lessons they—and the often painful history of social-democracy and communism (Chapters 3 and 4)—have for those of us who seek to use Marxism as a tool for human liberation in the present.

## LAWS OF HISTORY?

Perhaps the most fundamental problem of Marxism arises when its purportedly "scientific" analysis of society is detached from its basic insight that human beings create themselves in history. With this separation, it is forgotten that the social structures described by historical materialism are the products of human action. Then the mode of production can be mistakenly thought of as something different from the actions of socially connected, living human beings. The mode of production seems to take on a life of its own, appearing to be a power or structure controlling human action "from the outside."

In one version of this position, our supposedly "scientific" analysis of the mode of production gives us generalizations that are like those of natural science. We think of them as embodying universal laws of human development rather than as what they in fact are: temporarily stable patterns of human action in particular social, technical, and cultural contexts. We see these laws defining the past and guaranteeing the future, working with "iron necessity toward inevitable results," (Marx 1967 I: 8) like the laws governing planetary motion. This flawed view asserts that since the law-governed economy determines social structure and historical change, *we may know the entire social future on the basis of an analysis of the present economy.* Experience, consciousness, and desire—in short, people—are products of something essentially inhuman.

In another variation, Marxism becomes a secular religion. The development of the mode of production is thought to express a Necessary Force of History, with Marxism as the key to understanding this Force. Human life is seen as a compulsive teleological growth towards the fulfillment of the human species, inevitably leading to a golden future in which all alienation and oppression are eliminated. As servants of the ultimate purpose of human existence, Marxists know that their politics are correct because they serve the God of History, as described by the one true Prophet: Marx.[1]

In still another form of separating the mode of production from the ongoing experience, beliefs, and values of human beings, Marxism claims to find a universal drive towards technological development. This drive is supposed to animate all societies and create an ever-present human tendency towards the development of the means of production. This tendency underlies local outbursts of class struggle and guarantees the eventual creation of a rational social order. As Marx put it in one of his least apt but most frequently quoted passages: "the hand-mill *gives you* society with the feudal lord; the steam-mill society with the industrial capitalist." (Marx 1963: 109 my emphasis).

These positions contain profound errors. They are also distortions of the most powerful elements of Marx's original position. To the extent that human beings *make themselves over time*, we should not interpret historical materialism as providing natural laws of social development, or a metaphysical History which guarantees the outcome of social life, or a universal drive towards technological development. Yet while these views do not dominate Marx's work, they can all be found in it. Thus, subsequent distortions of Marx are not without some foundation in the original theory.

The quasi-religious, Marxist trust in a guaranteed future is mainly of historical interest, and I will discuss it as part of the communist betrayal of Marxism in Chapter 4. The claim that there is a universal human drive to develop forces of production will be assessed in Chapter 8. The version which claims scientific status for Marxism is the most important and most dangerous of the above tendencies, and I will focus on it here.

This view replicates in Marxism an intellectual tendency endemic to much of modern social life, one often referred to as positivism (or scientism).[2] For positivism, natural science is the sole or preferred form of knowledge. Therefore, a "scientific" or "rational" account of the social world should have the same form as our knowledge of nature; i.e., it should have an "objective," value-free stance; produce universal, exceptionless generalizations describing the behavior of the objects in question; and explain those generalizations by reference to universal laws which themselves are the products of a hidden or unseen "deep structure." For example, our theory of molecules allows us to explain the wide range of behavior of common objects (freezing, boiling, burning, rusting, etc.) by referring that behavior to a structure hidden to the naked eye and paradoxical to the commonsense understanding of solid objects. Newton's laws of motion show how the movement of footballs, cannonballs, billiard balls, and planets are all effects of the same universal forces. For positivist Marxism, the laws of capitalist development explain social life in a comparable way. They describe the underlying structure and provide laws of change for human action. Like Newton's laws or molecular theory, this knowledge can be had in abstraction from human self-understanding or desires. They allow us to explain and predict without knowing what people believe or feel.

We should first note that the general positivist understanding of natural science has been under serious attack for nearly twenty-five years. Philosophers and historians of science have pointed to the way natural scientists do not simply record or understand "nature" but function within traditions defined by ingrained suppositions or paradigms. Critics have also argued that particular sciences and technologies are influenced by cultural values or class biases. Moreover, it has been pointed out that far from being value free, science requires ethical norms of free inquiry and criticism, and that its understanding of the natural world as simply a collection of objects to be used up is a premise for which no final justification can be offered.[3]

Positivist Marxism is also deeply flawed because of the essential differences between human beings and physical objects, and therefore between social theory and natural science. For one thing, understanding and belief play no part in the behavior of the physical systems described by science. Yet the situation for social life is dramatically different. Social life is partly made up of—constituted—by what people believe and want. Human beings *experience* social life, learn from it, and have their understanding and intentions altered in the process. The feel of permanence and solidity which surrounds systems of ownership and political power arises because these are long-term, widely accepted forms of human life. They may therefore appear to be distinguishable from the persons who create them. But they are in actuality sustained by the repetition of human activities and the reproduction of human relationships. We fabricate our world through our passive acceptance of what we have and our active participation in particular activities and institutions. We understand ourselves as capitalists or workers; we accept those roles; and we devise forms of popular culture, political ideology, and self-conception to make it all work. Without particular forms of human self-understanding, the mode of production does not exist. What we do stems partly from what people think is justified, fair, or desirable.

Human consciousness is thus not a consequence of the mode of production but part of it. Of course our beliefs, desires, and values should not be thought of as separate from and determining concrete social relations (as in Hegel). Our ideas do not magically emerge from our minds, but are produced by—and produce—our society. Positivist Marxists simply inverted Hegel when they mistakenly interpreted historical materialism as sharply distinguishing between physical reality and immaterial consciousness. Social structures are human products and as such embody human consciousness. The "material" in historical materialism is meant to refer to conscious, collective human activity, especially social labor. This activity may at times be predictable, or misunderstood by the agents, or described in a distorted way; but it is nevertheless ultimately susceptible to the understanding and control of the people involved. Thus, when human experience and understanding are altered, past "laws" of social life become simply the outworn habits of the past. Without truly timeless laws, social life is fundamentally different from the natural world, and Marxism cannot be a "science."

In concrete terms, this means capitalist development takes the form of a law-governed historical process only *until* collective social agents begin consciously to alter it. Present capitalism is different from earlier capitalism not because one mechanical, law-governed process replaced another. Rather, it has changed partly because capitalists, workers, politicians, bureaucrats, and intellectuals have subjectively experienced and responded to past events. For instance, during and after the Depression of the 1930s—in which virtually all the developed capitalist world was wracked by crushing unemployment, dire poverty, and the collapse of major industries—leading capitalists, government managers, and organized workers developed strategies for changing society. The result was a fundamentally different kind of capitalism, one in which the economic role of the government and the political influence of the working class were now central factors. Since capitalism was no longer at the mercy of the business cycle, the rigidities of its development were softened by political struggle. No set of laws could predict this outcome. It came from a creative response to the crisis.

Another critical flaw in the positivist version of Marxism is that it cannot see that what gives "impersonal" historical events significant historical meaning is the way people relate to them. In particular, the social meaning of economic changes—for instance, a depression—is determined by the consciousness and political organization of classes. Now Marx never denies that human beings act in terms of their understanding and desires. He does not see people as automata, and he frequently chronicles the workers' political struggles.[4] But his (and his followers') positivist versions of historical materialism imply that *we can confidently predict just what our future understanding and desires will be, for they are in broad outline the product of the mode of production.* Working class political consciousness and action come from the workers' economic position, and the long-term political behavior of economic classes is a more-or-less predictable outcome of the economic system.

Consider, for example, Marx's comments on how the working-class movement to limit the working day "had grown *instinctively* out of the conditions of production themselves." The worker "*comes out of the process of production other than he entered. . . .*" (Marx 1967 I: 301, my emphasis) On the contrary, however, history has clearly shown that the social meaning of economic experiences *depends* on how they are experienced by the human beings who are living them out. A new production process, unemployment, or struggles with owners may all change the workers. But no pre-given schema can tell us what that change will be. The Great Depression led to fascism in Germany, welfare state liberalism in England, the New Deal in the U.S. There was no common, given, predetermined meaning. Rather, while the "laws" of capitalist development created the economic crisis, the different social consequences of that crisis were determined by how people understood and responded to it. That understanding and response, in turn, cannot be known simply from an analysis of the mode of production. The kind of certitude Marx frequently expressed is simply not justified. It stems from a crude economic determinism which offers an ultimately unjustified political confidence based on the economic present. In this passage, he claims that with the growing concentration of capital following each depression:

grows the mass of misery, oppression, slavery, degradation, exploitation; but with this too grow the revolt of the working-class, a class always increasing in numbers, and disciplined, united, organized by the very mechanism of the process of capitalist production itself. The monopoly of capital becomes a fetter upon the mode of production. . . . Centralisation of the means of production and socialisation of labour at last reach a point where they become incompatible with their capitalist integument. This integument is burst asunder. The knell of capitalist private property sounds. The expropriators are expropriated. (Marx 1967 III: 763)

Such frequently expressed confidence in the inevitability of a socialist revolution may have been part rhetorical political overstatement. But it also suggests that Marx retained a Hegelian perspective: while Hegel trusted in the hidden force of God, the historical materialist has faith that Progress will inevitability lead to secular Enlightenment.[5]

We must further recognize that intellectual assessments of social life can fundamentally alter the behavior of people who come to accept them. Past regularities are not indefinitely repeated; rather, collective awareness of such regularities leads to their transformation.

Consider the following two cases.

Before the Russian Revolution, government leaders and the rich in Russia watched as the more developed capitalism of Western Europe gave rise to leftist parties and trade unions. Russian capitalists were therefore wary about making common cause with workers and peasants in pursuit of the kind of "bourgeois revolution" which had occurred in more developed capitalist nations. The revolutions of France, England, and the U.S. sought to replace the inherited privilege and monarchies of pre-modern societies with the rights and relationships of liberal democracy. In the absence of a capitalist-worker-peasant alliance for a democratic, capitalist revolution, the working class and peasantry of Russia could seek rights and land reform only under the political and ideological leadership of socialists, anarchists, and communists. The end result was a revolution led by self-proclaimed Marxists in a country in which capitalism was at a very primitive stage. This outcome was very different from the Marxist scenario in which capitalist development paved the way for socialism. Thus, Soviet history is partly the consequence of an awareness of earlier events, and *not* a law-governed repetition of them.

After the revolution, the ruling classes in Western Europe and the

U.S. had to take account of the self-proclaimed socialist or revolutionary forces in the Soviet Union and abroad. Struggles with workers, responses to the business cycle, foreign policy—all these came to follow a logic not just of capitalist accumulation but of political reactions to (real or imagined) political threats. These developments are not seriously considered in Marx's original theory.

Two major conclusions follow from our rejection of positivist Marxism. *First*, there is nothing fixed or final about the course of capitalist development or its transition to socialism. In its early phases, the capitalist economy was liberated from the control of politics, tradition, religion, and community. People were free to sell, invest, and trade as never before. And the logic of the system compelled them to do so in the ways Marx described. Yet as time wore one, people's experience of capitalism made it possible for them to alter it. The "laws" of capitalist development could exist only as long as people failed to see their consequences and act to change them. And in fact, capitalism is no longer subject to laws of development. Since political alliances, organizations, and struggles now partly dictate how the economy unfolds and what social changes economic developments will bring, *politics now joins the mode of production as socially primary.*

*Second*, even if the capitalist economy remains subject to the business cycle, this fact tells us little about the political future of bourgeois society. The historical importance of economic facts stems from the way people understand them, feel them, and respond to them. A depression cannot motivate people to revolutionary action if they blame themselves for being out of work rather than the weaknesses of an economy controlled by large corporations. Public evidence of government incompetence is politically irrelevant if people have no self-confidence in their own ability to control basic economic/political processes. The failures of capitalism are irrelevant if people believe that there are no feasible alternatives. If the ideological universe poses only the United States or the Soviet Union as possibilities, who in their right mind wouldn't choose the U.S.? Therefore, any attempt to change society is politically insignificant if people are socialized to be unable to cooperate or cannot imagine a society not dominated by competition, greed, and consumerism.

Whatever the economic development of capitalism may be, there can be no historical assurance that it will create a radical political consciousness. People's self-understanding, desires, and ways of inter-acting are thus essential to the process of revolution. Without funda-mental change in consciousness, strictly economic changes may as easily serve the continuity of capitalism or the emergence of another form of class power as they are to give rise to human liberation. Like politics, then, the socialization processes which shape our conscious-ness have become socially primary.

Our final criticism of positivist Marxism has to do with the way it has been used to justify political repression, one-party rule, and dogmatism. When historical materialism is viewed as a science, then the consciousness of social agents can be seen as a predictable outcome of impersonal social processes. The self-proclaimed "masters" of Marxist theory have at times used this view to justify exercising power over workers rather than awakening their political consciousness. The result has been insurrections led by an elite or totalitarianism dominated by a narrow clique of entrenched bureaucrats.[6]

In sum, my rejection of positivist Marxism has stressed the follow-ing: there are no laws of social life; persistent social regularities exist only as long as they are not seen or understood by members of society; and, therefore, the evolution of society towards liberation, freedom, and reason depends on our shared understanding of social life and our capacity to act collectively on that understanding. The political implication is that the creation of socialism is, in fact, exactly the same thing as the increase in consciousness and political organization of the mass of the population.

## REPRODUCTION, IDEOLOGY, AND SOCIAL DIFFERENTIATION

We have seen that positivist Marxism ignores the dimension of human self-creation in favor of "laws" of social life. Our next criticism, which will be developed in greater detail throughout the book, focuses on flaws in Marx's conception of what the process of self-making is. The difficulties stem from the fact that Marx and many of his followers understood human identity and history mainly or exclusively in terms of the economy: the development of production techniques, the labor process, control of the final product, the social struggle over the surplus.

The first critical absence in this picture has to do with the biological and emotional reproduction of human beings themselves; with the processes of pregnancy, childbirth, child rearing, and emotional nurturance. Since these processes are biologically or culturally the concern of women, the Marxist model of social life and historical change is inadequate to women's experiences and interests. The traditional Marxist position has been that women's oppression is a consequence of the mode of production; that women's entry into paid labor will end women's special oppression and gather them into the same work and political situation as male workers; and that therefore women ultimately have the same political needs and interests as men. This position (see Chapter 6) has been effectively challenged because it trivializes the exploitation of women, the special contribution of women's household, reproductive, and relational labor, and women's corresponding political *interests*. While Marx was in fact sensitive to certain forms of women's oppression, he never seriously asked whether women's social inequality might have roots in anything other than the "public" mode of production; e.g., that it might be rooted in male domination in family and cultural life as well. Nor did he consider the central role child-rearing practices and family life might have on the consciousness and political development of the working class. The way attachment to male domination distorts radical politics both within the working class as a whole and in purportedly radical political groups and movements was similarly ignored. The traditional Marxist framework simply could not raise some key questions. For example: Could childhood exposure to an authoritarian, male-dominated family create a psychic attachment to authority which is incompatible with truly liberating politics? Could a healthy rather than a repressed sexuality be central to our individual personalities or our capacity to create a politically non-repressive society?

Just as Marx thought gender identity would diminish in importance with the growth of capitalism, so he felt that differences of ethnicity, nationality, race, and religion would also become politically unimportant. Since consciousness derives from the mode of production, and the mode of production was becoming homogeneous, so the consciousness of workers would become increasingly similar. The failure of this claim is shown by daily headlines indicating continuing racial, ethnic, or religious strife; as well as by the two cataclysmic world wars which shaped the twentieth century. It is true that certain national differences have lessened—e.g., among successive waves of white, European immigrant groups in the U.S. or within Europe itself. Yet a host of antagonisms remain; for example, racism against blacks in the U.S., conflict between Catholic and Protestant in Northern Ireland, and separatist movements in France and Canada. With the collapse of the Soviet Union and a reunified Germany, anti-Semitism *again* surfaces, and ethnic antagonisms in Eastern Europe threaten massive violence. People live in societies structured by commodity production. Yet they still think and act in terms of different national, racial, religious, and ethnic bonds.

How could Marxism have been so wrong about these issues? How could it have misinterpreted the *interaction* between the economy and the forces of racism, sexism, anti-Semitism, nationalism, etc., as a simple *dependence* of the latter on the former? The problem lies in a very restricted view of what people are. While our class identity is essential, so too are factors such as our gender, race, nationality, or ethnicity. Focusing so much on material production, Marx made light of the way these other elements determine personal experience and political consciousness. For a traditional Marxist analysis, a black worker and white worker, a Jewish tailor and a Polish one, a steel-worker and his wife, are economically—and therefore politically—pretty much the same. But these people will often experience social life, use cultural resources, and feel social solidarity in quite different ways. In terms of personal and political identity, they may often lead very separate lives. These separations—which I will now call forms of "social differentiation"—are essential to personal identity and must be factored into any political prediction or program.

This point requires that the concept of "ideology" be dramatically extended. Traditionally, the term referred pretty much exclusively to consciously held beliefs which reflected and/or supported existing social relations. Subsequent social developments and the failures of leftist movements indicate that this conception is too limited. Our identity involves much more than conscious beliefs about what is true or false. We are socialized as children and continually molded as adults not just by false beliefs, but by learning to feel certain emotions and to express them in particular ways, developing exploitative or deferential attitudes towards other people and nature, repressing physical and sexual spontaneity and intellectual creativity, and identifying particular figures as role models or authority figures. In other words, ideology involves not just conscious beliefs but an *entire personality*. Capitalist society creates particular types of people as well as the acceptance of particular beliefs. To fit with capitalism, we must be more comfortable with authoritarian social relations than with equality, dependent on consumption to measure self-worth, seek competition rather than cooperation, and be individualistic and/or narrowly chauvinistic in our relations with others. Conversely, *the overthrow of capitalism requires the creation of a new personality structure*. If this is not part of the revolutionary process, the contradictions of capitalism may lead to a new social form which is no closer to human liberation than what it replaced. Simply changing private ownership for state ownership and calling ourselves "socialist" is not nearly enough. We need corresponding changes in our sense of what it is to be men and women, in our interactions with others, and in our sense of self-worth. These characteristics help shape our responses to the economic instabilities and injustices of class society and will be central in determining to what extent we can form effective and liberating political movements. They need to be recognized intellectually and *also* internalized. The failures of socialist and communist movements indicate what can happen if this transformation does not occur. Leftist movements have often been totalitarian, dogmatic, and self-interested. Leaders have often been on extended, macho power trips. These possibilities were not considered by Marx, but they became realities when people tried to put his theories into practice.

## IMPERIALISM

Marx was quite aware of how European colonialism generated wealth to fuel the early expansion of capitalism. "Primitive accumulation"— the basis of capitalist development—has two elements: creating a landless proletariat by driving peasants off the land, and generating concentrations of wealth. Tremendous resources came to Spain, Holland, France, and England, the first capitalist or proto-capitalist powers, by direct exploitation of colonies. Yet Marx also believed that capitalism's penetration of the non-capitalist world generally led to progress. Despite the enormous misery it caused in the short run, he claimed, it would eventually break down the comparatively primitive local economy, integrating it into a worldwide capitalist market and productive system.

Beginning with Lenin, however, many later Marxist theorists have seen a different picture. They have transformed the analysis of advanced capitalist *nations* into an analysis of a capitalist or imperialist *world-system*. From the late nineteenth century to the present, this view contends, capitalist nations have used the Third World for access to investment, cheap raw materials and labor, favorable conditions of trade set by force, and accessible markets. These factors condition the spectacular growth of Western capitalism and make possible the high standard of living which "buys off" workers in the West from revolutionary politics. This worldwide division of labor linked industrial capitalism to stagnation and economic distortion of much of the Third World. The development of Europe was made possible by the underdevelopment of other areas, and the initial development of capitalism precluded its own repetition elsewhere.

In this view, social contradictions between capitalists and workers have been shifted to conflicts between capitalist nations and the Third World. Since wealth in capitalist countries depends on the exploitation of underdeveloped countries, we find a potential *antagonism* between these groups, an antagonism not seriously addressed in original Marxism. Alliances between First World workers and capitalists in support of continued domination of the Third World can result.

This picture suggests political strategies not tied to the industrial working class. Third World peasants and workers may become the revolutionary, anti-capitalist vanguard. To the extent that capitalist development depends on unequal exchange, the ending of imperialist relations—not internal overproduction/underconsumption—may be the cause of economic crisis in developed nations. It is also hoped that Third World movements will serve as examples of and catalysts for political activity in advanced nations.[7]

## MORALITY AND HAPPINESS

The motivation for revolutionary change, Marx claimed, is based on two conditions: the tendency of capitalism to exploit workers; and the contrast between the possibilities created by capitalism and the realities of an unstable economy, concentrated wealth, and the organization of production for profit rather than human needs.

Yet this picture is challenged by the facts. A reformed capitalism has made the business cycle less severe and provided a more than adequate material life for the majority of the working class. In the words of French socialist André Gorz: "The working class will not unite politically or man the barricades for the sake of a 10 percent wage increase or an extra 50,000 dwellings." (Gorz 1973: 135)

If revolution is not linked to material betterment, what vision of human life *will* inform an overthrow of capitalism? This question was answered very inadequately by Marx. I doubt that he had the theoretical resources to approach it. His theory of ideology typically analyzed ethical values as direct consequences of class relations. While he himself was clearly outraged by the exploitation and oppression of workers, the origins of his own sense of morality are pretty obscure.

As Allen Buchanan (1982) observes, there is even a reasonable question about whether it is ever rational for any member of the working class to participate in a socialist movement. An individual worker may weigh the drawbacks and dangers of becoming a revolutionary and then simply wait for others to do so and reap the rewards of their actions.[8] A similar point is raised by Georg Lukács (1975). Writing immediately after the Russian Revolution, he asks how workers and peasants in backward countries will respond to the necessary self-sacrifice of the early years of industrialization. How will they willingly pay the price of restricted consumption as they produce the infrastructure of a new economy? Workers of capitalist countries had to be forced to do so by the inequality of class power. In a post-revolutionary society, however, power is supposedly in the hands of the masses.

Jürgen Habermas makes a related criticism when he suggests that there is something of a tendency for Marx (and his more traditional followers) to reduce problems of human interaction to simple conse-quences of the structure of production; that is, to believe that overcom-ing exploitation and oppression is simply a matter of making social production truly efficient. Rational production may be part of a liber-ated society, argues Habermas, but there is more to it than simply collective control of the means of production.[9] We need to free human interaction as well as eliminate the business cycle and meet material needs. While Marx is not consistent on this point, he does sometimes write as if oppressive work relations are the basis of all other oppres-sion, and that capitalism will destroy itself simply by its own ineffi-ciency.[10] He often seems to view debates about the values governing human interaction as secondary to questions of class power and eco-nomic organization.

On a more philosophical level of criticism, we can question Marx's notion that human fulfillment depends ultimately on conscious and controlled activity. His model of happiness, as we saw in Chapter 1, is free creation. He often took the artist's activity as the most complete or satisfying form of life. Yet we may ask (briefly, anticipating a more extensive discussion in Chapter 9): Are there not other dimensions of human existence that may be as essential to human fulfillment? Could Marx's ideal itself be ideological, stemming from a limited view which sees work as the central category of human life? In fact, the ideology behind Marx's position has affinities to a capitalist mentality which views production and the acquisition of money as the most important of human activities. It is also a *male* perspective. Work is central to the life of most men: either alienated toil which must be performed because we need money, or creative work which fuels our self-respect and self-image. Yet this is often not the case for women, who typically find as much (or more) of their self-identity in relations to other people as they do in labor.[11] While these relationships may occur in the context of earning a living, there is an aspect which has to do with unmediated emotional connection to other people. This connection is not focused on making a product or expanding knowledge. It is person rather than task oriented, and has to do with creating a bond based on a shared situation of experiencing the world as feeling beings. Our model of a fulfilling society is clearly incomplete and male-biased when this dimension of human life is left out.

These problems reveal central dilemmas for Marx's theory of revolution and for any Marxian perspective on ethics and human fulfillment. Three general conclusions may be offered.

First, as Jean-Paul Sartre pointed out, Marxism needs to accommodate itself to some of the central intuitions of Existentialism; i.e., it must understand the continuing importance of individual choice as a determiner of the fate of particular human beings. The explanation of human action in terms of the *situation* of class society must coexist with a recognition of the human *project* (to use Sartre's [1963] terms) of determining through personal choices what the ultimate meaning of that situation will be. Our objective class or group interests must ultimately be validated by our subjective commitment to those interests—as opposed, say, to our attempt to escape into another class or group, or sit idly by while others struggle. We cannot take this ethical commitment for granted.

Second, we need to understand revolutionary motivation and images of a liberated society in a manner informed by feminist understanding of the importance of emotionally based solidarity. The revolutionary process may not stem from a rational calculation of individual betterment, but from a felt need to join with others to create collective satisfaction, or save the Earth, or protect our children's future. We may have to recognize that socialism simply cannot be created by people who experience themselves as separate individuals seeking a higher standard of living.

Third, we should see that sustained argument over conflicting concepts of goodness, justice, and human satisfaction continue to be necessary even "after the revolution." Traditional Marxism had a tendency to dismiss such discussions as irretrievably ideological, bound by values and forms of reasoning which are the product of class interests. While the role of ideological distortions may, in fact, always be substantial, we still need to confront, as humanely as possible, individual differences in our vision of a liberating society. Such discussion must examine in critical detail Marx's supposition that the essential constituent of a good life for human beings is creative objectification. Feminist theory has stressed the importance of the affective and relational dimensions of human existence. The continuing role of religion shows us that spiritual pursuits have a surprisingly lasting importance, even after the development of modern technology, science, and mass society.

# II

## BETRAYAL

# 3

## SOCIAL-DEMOCRACY: THE PLAGUE OF POSITIVISM

Marx died in 1883, Engels in 1895. Between these dates and the start of World War I, Marxist theory dominated the world socialist movement. The rise and fall of this movement reveals some of the essential strengths and weaknesses of Marxism. A series of critical questions emerged when actual human beings, involved in real political struggles, attempted to guide their actions by Marxist theory. Among these questions were the following:

1. Is capitalism following Marx's predictions towards self-destruction and replacement by socialism—or can the capitalist economy transform itself in ways not expected by Marx?

2. What political strategy will lead to socialism? How do economic struggles for an increased standard of living and political struggles for increased political rights affect each other? How should socialists connect *immediate* attempts to improve the lives of the working class with the *ultimate* goal of the fundamental transformation of capitalist society? That is, how do we balance *reform* and *revolution*?
3. Does a Marxist-oriented class consciousness arise spontaneously, or does it have to be brought into the working class by others? As we build toward the overthrow of capitalism, do some sources of socialist consciousness exist outside and independent of political parties guided by experts in Marxist theory? After the revolution, are there independent sources of theory and political power outside the party-dominated state?
4. How should we understand the concept of revolution itself? Is it simply taking political power and nationalizing the forces of production, or are other changes essential? When is control by the state and elimination of private ownership really an expansion of collective freedom, and when is it simply the transfer of wealth, power, and privilege to a new ruling class?
5. Is the industrial proletariat the sole or leading class of the socialist movement? Is it, as Marx predicted, becoming homogeneous in social position, interests, and political orientation? What is the relationship between the proletariat of one country and those of other countries?

I will respond to these questions by describing some of the key institutional developments of the leading parties and international organizations between Marx's death and World War I, and by sampling some of this period's major Marxist voices (Engels, Kautsky, Bernstein, Luxemburg). I shall be arguing that the betrayal of Marxist theory, while clearly not the sole cause of the leftist failures of this period, contributed a misguided trust in agencies outside the awareness, capacities, and powers of the working class itself. Whether that "outside" force was universal laws of history, uncontrollable tendencies of capitalism, the expertise of leaders, or the evolution of purely political democracy within capitalism, most Marxist leaders viewed workers as essentially passive. There was also little recognition that the ruling class could learn to manage the contradictions of capitalism. Finally, the full scope of the nationalism which developed into World War I was veiled, as was the full complexity of the socio-psychological forces which bound the working class to bourgeois society.

## POSITIVIST MARXISM IN EUROPEAN
## SOCIAL-DEMOCRACY

Marx wanted to change the world, not just understand it. Since his death, numerous political parties, international organizations, and governments have claimed that they were putting his ideas into practice. German Social-Democracy and the Second International and Russian Communism and the Third International (Chapter 4) were the most institutionally developed and historically significant of those attempts.

In 1875, German socialists created the German Social-Democratic Party (SPD). Though not yet dominated by Marxist ideas, the SPD began defining itself against other radical political groups by staking out positions on four critical issues. It affirmed the central political role of the *industrial* proletariat, opposing perspectives which stressed the importance of the more highly skilled artisans or the peasantry. Against political reformers, it claimed the necessity of overthrowing rather than modifying the state. While cooperation with the government could at best lead to temporary improvements in workers' lives, these changes were granted by an ultimately hostile political power. It was also necessary that the workers' movement be independent from the progressive middle classes. Coalitions with non-working-class groups could be at best temporary tactics to better the conditions of the working class, not long-term strategies. Finally, the central agent of political change was defined as a broad, democratic party rather than a small, conspiratorial one.

Between 1878 and 1890 the government systematically persecuted the Party. But it continued to grow and by 1890, with the repeal of the anti-socialist laws, it controlled thirty-five seats in the legislature and close to one and a half million votes (almost 20% of the total). Its size and influence made it a model for the smaller and less influential social-democratic parties of Europe. With the exception of France, continental socialism looked to Germany for leadership.[1] During this same period, the SPD adopted an explicitly Marxist perspective. Karl Kautsky founded the Party's main theoretical journal on Marxist principles, with Engels as a frequent contributor. In 1890, Kautsky was commissioned to draft the Party platform for its 1891 convention at Erfurt.

The Erfurt Program embodied the central dilemmas of theory and practice facing both the SPD and the Second International, the umbrella organization of European socialist parties and left trade unions. The program began with a clear theoretical statement based on an "orthodox" understanding of Marxism: capitalism was creating larger and more concentrated firms and intensifying class struggle. Private ownership would become increasingly incompatible with the development of new technology and create ever larger economic crises. Workers of all countries shared interests in overthrowing the system, and their struggle for democratic reforms, increased rights, and better living conditions foreshadowed the eventual revolt which would socialize production and transform society to meet human needs.

Following the discussion of theory, we find the Party's immediate, practical objectives: universal democracy and representative government, women's equality, freedom of speech and assembly, separation of church and state, free medical care, and the end of child labor. (Kolakowski 1978: 11–12).

The central problem facing social-democracy was the relation between the two parts of this program: between the expectation of inevitable socialist revolution and the day-by-day attempts to reform parts of the system to make it more livable and just.

Engels and Kautsky (who on Engels' death in 1895 became Marxism's leading theorist) tried to connect reform and revolution through a positivist Marxism which saw the breakdown of capitalism and the socialist revolution as inevitable. This "orthodox Marxism" took Marx's *occasional* suggestions that capitalist development was governed by universal laws of historical development to be *definitive* of the theory as a whole. People's actions were reduced to predictable responses which could be known in advance by a quasi-scientific theory of history. The economy was viewed as a structure which circumscribed and caused human action. The replacement of capitalism by socialism was part of an age-old historical process whose course Marxist theory had mapped:

Just as Darwin discovered the law of development of organic nature, so Marx discovered the *law of development of human history*. . . . Marx also discovered the *special law of motion* governing the present-day capitalist mode of production and the bourgeois society that this mode of production has created. . . . (Engels, "Speech at Marx's Graveside" in Tucker 1972: 603, my emphasis)

The course of history is governed by inner general laws. . . . That which is willed happens but rarely; in the majority of instances the numerous desired ends cross and conflict with one another. . . . Thus the conflicts of individual wills and individual actions in the domain of history produce a *state of affairs entirely analogous to that prevailing in the realm of unconscious nature*. . . . Historical events thus appear on the whole to be . . . governed by chance. But where on the surface accident holds sway, there actually it is *always governed by inner, hidden laws and it is only a matter of discovering these laws*. (Engels 1941: 48–9)

Kautsky continued this strain in Engels' thinking. He believed that socialist class consciousness among workers was an inevitable outcome of a social process over which human beings had no control. Human history, he contended, is a natural process, not essentially different from natural history and capable of being explained by laws of the same type. Socialism was for Kautsky a historical "necessity," impelled by the development of large-scale, interdependent production. (Kautsky, *The Class Struggle* in Howe 1976: 163–8)

The second dimension of the orthodox Marxist connection of theory and practice had to do with the relations between socialist intellectuals and the mass of the working class. Kautsky argued that the historical development leading towards socialism was a natural process best understood by intellectuals. Comprehension of the necessity of capitalist evolution, crisis, and replacement derives *not* from the inner experience of the working class, *but from the intellectually sophisticated theoreticians of socialism*. Class consciousness must be imported into the proletariat from outside, by its leaders, who can transcend the educational limits, alienation, and false consciousness imposed on workers.

This position effectively separated radical political action from the experience and understanding of the mass of the working class. On the one hand, the revolutionary process is a "historical necessity," which will occur whatever people want or believe—or which will determine those wants and beliefs in predictable ways. On the other hand, the workers, for whom the revolution is supposedly to occur, need to be tutored about its necessity and shape. On both counts, workers' consciousness of their interests is a secondary phenomenon. It is *part* of the revolutionary process, to be sure, but it is a *dependent* part. It follows from universal laws of historical development, laws that are revealed to the masses by the leadership.

This theoretical perspective had disastrous effects on day-to-day political life. Seeing the breakdown of capitalism as an inevitable consequence of systematic laws of development, the SPD could reasonably trust in democracy, the increasing size of the proletariat, and its own well-protected organization. The leadership expected the economic contradictions of capitalism to pave the way for an easy socialist victory. As long as workers followed the Party and mouthed the ideals of socialism, cultivating a politically conscious and militant mass movement was thought to be unnecessary. The importance of profound personal changes in the mass of workers, expressed in vibrant and activist politics, was not seen.

Consequently, while its leaders claimed to seek the overthrow of capitalism, the SPD's politics were essentially reformist. In the Preface to an 1895 reprinting of Marx's *Class Struggles in France*, Engels proposed to replace revolutionary violence of the 1848 or 1871 variety with electoral activity by a mass party. He continued:

> The two million voters whom [German Social-Democracy] sends to the ballot box, together with the young men and women who stand behind them as non-voters, form the most numerous, most compact mass, the decisive "shock force" of the international proletarian army. . . . We, the "revolutionists," the "overthrowers"—we are thriving far better on legal methods than on illegal methods and overthrow. (Tucker 1972: 421)

Though Engels may have intended such strategy as a prelude to an eventual violent confrontation, it became for the SPD (as for the Second International as a whole) a long-term strategy. Like other German political parties of the time, the SPD had a theoretically sophisticated Party statement. But it no more threatened the government than its liberal or conservative competitors. Social-democrats cultivated their Party organization, instructed the workers (whom they saw as an essentially receptive mass), and tried to win reforms that would improve the workers' lives and create Party loyalty. As Kautsky argued: "Our task is not to organize the revolution but rather to organize ourselves for the revolution; not to *make* the revolution, but to *use* it." The comfortable, well-oiled machine appeared to move with decisive efficiency. The Party became a life-world of schools, organizations, clubs, social events, and publications. And the strategy seemed to work; by 1912, the SPD won over one-third of the parliamentary vote and had over one million members. (Howard and Klare 1972: 38–9)

Yet this way of connecting theory and practice ignored some crucial questions: Is voting socialist really synonymous with a developed, politically radical consciousness? Can a revolution occur if workers don't fundamentally change the way they think, feel, and act? To their peril, the leaders of the SPD had no awareness of such issues.

We can put the matter slightly differently: in the transition from capitalism to socialism, what are the sources of political awareness, class solidarity, and institutional empowerment? In comparatively early writings, such as the *Communist Manifesto*, Marx emphasized the need to use state power in opposition to concentrated private property. At that time his answer to this question was: capture the state and use its powers against capitalism. In later writings, and especially after the experience of the revolutionary Paris Commune of 1871, he argued that the existing state was too geared to the needs of capitalists to serve workers. It had to be "smashed" and replaced by the "dictatorship of the proletariat." Despite the ominous ring of this phrase, he had in mind the domination by the *majority* of the *small minority* who wished to continue the old relations of exploitation. In this "dictatorship," there were to be elected representatives, recallable at any time, receiving no higher salary than the average factory worker.

Yet the Marxist tradition did not envisage *any* independent, i.e., non-state, sources of ideology, power, or organization. For Marx, as for the later orthodox Marxism of the SPD and the Second International, *there was no countervailing force to the state* after the revolution and no independent sources of working-class self-organization and activity before it. The capitalist state would be replaced by the socialist state through the inevitability of revolution. The revolution would be led by the politically correct social-democratic party.

*But what is the revolution?* My argument is that it can only occur if the mass of people in a society come to understand and control the social relations which govern their lives. Orthodox Marxism did not hold this position. As the "scientists" of the revolution, what need had they of the insights and developing capacities of the masses? The SPD thus unknowingly reproduced the hierarchical and expert-oriented model of human relations which permeated the society it was supposedly going to transform.

The sociologist Max Weber had argued that in capitalism, the centralized power of a modern, rationalized, state administration and bureaucracy is kept in check by countervailing forces of independent concentrations of wealth. Marx supposed that under socialism no countervailing force is necessary, for there will be homogeneity of social life based on the homogeneity of class. Since there are no exploiters, we all have the same interests. The state becomes purely an administrative force, no longer a repressive one. The Marxism of the SPD and the Second International, by and large, put a comparable faith in the role of the party and the growth of democracy: if everyone is voting, and the working class is getting larger and larger, and the SPD is its representative, then we are moving solidly in the right direction. As we shall see below, SPD radical Rosa Luxemburg subjected this trust in democracy to a devastating critique. Here I will point out that voting is the most passive of political acts. It does not involve people in actively changing fundamental social relations, does not develop any but the most elementary capacities for political action, and does not further working class capacity for self-rule. It merely designates others to act in our place.[2]

The cozy life-world of the SPD contained little that would help generate activist political awareness. It reproduced slogans supporting the ultimate revolutionary goals—but its day-to-day politics did practically nothing to reach them. There was no preparation for radically different relations of authority, gender, property, power, and consumption. There was no attempt to cultivate initiative, ideological independence, or freedom from control by "experts." Yet all these are essential for socialism. While the SPD's islands of leftist sentiment stayed intact for some time, they were incapable of reorganizing society. Perhaps in this historical period nothing else was possible. Perhaps the ruling class and the state were simply too well entrenched to be overcome. Perhaps workers had no real interest in revolution and were attracted to social-democracy only by the promise of immediate reforms. The point here is not to blame the leaders of the SPD, but to show how distortions in Marxist theory contributed to the SPD's failures.

Finally, Marxist orthodoxy of this period continuously asserted that "the working man has no country"; i.e., that workers should—and were coming to—identify solely with their class and not their nationality. This understanding went along with an economic theory that stressed the tendency of capitalism to promote increasing class polarization, isolating the working class from the rest of society. Yet the more political and economic reforms improved the conditions of workers' lives, the less workers were the despised and rejected of bourgeois society. Since they had gained, they now had something to lose. As comparatively apolitical trade unions increased wages and improved working conditions without inserting those changes into a socialist ideological framework, the dream of "revolution" appeared increasingly distant and unnecessary. Workers were part of society, and they accepted its patriotism and militarism. At least, they were willing to defer to the government in such matters.

The mechanical theory and reformist strategy of the SPD was largely consistent with the rest of the Second International, which had been founded in 1889. At that time, over four hundred representatives from twenty countries began a loose federation which would connect European socialists for the next twenty-five years. As in the SPD, most members chose a revolutionary strategy based on mass parties and parliamentary victories rather than one which stressed direct action, strikes, or revolutionary violence. Further, it was assumed that a European war would be prevented because the interests of the proletariat transcended national boundaries and workers would not support their governments' militarism.

As its largest and most successful party, the SPD usually dominated the Second International. The failure of the SPD-led organization showed most clearly in August 1914, when most of its leaders endorsed their countries' entry into World War I. While there were some exceptions, the socialist parties were by-and-large powerless against their members' support for war; and many famous, previously "internationalist" leaders, found "reasons" to justify their side against other nations. After the war, reformism came to be the Party's hallmark. When the rise of fascism spelled the violent repression of the SPD, effective activism was found on the Right, not the Left. The trust in capitalist democracy reached its logical conclusion: the end of democracy meant the end of the Party. In the absence of an active revolutionary mass, the SPD was only as powerful as its last electoral success.

## REVISIONISM

In the latter part of the nineteenth century, economic developments seemed to support the orthodox Marxist belief in the inevitability of revolution. From the mid 1870s to the 1890s, the European economy suffered a long slump. After the tremendous expansion of industrial capitalism of the previous fifty years, it now seemed that capitalism had exhausted its capacity for growth. Leaders of the SPD saw in this slump the telling forecast of capitalist collapse. Yet this was a distorted interpretation, itself prompted by the belief that mechanical tendencies of the economy would create an economic crisis that capitalism would simply be powerless to overcome.

Actually, the long slump was the prelude not to the collapse of capitalism but to its reorganization, the beginning of the transition from competitive to monopoly capitalism. (Colletti 1972: 45–110) Thousands of small enterprises were eliminated, and many industrial and commercial fields consolidated into small clusters of increasingly larger firms. The formation of cartels drastically diminished the price competition which had helped spark the slump by lowering the rate of profit. There was also a dramatic drive for colonies on the part of the European powers. Consonant with Marxist theory, capitalism was spreading to the rest of the globe in search of markets, raw materials, and areas of investment.

Yet Marxism had not anticipated a central consequence of this development: profits from imperialism and the economic stability of a now less competitive capitalism boosted the standard of living of the working classes in the European center. Conceived of simply as those who work for wages and have little or no control over their work, the working class did grow. Yet it *also became increasingly stratified.* Among propertyless wage earners there were highly significant differences in income, union protection, and working conditions. There developed in industrial Europe and the United States what Lenin was later to call a "labor aristocracy." These workers experienced improved living conditions and came to feel more, not less, identified with the nations and cultures of their birth. They had little interest in forging international revolutionary ties and for the most part were politically mobilized only in pursuit of their immediate material interests. Also, governments were slowly learning the lessons of a century of intermittent worker and peasant radicalism. They began (after considerable prodding) to extend democratic rights, political representation, and social welfare legislation. Thus, Marxism confronted not only the failure of the *working class* to take up a truly radical stance, but also a *ruling class* which was beginning to manage capitalist society in a self-conscious way.

These changes led to temporary political stability and economic affluence in Europe and the U.S. A comparatively privileged sector of industrial labor won (after bitter struggle in some cases) improvements in wages, working conditions, and political rights. Social-democracy served the short-term interests of these workers. Trusting their deterministic version of Marxism, leaders of the Second International were unprepared for the catastrophic social effects of a World War motivated by the pursuit of Third World markets and resources. Nor could they understand that workers, despite Marxist theory, identified with their nationality as much or more than their class.

Eduard Bernstein, editor of the SPD's main theoretical journal, diagnosed the contradiction between social-democracy's radical theory and its reformist politics. He initiated a fundamental "revision" of Marxism, challenging many of the theory's basic claims. Bernstein began by criticizing Marx for a Hegelian legacy of confidence in the inevitability of capitalism's collapse, a confidence based more in abstract philosophy than real life. In fact, capitalism had stabilized itself and was providing a steadily increasing standard of living. Small owners continued to exist, and therefore the industrial working class did not constitute the overwhelming majority of the population. Although violent revolution was clearly not on the agenda, claimed Bernstein, socialism would be created by slow-but-sure growth of socialist parliamentary power, trade unions, and consumer cooperatives. Given a climate of political democracy, these institutions would erode capitalist profits to the vanishing point. Incremental progress, not economic crisis and insurrection, would lead to socialism.

> Unless unforeseen external events bring about a general crisis, and as we have said that can happen any day, there is no urgent reason for concluding that such a crisis will come to pass for purely economic reasons. (Bernstein, *Evolutionary Socialism* in Howe 1976: 239)

> In all advanced countries we see the privileges of the capitalist bourgeoisie yielding step by step to democratic organizations. . . . The more the political organizations of the modern nations are democratized the more the needs and opportunities of great political catastrophes are diminished. (242)

> The most important problems of tactics which German social democracy has at the present time to solve, appears to be to devise the best ways for the extension of the political and economic rights of the German working classes. . . . (245)

The SPD formally rejected revisionism, criticizing Bernstein for misreading Marx and denying the labor theory of value. Critics also complained that Bernstein was blind to the fact that in the imperialist phase of capitalism the very cartels, trusts, and credit mechanisms which were guaranteeing its present prosperity would eventually cause a crisis.

In terms of the immediate future of capitalism, Bernstein *was* wrong. The economy-stabilizing imperialism plunged Europe into war. The political outcome of the social crises which followed the war was decided not by democracy, but by violence. Later still, politically unregulated monopoly capitalism was to produce the most extreme of capitalism's economic slumps in the Great Depression of the 1930s.

Despite these theoretical weaknesses, Bernstein's position did reflect the actual practice of the SPD. As an experienced Bavarian socialist wrote to him: "One doesn't formally decide to do what you ask, one doesn't say it, one *does* it. Our whole activity . . . was the activity of a Social Democratic reforming party." (Joll 1966: 94) Equally important, Bernstein *had* raised a crucial question for Marxist theory: What if capitalism was not going to create increasingly severe crises? What if it could regulate itself? In this possibility, the orthodox Marxist theory of revolution crumbles. We are no longer confident that a cataclysmic economic crisis will precipitate the final overthrow of capitalism. Instead democracy, increases in the standard of living, and its own self-protective organizations integrate the working class into capitalism. *Where then is the motivation for revolution?* For Bernstein, this was not an important question. The process towards socialism, he frequently stated, was more important than the final goal itself. As some of the more philosophically oriented Marxists of the period had it, the desire for socialism does not really emerge from the concrete experience of social life or from Marxist theory. It is an ethical ideal.[3]

In a sense, Bernstein was an orthodox Marxist without a theory of crisis. His revision of Marxism rested on the unstated confidence that, bit by bit, things would simply keep getting better. Yet Bernstein faces questions like those which perplex the orthodox Marxist: How do we know when we are progressing towards that goal of socialism— and not meandering endlessly on the terrain of the fundamental social inequality of capitalism? Does purely political democracy really lead towards socialism? Are all the present reforms necessarily going to be retained in the future?

These questions were posed for both Bernstein and the more orthodox Marxists with great clarity by the leading "radical" of the Second International.

## A CHALLENGING VOICE: ROSA LUXEMBURG

Rosa Luxemburg emigrated from Poland to Germany in 1898 and devoted her life to socialism and to radicalizing the SPD's perspective on daily political struggles. She contributed to the development of Marxism by making its theory of the political development of the working class much more sophisticated. Marx's simplistic confidence that the economy would radicalize the proletariat was one of the critical weaknesses of his original theory. It was perpetuated by orthodox Marxism's trust in the scientifically guaranteed inevitability of the revolution and the both orthodox *and* revisionist trust that uninterrupted democracy would break the power of the ruling class. Orthodox and revisionists alike trusted in political reforms: the orthodox because the revolution was certain; revisionists because the gradual progress of reforms would lead directly to socialism without the necessary intervention of a crisis. Neither perspective had focused answers to the question: in what fundamental changes of self-understanding and capacity for action does the radicalizing process consist?

Luxemburg's ideas on these topics are best expressed in "Social Reform or Revolution," a response to Bernstein, and "Mass Strike, Party and Trade Unions," inspired by the revolutionary uprisings of Russian workers in 1905.

The central theme of both essays is the relation between everyday political activities and the overthrow of capitalism. Luxemburg argued forcefully that the mechanisms of reformist politics—trade union action, parliamentary victories, extensions of democratic rights—do not, in and of themselves, pave the way for socialism. Accepting the basic premises of capitalism, trade unions are defense organizations, geared to increasing workers' standard of living under conditions of wage labor. A union perspective does not envision a socialist society; and as organizations, unions are ultimately powerless against the business cycle, capital mobility, or technical developments which lower the demand for labor. Moreover, the same mentality that allows union leaders to gain a measure of economic well-being for their members makes unions liable to atrophy as organs of social change.

The specialization of their professional activity as trade-union leaders, as well as the naturally limited horizon which is bound up with the disconnected economic struggles in a peaceful period, lead the trade-union officials only too easily to bureaucratism. . . . Especially important here is the overestimation of the organization, which is changed from a means to an end, gradually to an end in itself. . . . The trade-union leaders gradually lose the power of seeing the larger connections and taking survey of the whole situation. (Luxemburg 1971: 262)

Similar problems plague consumer cooperatives, which Bernstein also thought would help erode capitalist prerogatives.

Luxemburg mounted an analogous critique of the limitations of reforming the government. While capitalists will make some concessions in the interests of social peace, she argued, they will not surrender their power. Getting laws which benefit workers is very different from exercising control over the state itself.

As for democracy, the fundamental mistake of both the orthodox and the revisionists is to abstract the *political* form of democracy from the *class structure and class interests* of the society in which it appears. Democracy has a historically progressive effect when the emerging bourgeoisie struggles against the inherited privilege of the aristocracy. In that context, it is a demand for freedom of economic activity masked as a commitment to "universal" human rights. But there is no guarantee that monopoly capitalism, especially as it confronts the later emergence of an organized working class, will tolerate democracy forever. Since political life expresses class interests, the uses of democracy ultimately depend on the balance of power between contending classes. Given the subsequent rise of Nazism—which eliminated democracy and violently repressed the SPD—this is one of Luxemburg's most prescient observations.

Luxemburg was not arguing that trade union, cooperative, or parliamentary/electoral activity should be abandoned and that we should save all political activity for the overthrow of the state! She was not against reforms. Rather, her position was that reforms had to be evaluated by reference to a standard outside themselves. To find out whether this or that union, reform, or electoral campaign serves the ultimate interests of the working class, we must ask: to what extent does it prepare the workers for the ultimate confrontation with capitalism, cultivate workers' capacity for action, and raise the level of their understanding of both the inner dynamics of the society they live in and their own essential interests?

> The socialist significance of trade-union and parliamentary activity is that it prepares the proletariat—that is, the *subjective* factor of the socialist transformation—for the task of realizing socialism. (Luxemburg 1971: 85)

Using this criteria, Luxemburg saw critical strategic implications in the mass uprising in Russia in 1905. The small but politically active proletariat took to the streets, engaged in mass strikes, and even created organs of self-rule (the "soviets," or councils). Luxemburg saw this activity as a product of years of political organizing and also as a decisive experience in organizing and training workers for future conflicts. Here the political contest for state power and the economic struggle of unions had fused. The SPD needed to learn this lesson, instead of trying to separate them neatly into parliamentary elections and limited strikes. Without a unity of political and economic struggle, there could be no decisive social change.

> The economic struggle is that which leads the political struggle from one nodal point to another; the political struggle is that which periodically fertilizes the soil for the economic struggles. . . . The economic and political moments in the mass strike form only two interlacing sides of the proletarian class struggle. . . . And *their unity* is precisely the mass strike. (Luxemburg 1971: 241)

The role of the Party during the revolutionary upsurge, therefore, is to be in active connection to the political power and energy which is flowing from the working class. Far from accepting Kautsky's notion that socialist consciousness must be imported to the proletariat from the outside by intellectuals, Luxemburg insisted that the proletariat's freely emerging political activity is the actual creation of the revolutionary process.

There are quite definite limits to initiative and conscious direction. During the revolution itself it is extremely difficult for any leading organ of the proletarian movement to foresee and to calculate which occasion and moments can lead to explosions and which cannot. . . . In short, the element of spontaneity plays such a prominent role in the mass strikes in Russia not because the Russian proletariat is "unschooled" but *because revolutions allow no one to play schoolmaster to them.* (Luxemburg 1971: 245, my emphasis)

To give the slogans, the direction of the struggle; to organize the *tactics* of the political struggle in such a way that in every phase and in every moment of the struggle the whole sum of the available and already released active power of the proletariat will be realized and find expression in the battle stance of the party . . . to see that . . . the tactics of Social Democracy never fall *below* the level of the actual relation of forces but rather rise above it—that is the most important task of the "leadership" in the period of the mass strike. (247)

Luxemburg tried to return Marxist theory to the critical starting point of Marx's conception of human beings as self-acting, self-transformative beings. The key to the revolutionary process is the way in which the "subjective" factor is prepared. This preparation is not training in obedience to revolutionary experts, but developing workers' capacity to act on their own behalf. Realistically, Luxemburg did not reject leadership altogether; nor did she see revolutionary activity springing magically from the oppressed. The capacity to act, she argued, is itself always the product of long years of parliamentary and trade union activity, ideological struggle, and limited skirmishes. Yet this critical capacity is *not* going to be cultivated by any self-proclaimed leftist politics which takes the preservation of the organization as its highest goal. Nor can it be developed by a leadership which sees the masses as passively waiting for direction from experts. Luxemburg's criticism of trade union bureaucrats, quoted above, applied to the SPD as well. One need only change "disconnected *economic* struggles" to "disconnected *political* struggles."

Although Luxemburg stressed the self-activity of the masses, she too suffered from a tendency to overestimate the determining effects of economic development on political life. In her economic writings (1970), she provided a complicated "proof" that capitalism would eventually collapse when it exhausted non-capitalist markets. Without a belief in the final crisis, she claimed, there was no function for working class consciousness; capitalism would just continue forever. She failed to see that in the absence of a particular form of working class consciousness, there *could not be* a crisis. A crisis only occurred when a particular economic or social development was understood and acted upon by the mass of people in the society. No mathematically defined loss of income, fall in profit, or rate of unemployment has a *political* meaning in and of itself. This last fact was not understood by any of the major voices of this period: neither the orthodox, the revisionists, nor the radicals. It remained for the Western Marxists— whose contributions we will trace in Chapter 5—to redefine the significance of economic life partly in terms of people's consciousness of and response to it.

The First World War signaled the end of the political influence of social democracy—at least as in any sense a radical political movement—for the next sixty years. The working classes followed their governments into war and most socialist leaders trailed along. While some social-democratic leaders led European governments between the wars, they made no attempt to seriously challenge capitalism.

World War I, however, destabilized the existing balance of power: America rose to world economic dominance; the Austrian and Russian monarchies were overthrown. In the period immediately following the war, the national and democratic struggle merged with a Marxist-oriented attempt to create a socialist society. In this struggle, international leadership passed from the evolutionary reformism of social-democracy to the revolutionary politics of Russian communism.

# 4

## SOVIET COMMUNISM: THE DEATH OF MARXISM

Russian communism was the first movement to take state power under the banner of the ideas of Marx and Engels. It faced enormous difficulties—both in Russia's own lack of economic and cultural development and in the hostility and pressure of the capitalist world. In response, this initially progressive movement degenerated into a monstrous tyranny that had virtually nothing in common with Marx's vision of socialism. Yet if social backwardness, economic underdevelopment, foreign pressure, or even personality quirks (Lenin was arrogant and intolerant, Stalin was a paranoid egomaniac) are the cause of this failure, then the Russian Revolution has little meaning for the study of Marxism.

We are directed, therefore, to the following questions: What does the Russian Revolution tell us about whether Marxism can be useful for contemporary struggles for justice and human fulfillment? To what extent did the ideas of Marx—or their adaptation by Lenin and Stalin, the major architects of first the revolution and later the Soviet state— betray the attempt to create a just and humane society? Are Lenin's ideas (what many call "Marxism-Leninism"), dominant in the Russian Communist Party until 1923, the catastrophic break with Marxism? Is it Stalin who simplified and distorted the noble ideals of Marx and the dedicated revolutionary spirit of Lenin? Or does the Stalinist dictatorship simply reveal the ultimate bankruptcy of Marx?

The discussion will show, I hope, that the tragedy of the Soviet Union is neither totally unconnected to Marxism nor its inevitable product. Rather, the evolution of the Russian Revolution looms as a vital warning against the positivist strain in Marxism criticized in Chapter 2.

Interestingly, this pernicious strain of Marxism not only infected the revolution in undeveloped Russia, but also has affinities with ideas and practices in advanced industrial societies today. The failures of Marxism are not completely unlike the failures of bourgeois society, popular culture, and intellectual life. Ultimately, all rest on an exaggerated respect for pretentious authority and a corresponding disrespect for ordinary people. The ultimate lesson is that the flaws of both communism and advanced capitalism can be overcome only if ordinary people achieve sufficient power and self-knowledge to shape social life in terms of the wisdom of their own experience and the demands of their own true needs.

## LENINISM AND RUSSIA

In economically and politically undeveloped Russia, socialists faced the persecutions of the secret police and a complete absence of democracy. It was an overwhelmingly rural society, with a few centers of large-scale, usually foreign-owned industry and some militant workers' organizations. This Russia was very different from the developed capitalist country in which Marx thought the revolution would take place. In organizing the working class, Russian Marxists faced what was for the most part a *pre-capitalist* society.

Yet Russia was not just pre-capitalist; it was also shaped by the history of capitalist development elsewhere. History was not unfolding according to "laws" of development. Rather, the earlier rise of capitalism—which itself created Marxism, workers' movements, modern technology, and capital which could be invested abroad—made it impossible for the pattern to be repeated again. In particular, the class alliance of the capitalists and workers in making a democratic, modernizing revolution—as in England, the U.S., or France—was not on the Russian agenda. The small Russian bourgeoisie had enough political insight to see the danger of allying itself with a potentially revolutionary proletariat. On the other hand, social and economic crises provoked by World War I made it impossible to wait for the slow development of a mass, majority working class. For all these reasons, Russian socialists would find it very hard to employ an SPD strategy dependent on bourgeois democracy. The political tactics of the Second International simply could not work in Russia.

Of the various socialists who attempted to synthesize Marxism for these social conditions, Lenin was the most successful. It was his theoretical and political vision that dominated the politics of the Bolshevik[1] wing of Russian social-democracy, the group that took power in October 1917.

My concern here is not with Lenin's vast and not always consistent writings.[2] One of the most important political figures of the twentieth century, influencing political movements throughout the world, he has been exhaustively analyzed. My goal, rather, is to describe the central ways in which Lenin transformed Marxism to fit Russian contours and what happened to Marxism as a result.

Lenin's theory has three main elements: the central importance of the vanguard political party; the alliance between peasants and proletariat under the latter's leadership to make first a democratic and then a socialist revolution; and a global perspective which sees capitalism as a world system of imperialism rather than as a series of isolated capitalist nations.

Lenin believed the struggle for political rights and better wages was part of the socialist program, but it was ultimately aimed at the more militant struggle to overthrow both Czarism and capitalism. To reach this goal, he argued, the leadership not of a mass but of a "vanguard" party was necessary. Between 1901 and 1907, Lenin defined the vanguard party as a group of disciplined, highly trained, professional revolutionaries. Only such a party, he believed, could coordinate diverse struggle in the face of state repression and inject socialist class consciousness into a working class dominated by bourgeois ideology. (Lenin 1943, 1960, 1970) The Party was central because by themselves the majority of workers would develop only a limited political consciousness of their own immediate economic interests (a "trade union" consciousness). Adopting Kautsky's view, Lenin claimed that a comprehensive class consciousness had to be brought from outside, by intellectuals and revolutionary leaders. Since Russia had few literate people and was autocratically ruled, however, the Party which did this would have to be small, tightly organized, and secret. Further, the tendency of mass organizations to seek compromise with the limited political horizons of their members, and of trade union bureaucrats to promote their own limited ends, demanded that the revolutionary cadre be disciplined, totally committed, and unwavering in its dedication to the revolution.

Russia was essentially a peasant society. Therefore, observed Lenin, any workers' movement with broad goals had to ally with the peasantry. This alliance, he thought, would take two forms. Challenging traditional social-democratic views, he asserted that the moderate and poor peasants shared an interest with the workers in overthrowing the Czar. This partnership would secure them land, their chief concern. After the downfall of the Czar and the establishment of the basic conditions of modernized democracy, however, the workers' party would split the peasantry and unite with the poorest segment to build a socialist society.

Even in such a situation, socialist forces in backward Russia would stand vulnerable to class conflicts and the opposition of surrounding capitalist countries. The third ingredient of Leninism thus had to do with an analysis of international capitalism as a system of imperialism and with the prospect of foreign aid for a post-revolutionary Russia. Imperialist capitalism, Lenin believed, was based on monopoly rather than competition. Furthermore, concentrations of bank and industrial capital had merged to form "finance" capital. This capital was driven overseas to compete for colonies, foreign raw materials, and investment. On the home front, immense profits from imperialist ventures and monopoly firms helped create an "aristocracy of labor"—a segment of the working class whose material position led it to ally with the bourgeoisie. The internationalization of capitalism in some respects shifted the struggle between workers and capitalists to that between colonized and colonizing nations. Ultimately, however, no enduring stabilization of the system was possible. The very mechanisms of national monopoly and international exploitation which supported the aristocracy of labor worsened the inequalities between different capitalist nations. These inequalities *guaranteed* conflict and would cause fatal economic and social crises. Imperialism was the final, parasitic, "moribund" stage of capitalism. Further adaptation could not occur. Since capitalism had formed a world system, it was possible to attack that system at its weakest—or at least weaker—points, and to hope that the shock of one revolution would cause the whole rotten edifice to crash to the ground. With that collapse, the proletariat of the developed capitalist nations would join forces with the revolutionary vanguard in Russia.

Before we can evaluate Lenin's ideas, we must briefly examine his "success."

## THE COURSE OF THE REVOLUTION

The February 1917 revolution which deposed the Russian Czar and ushered in a liberal coalition government had many causes: the protracted social suffering produced by the First World War; the reemergence of the councils ("soviets") of workers, peasants, and soldiers which had arisen previously in the 1905 uprising; the political ferment of these same groups ignited by a plethora of socialist and populist-peasant political parties; the growing attempt of the bourgeoisie to usher in a regime of modern political rights; and the peasants' demand for land reform. In the aftermath of February, a central coalition government shared "dual power" with the soviets. The political question all socialists then faced was: Should we stop with a liberal, democratic, capitalist-supporting government? Or push for full soviet power and attempt to construct socialism?

The Mensheviks, Lenin's major opponents among urban socialists, were caught in an impossible situation. In their perspective, feudalism necessarily led to capitalism, which would inevitably create socialism. This mechanical theory directed them to ask the workers to make a revolution *for* the bourgeoisie and then wait for a worker's government *after* the full development of capitalism. Not surprisingly, this position had little appeal for the most radical, activist workers. Lenin's position appealed to a broad spectrum of workers and peasants: immediate end to the war, land for peasants, and a strong worker's voice in the government. In October 1917, Lenin took advantage of the vigorous Bolshevik support among workers in the capital and decided the time was ripe to end the dual power of parliament and soviets. The provisional government was dismissed, and the soviets—under the tutelage of the major left parties—took power.

Following on the seizure of power, the Russian Communist Party[3] came to dominate the nation's political and social life. Other political parties were eliminated and councils, trade unions, and peasant cooperatives were destroyed or turned into puppets of party power. All independent political expression was made impossible. From a government of soviets in which the communists had a leading role there emerged a communist government.

The Party claimed its repression was a justified response to both internal and external problems. First among these was Russia's economic underdevelopment, which worsened after a civil war against counterrevolutionaries and foreign forces crippled agriculture, industry, and distribution. Soviet industrial output was not to reach pre-war levels until the late 1920s. Far from inheriting an economically and socially modernized country, as Marxist theory forecast, Lenin's

Marxist party had to modernize and industrialize and to demand that Soviet citizens sacrifice immediate consumption to develop future industrial capacity.

Second, internal political struggles lacked any democratic traditions. The outlawing of opposition parties is often taken as evidence of Leninist "dictatorship." Yet it should be remembered that some of his opponents attempted to kill Lenin and others allied with hostile foreign powers.

Third, the international revolution did not occur. After a series of uprisings, the post-war tide of European radicalism ebbed. Instead of sparking—and receiving aid from—European revolutions, Russian communists found themselves surrounded by antagonistic capitalist powers. They had become the lonely vanguard of history instead of the inspiration of a new world order.[4]

Finally, the original social base of the Bolsheviks, the peasant-worker alliance, collapsed. By 1921 the Russian working class, as an organized group capable of exercising some controls over its political representatives, had ceased to exist. A significant percentage of the originally class conscious, activist workers had been killed in the civil war, returned to the countryside as industry broke down, or had risen into the ranks of the new bureaucracy.[5] They could no longer serve as organized opponents of the government's monopoly on social power. In the absence of a self-active proletariat, the Communist Party became an autonomous force.

To the extent that the peasants supported revolutionary aims, they sought to develop their historic communes into autonomous rural organizations, not to serve a centralized communist state. While the Party briefly supported peasant profit during the New Economic Policy of 1921–8, it would not long allow peasants any independent political power. For Leninism, Russia's population had to be subordinate to the (supposed) representatives of the tiny working class. With the stabilization of communist rule by the late 1920s, the CP-peasant alliance turned to violent struggle. Punished for their resistance to Stalin's forced collectivization, some variously estimated five to fifteen million peasants were killed or allowed to starve, and non-communist peasant leaders were executed. While some efforts were made to win the poorer peasants to socialist ideology, no serious consideration was given to sharing power with progressive peasant forces. (Kingston-Mann 1983)

Some who made the original revolution resisted communist domination. In 1921, with the end of the civil war, the "Workers' Opposition" demanded increased power for independent soviets. True to its belief in the role of the Party, the CP answered:

> Only the political party of the working class, i.e., the Communist Party, is in a position to unite, educate and organize such a vanguard of the proletariat and all the laboring masses as will be able to counteract the inevitable petit-bourgeois wavering of the masses, to counteract tradition and unavoidable lapses of trade union narrowness . . . to direct all sides of the proletarian movements. . . . (Daniels 1960 II: 210)

Responding to an uprising by the previously supportive sailors of the Kronstadt navel base, the Party passed a resolution banning factions and demanding strict unity. The democratic reforms of 1920 were curtailed and greater power accorded to the Party's organizational structure. By 1928 the defeat of the "joint opposition" (led by Leon Trotsky) marked the end of serious inner-party struggles. Justifying its dictatorship by appeals to security, the CP eliminated all opposition, modernized agriculture, and initiated the fastest industrialization in world history. It also created a new class of privileged bureaucrats and technical experts.

Politically, Leninism blossomed into Stalinism. Far from imbuing the working class with socialist consciousness, this new ruling class took Russian society as an object to be controlled. Unlike the early years of the revolution, women's and homosexual rights, progressive education, and collective child rearing were attacked. There was a resurgence of narrow nationalism, anti-Semitism, and support for traditional family structure (even as women were increasingly entering the work force). In the 1930s a Stalinist reign of terror killed millions, including many (perhaps most) of the dedicated Party members. False confessions were extracted by torture and history was knowingly distorted. (Medvedev 1973)

At the same time, Soviet citizens and the world at large were assured that communists were building "socialism in one country." Just as traditional Marxism had been unprepared for revolution in backward Russia, so Marxism-Leninism equated socialism with central planning and government ownership of the means of production. Schooled in orthodoxy, most Marxists of Russia and the world could not see how powerless masses and the absence of democracy made the Soviet Union a new form of class society rather than a "socialist republic."

The "success" of Leninism led to the formation of communist parties throughout the world. Affiliating together in the Third or Communist International (Comintern), these parties agreed to unconditional support of the Soviet Union, obedience to the Executive of the Comintern on penalty of expulsion, the splitting of previously existing parties on lines defined by the (Soviet-dominated) Executive, and acceptance of the Soviet model of revolutionary strategy and organization.[6] As European revolutionary movements faded, Soviet leaders demanded that the policy of all foreign communists be dedicated to the interests of the Soviet Union.

> For whoever thinks of defending the world revolutionary movement apart from, or against, the U.S.S.R. goes against the revolution and must inevitably slide into the camp of the enemies of the revolution. (in Leonhard 1971: 115)

Not only a shifting theory, but self-interested Russian nationalism motivated this strategy. A poverty of theory combined with an unfortunate "wealth" of narrow national and bureaucratic self-interest masquerading as universal revolutionary morality. Communist parties justified opportunistic deals between the Soviet Union and capitalist nations, allowed themselves to be pushed into catastrophic alliances with bourgeois nationalist forces in colonial countries, and rejected cooperation with social-democratic forces during the rise of Fascism. On the level of theory, independent thinking and creative scholarship were replaced by dogmatic justifications of Soviet policies.

## LENINISM AS DOMINATION

What are we to make of Leninism?

First, notice that Lenin's model of the revolutionary process—his belief that revolution was even a real option in Russia—constituted a fundamental break with traditional Marxism. He was making a revolution, as the Italian Marxist Antonio Gramsci observed, "against *Capital,*" i.e., against Marx's claim that full capitalist development was the pre-condition for socialism. Since the evolution of capitalism was not creating class consciousness, that consciousness had to be brought from outside, by the Party. The disciplined, perfected Party would make up for the political and intellectual limitations of the working class. It would step into the economic crises of imperialism and the social crises of the disintegrating monarchy and produce a revolution. History had not made the Russian workers a majority, and social life had not made very many of the Russian people socialist revolutionaries. But it had given Russia Marxism, a Social-Democratic Party, and Lenin. No wonder that "orthodox" Marxists from both Russia and the rest of Europe were shocked by Lenin's ideas. He was, in Lukács' phrase, replacing laws of history with the "actuality of the revolution"—making history instead of waiting for historical inevitability to grind out socialism in the hazy future.

How could Lenin fulfill a Marxist end without Marxist means? Give leadership to the Party, use the peasantry, and hope that the revolutionary sparks from Russia would ignite the rest of the world's proletariat. The revolutionary process could preempt the course of history by taking advantage of temporary political conditions in the balance of power between classes. Therefore, political struggle could take the form of a minority insurrection. 'Out of this act, the mass movement could be created at a later time, when the vanguard had the power of the state at its disposal. (Leonhard 1971: 358)

The brilliance of Lenin's synthesis should not be underestimated. He explained the political passivity of the working class of more advanced capitalism, and his theory allows the workers of undeveloped countries to share historical center stage with those of western Europe and the U.S. His concept of revolutionary organization (the Party) and strategy (alliance with the peasants) made Marxism-Leninism the model for dozens of anti-imperialist, anti-feudal, and anti-colonial revolutionary movements. From China to Cuba, Yemen to North Korea, many of these movements were ultimately successful—at least in the sense of eventually taking political power.

Whatever our admiration for its brilliance, however, we must acknowledge Leninism's basic flaws. To begin, remember that Lenin believed that a proletariat and peasant alliance could hold power and begin to build socialism in Russia only with aid from a post-revolutionary Europe. But what if the European upheaval never occurred? This possibility, after all, was raised by Lenin's own theory. He had claimed that imperialism made workers in the advanced countries reactionary and had shown that the world proletariat was stratified and divided by nationalism, income, and differences in political strength. The imperialist stage did give rise to intra-imperialist competition, wars, and economic crises. Yet without a radicalized and unified working class, socialist forces could not make use of these crises. Russian revolutionaries would get no significant help from abroad.[7]

In the absence of world revolution, then, what would sustain the alliance between the proletariat and the peasantry? Many peasants wanted land for their own families or local communities, or they wanted to retain their own communal institutions. But neither family, village, nor peasant commune had a place in Lenin's model of proletarian social dictatorship. As support from peasants melted away and aid from abroad never arrived, the revolution lacked the necessary cultural, economic, and political resources. The Party controlled the state, but it was state power *without* a revolution.

Lenin's vanguardism was in some ways an improvement over the positivism of the Second International. Yet his faith in the knowledge and virtue of "the Party" sowed the seeds of future dictatorship.[8] The small, professionalized Party became a power elite, a privileged bureaucracy rather than a selfless revolutionary leadership. It is obvious, now at least, that the very same conditions which made it seem reasonable to require a centralized, professional Party to serve as a vanguard *before* the revolution could lead the Party to become a tyranny *afterwards*. The working class had a comparatively undeveloped sense of its socialist self-interest, constituted a tiny minority of the population, and could rely on the peasants only to a limited extent. Therefore, while workers did form independent centers of power, they could not sustain them against the Party.

The peasantry did support the overthrow of the Czar, ending the war, and the distribution of land, but they had no interest in a society-wide reorganization of wealth. And the Leninist commitment to central power and direction could not allow any independent source of self-direction. Eventually, all the peasants who resisted centralized control were allowed to starve or were driven into collective farms directly under Party control. Similarly, when workers or soldiers challenged the Party, the Leninist response was that opposing the Party is always wrong. Correct class consciousness comes from experts. There are to be no *other* sources of revolutionary transformation. As the Party is centralized and hierarchical, so is revolutionary society. Thus the fundamental flaw of Leninism, of much greater importance to us than any particular miscalculation of the balance of forces in Russia or the world in the early 1920s, is its primary commitment to a hierarchical, centralized social order.

Of course in *State and Revolution*, written between the fall of the Czar and the Bolshevik seizure of power, Lenin supports a political form in which the masses take a direct role in governing. But the history of Leninist practice shows that he wanted others to share power only when they believed exactly what he did. Until the masses are just like the Party, they are not included but dominated. Lenin never supported movements towards the development of other centers of power or self-organization. As Herbert Marcuse observed, "Lenin tried to counter the isolation of the revolution in a backward country by establishing the priority of industrialization over socialist liberation. . . ." (Marcuse 1958: 58) He saw the development of the Soviet economy in terms of efficiency, industrialization, central planning, and modernization. Socialist social relations of mutuality, self-management, equality, and workers' democracy receded into the hazy future. In 1921 he claimed:

> In reality, state capitalism would be a step forward for us. If we were
> capable of attaining state capitalism in Russia within a short time, this

would be a victory. . . . I said that state capitalism would be our savior. If we would have it in Russia, then the *transition to full socialism would be easy and certain*. For state capitalism is a system of *centralization, integration, control, and socialization. And this is precisely what we lack*. (in Marcuse 1958: 29)

And, presumably, just what was needed. But of course this need had little to do with socialism as envisaged by Marx and everything to do with the creation of an industrialized economy and a modern, administrative, dominating state. And it is just because "centralization" and "control" are so endemic to capitalism and so antithetical to human liberation, that the transition from such "state capitalism" to socialism is neither "easy" nor "certain."

Shortly after the revolution, the economy was placed under the control of commissions over which workers had no direct authority. In 1919 Lenin argued that before the workers were capable of taking part in government, their consciousness had to be completely changed. Until then, government institutions would be *for* the workers, not *by* them. Cultural change would occur after the revolution. In short, the Party knew what workers needed better than the workers themselves. Lenin had no problem with Trotsky's 1921 statement: "The Party is entitled to assert its dictatorship even if that dictatorship temporarily clashes with the passing moods of workers' democracy."[9]

Further, if we try to find out what the development of class consciousness is in the Leninist tradition, we find that it means essentially developing the right kind of opinions, the ones which will lead the class to follow the Party's lead. In this Lenin was in the tradition of the most limited kind of Marxist thinking. As Engels wrote in 1880:

To thoroughly comprehend the historical conditions and thus the very nature of this act of universal emancipation, [i.e., revolution,] to impart to the new oppressed proletarian class full knowledge of the conditions and of the meaning of the momentous act it is called upon to accomplish, this is the task of the theoretical expression of the proletarian movement, scientific socialism (Engels 1969: 75)

In other words, the essence of the revolution is known by the theorist-leaders, who have virtually nothing to learn from the workers themselves. Moreover, the "full knowledge" of the revolution is encompassed by purely *intellectual* knowledge that can be transferred from one group to another as mechanical and objective lessons can be taught by teachers to students. This misses the point that revolutionary transformations require an essentially subjective alteration of the people involved. It also calls on an overly abstract and (as we shall see in Chapter 6) a culturally male view of how people understand the world, themselves, and how they change both. Most important, it enshrines at the heart of Marxism—and then of Leninism—a relation of power and authority between Party and class, leaders and led. Whatever its intentions, this view privileges a kind of "knowledge aristocracy" over the ignorant masses.

For the Leninist, then, workers can have either of two types of class consciousness: a limited and self-interested "economism," which requires Party direction to expand its horizons and combat its selfishness; or exactly what the Party believes to begin with. Anything else can only be counter-revolutionary ideology. In the social instability which followed the war, the Bolsheviks tried to jump over these alternatives, to use the centralized state as a substitute for the historical development of social conditions and for the emergence of the self-active mass. When the gaps between what they wanted and what they had became too great, they had to choose either surrender of power or its increased use. They opted for the latter and created a self-aggrandizing ideology of the purity of the Party and its state to justify their crimes.[10]

Finally, we must make some mention of the Leninist written and personal style of interaction. There can be no question of Lenin's complete devotion to the goal of revolution. Self-interest or selfishness in the narrow sense had virtually no part in his character. Yet his utter confidence in his own expertise and that of the (actual or ideal) Party led to a terribly self-righteous, arrogant, and hostile way of relating to other people. Marx had his own tendencies toward exaggerating differences, discrediting opponents, and painting conflicts in absolute shades of black and white. Lenin raised these to a high art which has characterized Marxism-Leninism ever since. This cognitive and emotional framework eased the transition from invective to murder when the Leninist Party became the Stalinist state machine.

## STALINISM

Stalinist state power was in many ways simply an expression of the self-interest of a new class of bureaucrats and managers in a backward country. Yet starting with the Leninist premise—that *this* Party and *this* state could fulfill the basic interests of the working class in particular and humanity in general—the Stalinist state developed its own sick logic. What were its main features?

First, by the mid-1920s it was clear that the international revolution had failed. In opposition to the tradition of all of Russian social-democracy, Stalin then proclaimed the doctrine of "Socialism in One Country." The Soviet Union would be all of the revolution. Socialism would happen here no matter what happened elsewhere. At the same time, however, Stalin also introduced the idea of "building socialism." This meant that while the Soviet Union was trying to be the world's sole socialist nation, the full benefits of abundance and equality were not to be expected until the future. Consequently, it was acceptable to continue economic inequality, enhance the privileges of the managers and Party members, and divide workers between planning and primitive labor, power and obedience.

Since socialism had not yet been achieved in this (supposedly) post-revolutionary society, Soviet citizens should expect a continued "intensification of class conflict." Failures of the economy were the work of saboteurs who sought to overthrow the state. Differences over policy were explained as counter-revolutionary plots. These ideological smokescreens justified decades of terror applied to an increasingly cowed population. Further, since the socialist paradise was encircled by hostile capitalist powers, the Soviet state could use these justifications indefinitely. The basic political goals of Marx and Engels—the withering away of the state, the wide sharing of political power, the replacement of politics by administration—were all deferred to the distant future.

In 1936 it was announced that socialism had finally triumphed in the Soviet Union. This *was* socialism, and anyone who didn't like it was therefore anti-socialist. Along with the now-inevitable purges which followed this incredible distortion of reality came the destruction of even the conception of communism. From a vision of real human fulfillment, Soviet theory now defined it with simple-minded truisms about meeting people's needs, raising the level of consumption, and maintaining the power of the Party.

These ideas justified the turns and twists of Soviet domestic and foreign policy. The forced and sudden collectivization of agriculture alienated even those peasants who might have been won over—and led to the decision to intentionally starve out from five to fifteen million middle and wealthy peasants who resisted. The many failures of industrial planning were the inevitable result of trying to run a modern economy on the basis of medieval beliefs and terror. On the eve of World War II, Stalin made the lunatic decision to purge one-third of Russia's generals. There were also consistent betrayals of revolutionary movements in other countries in order to serve temporary Soviet interests.

Finally, it must be noted that despite the constant appeal to Marx and Lenin, Stalinism was forced to invoke pre-modern ideologies to justify itself. The most crucial of these was the near deification of The Leader. Consider Stalin's speech at Lenin's graveside in 1924:

> We Communists are people of a special mold. We are made of a special stuff. We are those who form the army of the great proletarian strategist, the army of Comrade Lenin. . . . There is nothing higher than the title of member of the Party whose founder and leader was Comrade Lenin. (in Leonhard 1971: 95)

As Wolfgang Leonhard comments, these words show the embryonic forms of Stalinism:

> The comparison of the Party with an army, the marked emphasis on the leading role of the party whose members were of a "special type" . . . the

indirect though perceptible claim to infallibility, and the glorification of one person (at this point still Lenin) as the "leader." (95)

After taking full power by the late 1920s, Stalin exaggerated this pose to what later communists called the "cult of personality." All the forces of state propaganda represented Stalin as the most intelligent, devoted, and fearless of men. Virtually every topic in the state press had to have its obligatory comment from Stalin. Successes in any field were laid to his door—while failures were always blamed on his enemies. He was the "Father of the world—the Sun" to national and international communism. Since he was at the right hand of God in this officially atheistic society, his opponents could not simply be honorable citizens who disagreed. They had to be wretched sinners deserving nothing less than death. Thus, we see the utter bankruptcy of this version of Marxism: the philosophy of revolutionary freedom, collective control, and self-development devolved into the deification of a bloody tyrant and the entrenched power of a selfish and corrupt bureaucracy.

## WHY DID IT HAPPEN?

We can begin by taking issue with an interesting, but I believe essentially mistaken, position put forward by Tony Smith. Smith argues that since Marxism has no theory or understanding of independent state power, it is incapable of resisting Stalinism. For Smith, its theoretical stress on class forces and interests blinds Marxism to the possibility of domination and oppression stemming from a political elite as opposed to an economic one.

> Marxism would be obliged to deny that an accumulation of the kind of power Stalin wielded could exist, for the simple reason that the theory discounts the power and independence of things political . . . (Smith 1987: 93)

This seems plausible at first: Marxism does claim that the economy is socially primary. The concrete reduction of all forces in social life to class interests is a primitive—but not totally alien—form of Marxism. When Soviet leaders defined socialism as electric power plus soviets, or narrowly Marxist criticisms of the Soviet Union insisted that if it were not socialist it had to be capitalist, they had some basis in the tradition.

But this is surely not the whole story. For one thing, Marx's frequent denial of the autonomy of politics is focused on the bourgeois state, which typically represents itself as being above class interests when it in fact serves them. Since only in capitalism do we find a sharp institutional separation between political and economic power, only here can we argue that the former serves the latter. In feudalism and other pre-capitalist societies, as Marx observed, economic surplus is often extracted by "extra-economic" means, i.e., by force or tradition, not the hidden unequal exchange of surplus labor. The relationship of exploitation is not clearly economic or political but a fusion of both. In socialism, political and economic power will fuse again.

In other words, divisions between "economics" and "politics" do not exist in every society. Soviet society located class power in the Soviet state, the Party, and the managing bureaucrats. They controlled productive life, co-opted the surplus, directed investment, and controlled the labor process. And they did so in virtue of their political power. These authorities were not institutionally divided into public government and private property. The two functions were not separate, with priority going to the political, as Smith suggests. Rather, they collapsed into one central power.[11]

That Marxists can recognize the dangers of one-party domination is also shown by the fact that Leninism and Stalinism have been widely criticized by other Marxists. When Lenin first promoted his vision of the vanguard party, he encountered much resistance from other social-democrats. At the 1903 Russian Social Democratic congress, Trotsky issued a terribly prophetic warning about a situation in which, after having substituted the Party for the class

the party organization is substituted for the party, the Central committee is substituted for the party organization, and finally a single "dictator" is substituted for the Central Committee. (Daniels 1960 I: 31)

Similarly, Rosa Luxemburg criticized Lenin for confusing "the corpselike obedience of a dominated class and the organized rebellion of a class struggling for its liberation." (Luxemburg 1971: 191) These reasonably orthodox Marxists clearly saw that the Leninist vanguard could become a power elite.

In the immediate aftermath of the revolution, Kautsky, another orthodox Marxist, sharply criticized the Bolsheviks for repressing democracy, relying on terror, and silencing the opposition:

> Even for the Russian revolutionaries it is a shortsighted policy of expediency, if they adopt the method of dictatorship in order to gain power, not to save the jeopardized democracy, but in order to maintain themselves in spite of it. (Kautsky 1964: 138)

Kindred concerns were expressed by the Bund, the Russian and Polish Jewish social-democratic party, which conceptualized the interests of the impoverished Jewish masses along Marxist and socialist lines. Bundists criticized Lenin for "blind bureaucratic centralism"; for overly stressing distinctions between leaders and followers, intellectuals and workers; and for the collapse of democracy in the Soviet Union (Tobias 1972, Johnpoll 1967, Weinryb 1970). Further, as we will see in Chapter 5, the beginnings of Western Marxism are found in Karl Korsch's (1971) critique of Bolshevism for creating a dictatorship "over, not of," the working class.

After Stalin achieved undisputed power, Trotsky—co-leader of the 1917 uprising and commander of the Red Army during the civil war—developed a series of critically dissenting positions. In 1928 he sought a reform of the Party through increased worker control and a return to political power for the soviets. By 1933, he advocated reforming the state by replacing the bureaucracy-dominated CP. In 1935, in *The Revolution Betrayed*, he supported a political revolution against the state bureaucracy as a whole—but still failed to see that the Soviet system had created a new social form which was neither socialist nor capitalist. Finally, in 1939, he acknowledged the possibility that the bureaucrats were not simply administrators caught between the socialist interests of the working class and the capitalist interests of the rich, but had evolved into a new form of class power in which politics and economics had fused.

These points—and many more could be offered—indicate that there is no necessary connection between Marxism and the tyrannical forms which evolved in the Soviet Union, its satellites in Eastern Europe, China, and other supposedly "actually existing socialist" countries. Because Leninism—and then Stalinism—triumphed, these betrayals came to define the public meaning of the ideologies they trumpeted. But this political history need not determine *our* assessment of the possibly constructive, liberating force of Marxist theory and socialist politics.

Yet we still need to reflect on the evolution of communism out of Marxism. I believe the essential lesson is that it is impossible to skip over the necessary forms of collective transformation which are essential to the transition from class to classless society. The distortion that allows for Marxism to become communism rests, then, in a denial of the fundamental necessity of the change from subjugation to freedom, obedience to empowerment, ignorance to awareness on the part of the mass of the population.

Herbert Marcuse (1958) claimed that the philosophical basis of Stalinist practice was a "new rationality"; i.e., a new—and highly distorted—perspective on how we are to evaluate social life. Marcuse argued that the rush to modernize in the Soviet Union necessarily skipped over the long development of individual legal, moral, and cognitive responsibility characteristic of bourgeois liberalism. In the West, this sense of responsibility had been embedded in a social order in which the economic structure denied it to the vast majority of people. It was a privilege of the wealthy, for whom individual choice was supported rather than crushed by class position. Yet despite its considerable ideological limitations, the notion of a subjective capacity to assess issues of truth and rationality provided a basis for a certain amount of independence in thought and action; a capacity, no matter how deformed by class inequality, to make judgments independent of authority. This capacity had never been widely generated in the Soviet Union.[12] To the extent that Party intellectuals retained it, Stalin successfully replaced them with loyal functionaries drawn almost exclusively from the working class. (Fitzpatrick 1982)

Revolutionaries were further threatened by the way developments in the Soviet Union violated their understanding of social life. A minority proletariat had taken power against the wishes of the majority of the country. After the brief years of revolutionary flare-ups in Europe, the workers of the world had not united for radical change but instead had abandoned the Soviets to their own fate. The economy was in a shambles and the first major economic policy—the NEP—based itself not on socialist economics but on capitulating to peasant greed in order to get food to the starving cities. Finally, the state did not command the respect of the mass of the people and so had to coerce them. What could the communists do? Either abandon their life's work or tell themselves and others that the work was succeeding. The essential notion of Marxism—that the working class could make a revolution and vest its interests in a revolutionary government—had to be proclaimed over and over again, *despite* the obvious reality that it was not so.

The ritualized language [of Soviet Marxism] preserves the original content of Marxian theory as a truth that must be believed and enacted *against all evidence* to the contrary: the people must do and feel and think as if their state were the reality of that reason, freedom, and justice which the ideology proclaims. . . . (Marcuse 1958: 73, my emphasis)

To cling to the revolution, the leaders themselves had to sacrifice the capacity for independent ideas. The state, directed by the Party, became the standard of reason and truth. In this new rationality, as Marcuse describes it, there was no need or justification for critical thought:

To transcend that which is, to set subjective reason against state reason, to appeal to higher norms and values, belong to the prerogatives of class society. . . . In contrast, Soviet society institutionalizes the real interests of the individuals—by this token it contains all standards of true and false, right and wrong. (Marcuse 1958: 70)

Is this description of Stalinist logic an unfounded exaggeration? Could otherwise intelligent, experienced, dedicated people believe this drivel? In fact, it *was* the mentality of many communists, from the leaders to the rank and file. As they had trusted the Party, now they followed the state. As Trotsky said in his pledge of obedience after being defeated on several policy issues in 1924:

> In the last analysis the party is always right, because the party is the single historical instrument given to the proletariat for the solution of its fundamental problems . . . . I know that one must not be right against the party, for history has created no other road for the realization of what is right. . . . (in Smith 1987: 94)

Why did the Party deserve complete allegiance? Because, devoted communists believed, it was the central agent of fundamental historical change, a change which would realize humanity's most essential goals. This unshakable foundation shaped their answers to questions of fidelity to the Party, the morality of political life, and the permissible uses of violence.

Is this glorification of the communist state and denial of individual ethical responsibility really part of the Marxist tradition?

On the one hand, Marx believed that most appeals to ethical principles were really ideological subterfuges. While appealing to universal standards of truth and goodness, moral claims actually reflected and reinforced existing class relations. The liberal theory of rights, as generations of Marxists have shown, was the philosophical expression of the capitalist need for free access to investment, buying, selling, and overcoming the entrenched privileges of the hereditary aristocracy. Supporters of the universal "rights of man" had no trouble co-existing with slavery, the inequality of women, or the exploitation of the working class.

On the other hand, however, a clear moral passion animates all of Marx's writings. It is in his earliest essays, which manifest a powerful commitment to ending all oppressive social conditions, as well as in the idea, running through his theory of exploitation, that the labor theory of value reveals a hidden form of unequal, unjust exchange.

More generally, it is clear that Marx believed that socialism would fulfill human capacities—and that it was good and right that this occur. Unlike the ideologically bound vision of bourgeois democracy, socialism would actually meet everyone's authentic interests.

Does Marxism in any way resolve the contradictions between these two viewpoints? And in that resolution, are there moral limits on the behavior of the revolutionaries? [13] In particular, does Marxism justify repressing all dissent, liquidating opponents, lying and distorting history to fulfill its goals?

My own view is that the essential Marxist position is that moral claims are ultimately justified by the interests they fulfill. There is no *absolute* justification, if by "absolute" we mean rooted in something other than human interests. The values of the communist, then, aim to fulfill the interests of the working class and other oppressed groups and are justified solely on that basis. Further, the Marxist perspective claims that only under certain social conditions can a truly moral social order exist. Economic underdevelopment, cultural backwardness, class domination, rigid hierarchies, pervasive division of subservient and managerial labor—these conditions make the fulfillment of ethical goals impossible. The ethical ideal of the "revolutionary," then, is to serve the interests of the proletariat *by creating the social conditions which make morality truly possible.* Any policy, political opposition, or moral scruple which gets in the way of this task deserves no protection or sanction. Building on this theoretical base, Lenin defined the "revolutionary" as the "communist party member." The Party would create a society without exploitation or domination, a social order in which human fulfillment is available to all, not just a privileged few.

Does this framework show that the roots of Stalinist terror lie in Marxism's fundamental lack of respect for the individual person and for universal human rights? Will Marxism just *have* to sacrifice innocent lives to some mythical higher purpose?[14] Does the absence of principles held without regard to final consequences mean that Marxist morality will always justify horrible means by utopian ends?

Before we jump to agree, let us consider two points confronting anyone making this criticism of Marxism. *First,* whenever socialists achieve state power non-violently, they are typically greeted with violence by socialism's enemies. Leftist, democratic, popularly elected governments took power in Spain in the 1930s and Chile in the 1970s. In Spain the Catholic Church, the army generals, and the wealthy—with the help of Italian and German fascism—initiated a civil war and eventually imposed a dictatorship. In Chile, the American CIA worked with the Chilean Army and the previous ruling class to engineer a rightist military coup in which close to fifty thousand trade unionists, socialists, community leaders, journalists, artists, and workers were murdered. The lesson from these events is that renouncing violence in defense of the revolution may mean submitting to the violence of the counter-revolution.

*Second*, however, to renounce violence in the revolution is also to accept the day-to-day violence of the established order.

> He who condemns all violence puts himself outside the domain to which justice and injustice belong. He puts a curse upon the world and human-ity—a hypocritical curse, since he who utters it has already accepted the rules of the game from the moment that he has begun to live. (Merleau-Ponty 1969: 110)

Virtually every social order and every modern staté was founded on a bedrock of violence: the genocide against Native Americans; religious and nationalist wars in Western Europe; colonial and anti-colonial struggles in Latin America, Africa, and Asia. The colonization of the Congo by Belgium and subsequent destruction of half its population in ten years was not carried out by atheist Marxists but by Christians and capitalists, those who proclaim their respect for the individual, human rights, and the soul. The two World Wars were initiated by capitalist nations in pursuit of economic interests. The abject conditions of the industrial working class throughout the nineteenth century, black slavery, the American bombing of Cambodia—these and count-less other examples show that whatever the many failings of commu-nism, it is no more attracted to violence than other modern social systems. As Merleau-Ponty put it:

> Communism does not invent violence but finds it already institutional-ized. . . . The question is not to know whether one accepts or rejects

violence, but whether the violence with which one is allied is "progressive" and tends towards its own suspension or toward self-perpetuation.
. . . (Merleau-Ponty 1969: 1)

The idea of revolutionary Marxism, then, is that certain acts of violence can help create a social order in which the present violence will be eliminated. Unlike those who bemoan the fate of the oppressed and do nothing, the communist tries to translate ethical ideals into actual social relations. The ideals of liberalism have coexisted with exploitation of workers, racism, sexism, slavery, imperialism, and war. The communist claims to be pursuing a social course which will end all of these. We should not contrast the liberal capitalist respect for persons and the communist penchant for violence. Rather, we should ask: do the communist tactics and strategy move, as Merleau-Ponty put it, towards self-perpetuation or dissolution?

The historical answer is clear: no less than capitalist liberalism, communism tends toward self-preservation. Whatever its stated goals, its actual conduct has been political tyranny.

There are many reasons for this, not the least of which is the constant outside threat posed by capitalist nations to any socialist state. There are also particular issues having to do with the personality of the leaders, the structure of the national culture, and the organization of local classes.

Yet in terms of my focus here, I believe one issue is paramount. *The failure of Marxist communism stems from the deep conviction of the most sincere[15] Party members that the possession of Marxist-Leninist theory provided them with infallible knowledge of the ultimate needs of the working class and— by implication—of humanity as a whole.* The reliance on theory and the interpretation of that theory as a scientific authority was used to justify tyranny. Did the workers and soldiers resist or disagree, as in the workers' opposition and the Kronstadt rebellion? Then they were wrong—for the Party, guided by the certainties of Marxism-Leninism, was the embodiment of Truth. Did previously brave, devoted communists disagree? Then they were no longer brave and devoted, but cowardly and traitorous—for they were opposing the doctrine which would protect the revolution and usher in the era of human fulfillment.

Were there doubts, questions, uncertainties? These must be banished, for only total commitment could protect the gains won so far and promote the future. Did the Party leadership—i.e., Stalin—radically change its position on central issues without explanation or apology? Then it had good reasons to do so, reasons not to be questioned by the rank and file any more than lay people questioned doctors or physicists. Was there any question whether communists were really working for the good of the masses? Then the doubters had to be silenced, for a communist party could insist (with a vengeance) that it was whatever it said it was.

The fundamental problem, in other words, was a belief that the revolution, this most basic transformation of human social relations, could be directed by experts—could be external to the self-understanding and self-transformation of the mass of people who make up a society. Lenin's nearly anarchist description of the acquisition of authority by ordinary citizens (in *State and Revolution*) offered a model of equality of power. Yet that model was ultimately foreign to all of Bolshevik practice, and always had been. Lenin and his Party virtually always met disagreement with vituperation, expulsions, splitting and—after the revolution—repression. The working class would share in power in the Leninist state only when it became exactly what the Leninists wanted it to be. If it was not that, or if it had been decimated by war and economic collapse, or if the peasantry preferred its own communal institutions to state collectives, or if nationalities wanted independence, or if revolutionaries in other countries did not see the wisdom of the Comintern's directives and the necessity to sacrifice their own standing to the whims of the Soviet leadership—then in all such cases they had to be defeated, discredited, expelled, or, if possible, destroyed. In the end, Marxist theory simply became the *ideology of the state bureaucrat*, justifying the central power of the Party while claiming to represent all of humanity.

The weaknesses of Marx, furthered by the mechanical Marxism of the Second International, blossomed into the Leninist/Stalinist absolute trust in a centralized authority. Therefore, Russian communism had no answer to the following questions. (In fact, it could not even ask them.)

—Given the inevitable tendencies of power centers to arrogate power, who will protect the working class from the state?

—Given the separation of the centralized state from the day-to-day working of the economy, as well as its tendency to appropriate wealth through force rather than productivity, what will keep the centralized state from eventually being simply a drag on the economy?

—What social structures other than centralized political power will embody the will, interests, experiences, and resources of the working class?

In the first decade of the revolution all independent or potentially independent sources of organization and countervailing power were destroyed: opposition within the Party, other parties, soviets, peasant communes, independent intellectual or cultural life. Marx's idea of a single, "universal" *class* whose political emancipation would liberate humanity was transformed into the notion of a single *political institution* which would force that emancipation in the name of, and as a substitute for, workers themselves. Violence was an inevitable result not of the idea of socialism or revolution, but of the substitution of a small elite for the mass of people who are to be liberated.

Our conclusion can only be that revolution cannot be made "in the name" of some other group, but only by the group itself. Further, we see that only the most complete freedom of self-organization and self-expression will allow the mass of people to determine whether or not the centers of political, economic, and social power actually fulfill their interests. Even if we could trust that "The Party" will make the revolution, we can never be sure that *this* party is the real one, and not some collection of bureaucrats, weak-willed reformists, or aspiring tyrants. The task of the genuine revolutionary is therefore to help generate capacities for self-organization and self-expression on the part of the mass of people in society, to foster many independent self-acting, self-conscious centers of power and awareness. Only through these resources can a revolution truly be made, and only in a society characterized by these resources can the terrible fall into brutal dictatorship be prevented.[16]

Finally, if we try to apply the lessons of the Soviet experience to our own society, we must ask: Given the power of the modern bourgeois state and the increase in general economic stability since the 1930s, do Marxists have any choice but to embrace the revisionism of Bernstein? Is the slow accretion of propaganda and electoral power the only route to power for non-communist socialists? Yet if we embrace this evolutionary socialism, how are the "independent" centers and the self-acting consciousness which I have described to arise in a mass society dominated by enormous hierarchical institutions, the presumptions of managerial and scientific expertise, and a deadening popular culture of mass consumption? In an emotionally repressive society which promotes all kinds of addictive behavior, spectacle, and violent acting out, how are we ever to find out what people's real needs or interests are? *These dilemmas remain at the heart of Marxist theory and practice.*

## POSTSCRIPT: THE FALL OF COMMUNISM

We are as yet far too close to the historical upheavals of communism in the Soviet Union and its former satellites to know what political, economic, and social order will emerge in those countries. From my standpoint, the Soviet Union passed beyond the realm of Marx's theory and values with the advent of Stalinism. While Stalinism does tell us something about the weaknesses of Marxism, we do not necessarily learn anything new about Marxism from the economic and political failures of the Soviet Union since that time, or from the associated failures of the rest of Eastern Europe. In my view, the recent developments simply confirm the criticisms of Stalinism that (as we shall further see in Chapter 5) Marxist theorists have been making for decades.

Ironically, the collapse of communism is in some respects actually a confirmation of Marxism. Marx, after all, did claim that when social relations of production block development of the forces of production, the relations would be swept away. The history of communism shows that you cannot develop and maintain a modern economy on the basis of totalitarian terror. Inserted in a competitive world market and structured by constantly improving technology, modern economies need a free flow of information, some reward for personal and small group initiative, responsiveness to the needs and capacities of regions, and an ability and willingness to identify and correct errors. Communist tyranny makes these functions impossible. Its economic failures led to its political demise. This is completely in keeping with some of Marx's most general statements about how social life develops.

And yet, at least one very concrete theoretical and practical dilemma is raised now. I will simply state it and leave detailed studies to other authors.

The dilemma concerns the role of markets in a socialist society. The failures of the so-called socialist economies have raised serious doubts for many about the economic viability of central planning as the basic mechanism for the allocation of goods/services. Some people have argued that in fact some kind of market mechanism is essential. If it is, we may still wonder whether there can be socialist markets, markets without enormous concentrations of wealth and power that characterize, with all its drawbacks, a capitalist economy. (Le Grand and Estrin 1989) When socialists demand "collective control" of the forces of production, then, what exactly do we mean? How is that control to be at once democratic, just, and efficient? How do we mediate between the ordinary citizens and the centers of economic authority? Between authentic human needs and the actual decisions concerning investment and production? What speculation Marx offers on these questions is generally by way of an abstract philosophical orientation or utopian speculation. It is clearly one of the tasks of socialist theorists to articulate, however tentatively or provisionally, answers to these questions. The failures of communism demand that of anyone who claims to be against capitalism.

# III

## REBIRTH

# 5

## WESTERN MARXISM: THE
## ROLE OF CONSCIOUSNESS

The triumph of Stalinism spelled the death of Marxism. The worst features of the original theory dominated the only "successful" revolution, while in Europe and the U.S. communist radicals coalesced into servile and dogmatic cliques. In the Third World, Marxism-Leninism became the program of nationalist, peasant-based, anti-imperialist movements. Whatever our estimation of the ultimate character of these movements, we of the industrialized world cannot take either their theory or practice as our models. Meanwhile, economic and social crises came to advanced capitalism, yet power and authority remained with the ruling class.

Even at the beginning of these catastrophes, Marxist theory was reborn in the writings of the "Western" Marxists. [1] The first of these thinkers had witnessed the political failures of European socialism around World War I, and later ones saw the Russian Revolution degenerate into tyranny. As time wore on, they further realized that capitalism was learning to manage its economic and political contradictions. Since they rejected both capitalism and Leninist communism, these writers had to re-think the relation between the mode of production and the rest of society, generate a much more sophisticated understanding of the control capitalists exercised over the working class, and offer new models of revolutionary social change.

In describing the basic ideas of Western Marxism, I will necessarily ignore very real differences which exist both among different thinkers and over the more than half century during which this tradition has developed. What all the thinkers on whom this chapter is based have in common—and what animates this book as well—is the effort to criticize both capitalism and communism without abandoning the truths of Marxism. While these writers never led mass movements, they kept the original spirit of Marxism alive in a very dark time, and many of their ideas foreshadowed and influenced radical politics of the 1960s and 1970s.

## MARXISM AND SCIENCE

Seizing on some (but clearly not all) elements in Marx's writings, the Second and Third Internationals understood historical materialism in a positivist framework. Since historical materialism offered a "science" of history, those who understood it could wield the authority of experts. Just as chemists and engineers could understand and manipulate the natural world, so Marxist experts could understand and manipulate people.

We have presented a number of arguments against this positivist understanding of Marxism in Chapter 2. The Western Marxist writers Karl Korsch, Georg Lukács, Max Horkheimer, Herbert Marcuse, Antonio Gramsci, Theodor Adorno, and Wilhelm Reich were instrumental in generating the perspective out of which those arguments came. They sought a theory which could be both rational and dedicated to human freedom, a "critical theory" of social life.

We may begin in 1923, with the German socialist Karl Korsch. Korsch responded to the theoretical failures of the Second International by denying that "scientific socialism" was scientific in the positivist sense.

> Nothing was further from [Marx and Engels] than the claim to impartial, pure, theoretical study, above class difference, made by . . . most of the . . . Marxists of the Second International. The scientific socialism of Marx and Engels . . . stands in contrast to these pure sciences of bourgeois society (economics, history or sociology). (Korsch 1971: 69)

> The correct materialist conception of history . . . is incompatible with separate branches of knowledge that are isolated and autonomous, and with purely theoretical investigations that are *scientifically objective in disassociation from revolutionary practice.* (32, my emphasis)

Far from being detached from values or interests, Marxist theory is actually directly connected to the practice of revolutionary politics. It is *motivated* by the commitment to alter social life fundamentally, it must be *integrated* into the political practice which aims in that direction, and it must constantly be *evaluated* in terms of its practical results. If these connections are severed, Korsch claimed, Marxism becomes simply another ideology. The mistakes of the leaders of the Second International—turning Marxism into a positivist science and waiting for the "inevitable" revolution—are lessons in this regard. The distortions of the theory mirrored the separation of that theory from an activist movement.

Georg Lukács described another problem which arises when Marxism is considered a science. A positivist model simply reproduces the passivity which flows from the social phenomenon of "reification." By this term he meant the way all aspects of society seem given or objective. Bourgeois society protects its unjust social relations by denying that they are the creation of—and therefore can be changed by—the people in the society. Further, attempts to think about how human beings actually create the system are frustrated by "rationalization"—the systematic tendency to think about only small parts of the social totality. The structure of capitalist society is also "rationalized" in this sense. While particular parts—a factory, a science, technological development—become increasingly sophisticated, the society as a whole becomes increasingly irrational. To understand this point, one need only think of how highly developed technology causes life-threatening pollution.

If, as in the positivist perspective, knowledge is the passive reflection of a pre-given reality, the knower can only adopt a passive attitude toward that reality. By contrast, revolutionary theory, Lukács argues, requires that social reality be seen as the product of action, an expression of the same subjectivity which possesses knowledge of it. Joining knowledge and reality—theory and practice—in this way is the essential feature of an authentic class consciousness. Any other sense of what Marxist theory is will simply leave workers as passive "observers" of a social reality they cannot alter.

Max Horkheimer, the German philosopher and socialist who in the 1930s founded what came to be called the Frankfurt School of Critical Theory, echoes Lukács' point:

> Theory . . . practiced in the pursuit of the specialized sciences organizes experience in the light of questions which arise out of life in present-day society. . . . The social genesis of problems, the real situations in which science is put to use, and the purposes which it is made to serve are all regarded as external to itself.
>
> The *critical theory of society*, on the other hand, *has for its object men as producers of their own historical way of life in its totality*. The real situations which are the starting-point of science are not regarded simply as data to be verified and to be predicted according to the laws of probability. Every datum depends *not on nature alone but also on the power man has over it*. Objects, the kind of perception, the questions asked, and the meaning of the answers all bear witness to human activity and the degree of man's power. (Horkheimer 1972: 244)

Theories which will contribute to revolutionary change must be shaped by a commitment to radical social change. They are "objective," if that implies a willingness to examine data, discuss alternative forms of understanding, allow criticisms, and alter previous conclusions. But they are *not* objective if that means "detached" from the struggle for a better world. They are not "value free" or "value neutral." Their fundamental purpose is to identify and overcome unnecessary suffering and injustice. Thus, the very concepts they use to describe social reality are "value laden." Does this make them "unscientific"? Only if the natural sciences are taken as the model of all knowledge[2] and if we abandon all attempts rationally to evaluate social life. But we could then only use our rational intellect to describe how things are and not to say why things are not as good as they could be or how to make them better. Nor would we be able to attempt to communicate rationally about *why* we think things are unjust and need to be changed. Our vocabulary—and our moral and political lives—would be crippled.

The mistaken aping of natural science, Korsch argued, was a presupposition of the communist dictatorship *over*, not *of*, the working class. Communist leaders had accepted Lenin's earlier claim that knowledge is "merely the passive mirror and reflection of. . . objective Being in the subjective Consciousness." Commitment to this crude materialism stemmed partly from the belief that the "truths" of materialism were politically progressive and that a "scientific" outlook would help defeat the political and social conservatism of religion, philosophical idealism, and tradition. For Korsch, however, not religion but a positivist conception of science was the reigning ideology.

> The dominant basic trend in contemporary bourgeois philosophy, natural science and humanities is the same as it was sixty or seventy years ago. It is inspired not by an idealist outlook but by a materialist outlook that is coloured by the natural sciences. (Korsch 1971: 129)

Any Marxist theory, such as Lenin's, which does not recognize this fact is "not theoretically capable of answering the practical needs of the international class struggle in the present period." (130)

For Western Marxists, a positivist orientation produces dictatorship, not socialism. In the end, a pretense to "scientific authority" will lead to blind dogmatism. The certainty that Marxism alone—and

this particular version of Marxism expressed at this particular time—
possesses the final truth will keep people from thinking clearly and
honestly about anything.

> For years the Marxist intellectual believed that he served his party by
> violating experience, by overlooking embarrassing details, by grossly
> simplifying the data, and above all, by conceptualizing the event *before*
> having studied it. . . . At the time [1956] of the second Soviet intervention
> in Hungary, each group [of Marxists] already had its mind made up before
> it possessed any information on the situation. It had decided in advance
> whether it was witnessing an act of aggression on the part of the Russian
> bureaucracy against the democracy of Workers' Committees . . . or a
> counterrevolutionary attempt which Soviet moderation had known how
> to check. Later there was news, a great deal of news; but I have not heard
> it said that even one Marxist changed his opinion. (Sartre 1963: 23)

If Marxist theory is disconnected from a politically developing
proletariat, that class becomes another "object" of knowledge to be
manipulated in the same way the natural sciences enable us to manipulate nature. As Korsch stated and the Frankfurt School argued at length,
this view of science was endemic not just to Marxism but to the
modern bourgeois world as a whole. Roles previously played by
religion, tradition, or the invisible hand of laissez-faire capitalism were
absorbed by the (supposedly) disinterested, objective power of modern
science and technology. Thus, the relevance of Western Marxism's
position here extends beyond the history of Marxist theory. Rather, it
shows a fundamental problem in modern consciousness and culture:
the advent of science as authority.

Continuing the discussions raised in chapters 2 and 4, it will be
useful to examine how Max Horkheimer, Herbert Marcuse, Theodor
Adorno, and Jürgen Habermas (all part of the Frankfurt School of
critical theory) criticized this ideology of science. From Plato to Hegel,
the argument begins, the traditional philosophical concept of reason
had been identified with the capacity to choose ends appropriate to
human nature or to existence as such. The bourgeoisie had constructed
a much more restricted concept. It came to identify "reason" with
"science" and use the latter term in an extremely limited way. Origi-

nally a critical concept in the service of the bourgeoisie's struggle against the feudal order, "science" now justified domination. In the form of what Horkheimer called "traditional" theory, or what Marcuse and Habermas called "instrumental" or "technological" rationality, the goal of positivist rationality is an ordered system of propositions which reveal the world "as it is." Interests, norms, and goals are now separate from reason, beyond the bounds of intelligent argument.

On this conception of reason, only questions about the efficiency of actions and the accuracy of information can be rationally assessed. While the "success" of science and technology are paraded as proof of their rationality, discussion of the ultimate worth of the goals of institutions and practices are banished from the realm of rational discussion. Rational critique of the effects of physically compelling but ultimately destructive technologies and institutions is not possible.

As this conception of the relation between science, technique, and rationality becomes more widespread, technical experts seem to be the bearers of truth.

> The objective and impersonal character of technological rationality bestows upon bureaucratic groups the universal dignity of reason. The rationality embedded in the giant enterprises makes it appear as if men, in obeying them, obey the dictates of an objective rationality. . . . Private power relationships appear not only as relationships between objective things, but also as the rule of rationality itself. (Marcuse 1941: 431)

This pretense to scientific "Enlightenment" rejects all forms of thought which assess or assert the quality of life.

> Bourgeois society is ruled by equivalence. It makes the dissimilar comparable by reducing it to abstract quantities. To the enlightenment, that which does not reduce to numbers . . . becomes illusion; modern positivism writes it off as literature. (Horkheimer and Adorno 1974: 7)

As a result, the critical capacity to question social norms and institutions is lost.

Thinking objectifies itself to become an automatic, self-activating process; an impersonation of the machine that it produces itself so that ultimately the machine can replace it . . . Mathematical procedures become, so to speak, the ritual of thinking. In spite of the axiomatic self-restriction, it establishes itself as necessary and objective; it turns thought into a thing, an instrument . . . (Horkheimer and Adorno 1974: 25)

In such a world critical questions cannot be raised. Engineers and bureaucrats, masters of physical power and administrative efficiency, seem the only possessors of reason. As science and technology lead to power without reflection, bureaucratic structures run "efficiently" towards Auschwitz.

It is not clear exactly what form a critical theory should have, and Western Marxists have often differed here. But we can identify three significant features which sharply distinguish a critical Marxist social theory from natural science or positivist social science. Theory here makes no pretense at detachment from human concerns, but is rooted in the commitment to creating a free, just, and rational society. This commitment shapes the theory's basic evaluative concepts and directs it to search not just to find out what "is" but what "can be." Second, the theory pre-supposes that people create social life in its most essential aspects. The realization of freedom, reason, and justice depend not on "objective factors" but on awakening a certain human capacity for collective action. Third, this awakening depends on identifying the ways in which human capacities for self-understanding and fulfilling action are blunted by human relationships. The theory seeks "emancipation"—the overcoming of false beliefs and social structures which make social conditions unnecessarily limiting.[3]

## PRIMACY AND HISTORICAL MATERIALISM

In two basic ways, Western Marxists have considerably altered the traditional Marxist stress on the primacy of the mode of production.

First, they denied that an analysis of the structure and dynamic of the mode of production could by itself tell us what the social future would be. In particular, Western Marxists rejected Marx's confidence that industrialization and recurrent economic crises would necessarily create a revolutionary class consciousness among workers. Marx's rudimentary social psychology was rendered suspect by the failure of revolutionary movements and by the rise of fascism, rather than socialism, out of the world economic crisis of the 1930s. These events led Western Marxists to focus on how personal experience in capitalist society obstructs the emergence of revolutionary class consciousness, and how the political structures of advanced capitalism—most important, the state—manage the system to preserve ruling class power.

Thus for Antonio Gramsci, leader of the Italian Communist Party during the 1920s, economic structure only "sets the terrain" on which political and cultural issues are decided, only creates a context for the posing of certain questions rather than others. (Gramsci 1971: 184, 410–2). The mode of production brought a wide range of possibilities into existence. Which possibilities were realized depended on political struggle, national culture, and the collective experience of the major classes.

As a corollary of this position, Western Marxists argued that the "mode of production" could not be thought of as an isolated set of quantifiable and purely economic activities and relationships. Korsch claimed that economics and ideology, matter and consciousness, base and superstructure, were "dialectically" connected. They conditioned each other causally and determined each others' identity. The classic Marxist division of social life into an economic system opposed to politics, ideology, and consciousness was a mistake.

> The material relations of production of the capitalist epoch *only are what they are in combination with the forms in which they are reflected in the prescientific and bourgeois scientific consciousness of the period; and they could not subsist in reality without those forms of consciousness.* (Korsch 1971: 88–9, my emphasis)

Economic ideas themselves only *appear* to be related to the material relations of production of bourgeois society in the way an image is related to the object it reflects. In fact *they are related to them in the way that a specific, particularly defined part of a whole is related to the other parts of this whole.* Bourgeois economics [i.e., economic theory] belongs with the material relations of production to bourgeois society as a totality. This totality also contains political and legal representations and their apparent objects. . . . It also includes the higher ideologies of the art, religion and philosophy of bourgeois society. . . . Their ensemble forms the *spiritual structure* of bourgeois society, which corresponds to its economic structure, just as its legal and political superstructure correspond to this same basis. (98, my emphasis)

Lukács (1971) was making the same point when he suggested, to the horror of traditional Marxists, that true orthodoxy in Marxism was not economic determinism, but the point of view of "totality."

If capitalist society is what it is only because of the particular coincidence of "material relations" and "consciousness," then there can be no simple, one-way causal relations between the former and the latter. There cannot be an economic system distinct from ideology and politics. Nor can there be laws of economic development which necessarily bring about changes in society as a whole.

Also, changes in economic life considered in isolation—for instance, a fall in the rate of profit, high unemployment, the development of technology—will be historically significant only insofar as they are connected to structural changes in ideology and politics. What traditional Marxism claimed for politics, law, religion, philosophy, etc.—that they had no independent history—is now being claimed for the economic structure as well.

This position faces some very real dilemmas. In the last phrase of the second quotation, Korsch again seems to confer some kind of primacy on economics. Echoing Marx, he describes the economic structure as the "basis" to which the "legal and political superstructure" "corresponds." But if all aspects of society form a totality, how can one part be basic?

Like other members of the tradition, Korsch does not wish to deny all primacy to the mode of production. While Western Marxists have typically denied the most simplistic versions of Marxism, they also find relations of property and the activity of production to be central to social life. They focus on *bourgeois* society and *its* characteristic forms of politics, religion, law, art, etc. They do not categorize societies according to music or architecture. Neither do they believe we can learn as much about a society by studying its leisure activities as we can from its social relations of production.

Further, until the 1960s at any rate, Western Marxists shared with traditional Marxism the belief that the source of revolutionary social change had to lie in the organized working class. Workers were seen as having a *potential* political destiny because of their *actual* role in production. Political strategy still depended on an analysis of economic structure.

Thus, this tradition rejects orthodox Marxism but remains Marxist. This uneasy balance leads to a wide range in the particular positions we find in it. There is, however, one critical implication which must be stressed here. In Korsch's words, given the way different aspects of society form a totality:

> All these forms must be subjected to the revolutionary social criticisms of scientific socialism . . . They must be criticized in practice . . . Just as political action is not rendered unnecessary by the economic action of a revolutionary class, so intellectual action is not rendered unnecessary by either political or economic action. (Korsch 1971: 96–7)

Each dimension of social life requires its own struggle. An understanding of economics does not guarantee an understanding of culture or psychology. Changes in economic relations will not automatically produce changes in political relations or consciousness. With this claim, Western Marxism brought the critical question of class consciousness to center stage.

## WHAT IS CLASS CONSCIOUSNESS?

Western Marxists saw clearly that historical change is more dependent on the beliefs, attitudes, and personality structure of the working class than Marx had supposed. They had to ask: if the mode of production merely poses certain questions rather than others, *what dimensions of social life determine how those questions will be answered?* Their first answer was: economic crises caused by the inherent instability of capitalism would be resolved in progressive or non-progressive ways *depending* on working class consciousness.

Antonio Gramsci's concept of "hegemony"—developed in the 1920s—illuminates this issue. Hegemony signifies the dimensions of class power that are rooted in consent rather than force. Typically, the rulers of capitalist society do not have to constantly use violence to maintain their rule. The dominated think, act, and live in ways that take capitalism for granted. An uncritical and largely unconscious way of thinking forms a "common sense" compatible with capitalism. Therefore, ending capitalism means that oppressed groups must not only unify their "economic and political aims, but also possess intellectual and moral unity. (Gramsci 1971: 181–2) In other words, they not only have to follow the same leftist party and challenge existing political powers, they must come to a new common sense which understands work and politics in socialist, rather than capitalist, terms. Since present control is internalized in the minds and hearts of workers and peasants, a counter form of socialization, a counter form of self-identity, is required to overthrow that control.

Marxists had always seen the necessity for the working class to overcome bourgeois ideology. This overcoming, however, was seen as a more or less natural response to economic crises and to the homogeneity of working conditions. Rejecting orthodoxy, Gramsci denied that there was a controlling or predictable relation between the economy and the rest of social life. The emergence of a new consciousness is not seen as a necessary product of capitalist development. Rather, it is merely *one* of the possibilities set by that development.

The political implications of this view are highly significant. If "scientific Marxism" could assure us of the inevitability of the revolution, then it would be enough for Marxism to reveal the "truth" of history to us—"us" being a small body of intellectuals sufficiently educated to be able to understand and implement it. But if there are no "laws" of history, then our theory can at best tell us what possibilities exist. Which possibilities are realized, in turn, depend on the values, self-understanding, and political strategies of contending classes and groups. The political focus of Marxists should therefore be on awakening consciousness, not waiting to take advantage of inevitable economic crises.

This concept of hegemony also counters Leninist formulations of the role of the vanguard party. In a party where leaders dominate followers, a political crisis could easily lead to the betrayal of the mass by the elite. Without the internalization of new values and a new "common sense" by the mass of the working class, economic crises or even mass radical action—such as the factory takeovers by workers in Italy after World War I—would not lead to the overthrow of capitalism.[4] Similarly, however, any Leninist attempt to make the revolution by experts and bring the masses along later is *bound* to fail. If the masses remain in the control of experts, there is, *by definition*, no revolution.

Gramsci's ideas raise a central question, which Western Marxists have been answering for the last half century. How can the typical, ideologically deformed class consciousness in capitalist society change towards the commitment and capacity for socialism?

Lukács provided an intriguing answer to this question. Class consciousness, he argued, has two forms. First, there is the "actual" class consciousness that is the sum total of people's thoughts, feelings and beliefs at a given time. Second, there is "real" or "imputed" class consciousness, which

consists . . . of the appropriate and rational reactions "imputed" to a particular typical position in the process of production. . . . The historically significant actions of the class as a whole are determined in the last resort by this consciousness and not by the thought of the individual. (Lukács 1971: 51)

In this real class consciousness, the proletariat has the potential to "see society from the center, as a coherent whole." This will enable it to "act in such a way as to change reality; [for] in the class consciousness of the proletariat theory and practice coincide" (69). It is not simply a "scientific" analysis which will serve here, but a knowledge which necessarily changes those who possess it. To achieve real class consciousness is at the same time to become a self-active revolutionary agent.

This real class consciousness, Lukács believed, would develop because of workers' experience of capitalist exploitation and domination. The kernel of his argument is that while members of the bourgeoisie (mistakenly) experience themselves as controllers of bourgeois society, workers experience themselves as passive commodities. By coming to grips with their existence *as* commodities, the working class achieves real class consciousness.

> The quantitative differences in exploitation which appear to the capitalist in the form of quantitative determinants of the objects of his calculation, must appear to the worker as the decisive, qualitative categories of his whole physical, mental and moral existence. (Lukács 1971: 166)

What is for the capitalist a quantitative change in exploitation—more or less profit, a longer or shorter working day, more or fewer labor-saving devices—is experienced by the worker as a decisive change in his existence as a person. This is true, for instance, in regard to changes in the length of the working day,

> for the worker labour-time is not merely the objective form of the commodity he has sold, i.e., his labour power . . . In addition it is the determining form of his existence as subject, as human being. (Lukács 1971: 167)

Since a worker finds in "every aspect of his daily life" (165) that he ceases to be a subject, he is

> driven to surpass this immediacy . . . In his social existence the worker is immediately placed *wholly* on the side of the object. . . . But because of the split between subjectivity and objectivity induced in man by the compulsion to objectify himself as a commodity, the situation becomes one that can be made conscious. (178–9)

If workers can *know themselves* as commodities, the basis for real class consciousness will have been developed. The subjective status of knower and the objective condition of commodification contradict each other. As they know the truth of their situation, that situation will change.

When the worker knows himself as a commodity his knowledge is practical . . . [It] brings about an objective structured change in the object of knowledge. (169)

If its own existence as a commodity is revealed, the working class can come to understand how commodification affects society as a whole, that is, it will see through the "fetishism" by which relations between people are masked as characteristics of objects. Workers will see that they are humans being treated like things. Just as their commodification is a product of capitalist power, so is the rest of social life. As they can overcome their condition, so can society as a whole be transformed. The contradiction between the commodification of human existence under capitalism and the proletariat's subjective experience of that objectification makes possible the class consciousness which is the key to revolution. "There is no doubt that the factors mentioned above are *the indispensable precondition* for the emergence of the proletariat as a class." (173)

Lukács' theory of class consciousness deepens the simplistic social psychology on which traditional Marxism based its expectation of a working-class revolt. The subsequent failure of the class to become politically radical will then lead us to examine how their immediate experience prevents—rather than leads to—the development of class consciousness; or, we will at least see how that experience contains both radical and conservative aspects.

Although they made decisive contributions to the rebirth of Marxism, Lukács, Korsch, and Gramsci remained bound by two flawed basic principles. First, their work from the 1920s took for granted that class consciousness was made up solely of conscious beliefs. The task was to find out what falsehoods workers' believed, why they were believed, and how to change them for the truth. Second, these thinkers assumed that the workers' beliefs came from and focused on labor and politics; i.e., the public realm of power, wealth, and work. To borrow Sartre's phrase, they acted as if workers were "born the day they received their first paycheck."

It was left to the Frankfurt School theorists (Max Horkheimer, Theodor Adorno, and Herbert Marcuse) and to Wilhelm Reich to

challenge these two principles by expanding the concept of class consciousness. The rise of fascism compelled these writers to investigate
the social forces that seemed to make the working class not only
politically passive but psychically attached to bourgeois or Stalinist
authority. These forces included not just conscious beliefs but unconscious personality structures; not just the experiences of work, but
those of sexuality and family life.

To explain how the social relations of bourgeois society were
internalized by the working class, the Frankfurt School utilized certain
elements of Freudian psychoanalysis. While this framework falsely
universalized human relations of a particular time and place, it did show
how the human infant acquired a personality structure compatible with
an unfree society.

The Frankfurt School and Reich accepted from psychoanalysis the
notion that early childhood experience was an unconscious adaptation
of instinctual drives to structures of affection and authority in the
family, and that much of adult life masks and expresses that unconscious adaptation of early childhood. Most important, they saw adult
behavior as centrally determined by the formation of an authority-
oriented super-ego. This super-ego was an introjection (a bringing
into the self) of parental authority figures in response to childhood
sexual and emotional conflicts. The critical teaching of psychoanalysis
is that much human action stems from *unconscious* loves and fears,
desires and aversions. Who we are is not defined simply by what we
know about ourselves, but also includes needs and wants we usually
do not let ourselves feel consciously.

Horkheimer, for instance, describes how family relationships contribute to working-class political impotence:

> The lack of independence, the deep sense of inferiority that afflicts most
> men, the centering of their whole psychic life around the ideas of order
> and subordination, but also their cultural achievements are all conditioned
> by the relations of child to parents or their substitutes and to brothers and
> sisters . . . The bad conscience that is developed in the family absorbs
> more energies than can be counted, which might otherwise be directed
> against the social circumstances that play a role in the individual's failure.
> (Horkheimer 1972: 109)

By creating personalities habituated to authority, the family thus helps produce the "cement" that holds an irrational society together.

In another vein, Horkheimer (1972) argued that as mass, industrial capitalism replaced entrepreneurial competitive capitalism, fewer men were able to serve as authority figures to mold their children's lives. The diminishing role of masculine authority in the family bred a hunger for that authority in society at large. In this way, the centralized capitalism which marginalizes all but the most powerful of men provides a psychological basis for the attraction to fascism. The working class is enticed to a Hitler or Mussolini, against its real interests, because of an unconscious psychic yearning for authority. Since workers yearn for authority, they are tied to domination when capitalist development stumbles. Unconscious processes prevent social crises from being revolutions. Until new or counter forms of socialization challenge the old, until workers and their purported leaders realize that the "enemy" is not just "out there" but also inside the psychic structure of workers, capitalism remains safe.

Wilhelm Reich, an Austrian socialist who tried hardest to combine psychoanalysis and Marxism (and was rejected by orthodox members of both camps!) developed a similar position. His central point is that capitalism is not sustained just by false conscious beliefs, but rather by a "character structure"—an entire personality, including an unconscious mental life.

> In class society, the ruling class accrues its position with the aid of education and the institution of the family, by making its ideology the ruling ideology. . . . But it is not merely a matter of imposing ideologies, attitudes and concepts. . . . *Rather it is a matter of a deep-reaching process in each new generation, of the formation of a psychic structure that corresponds to the existing social order.* . . . (Reich 1976: xxvii)

Sexual repression in the patriarchal family creates a passive population cut off from natural instincts for egalitarian human relations, sexual pleasure, and enjoyable work. (Reich 1946: 30)

> The moral inhibition of the child's natural sociality makes the child afraid, shy, fearful of authority, obedient, "good," and "docile". . . . It has a

crippling effect on man's rebellious forces because every vital life-impulse is now burdened with severe fear. (64–5)

Dulled by sexual inhibitions, people's creativity and learning ability are sapped. The result is workers' irrational political quiescence.

## NEW MODELS OF SOCIALISM

Horkheimer and the Frankfurt School injected psychoanalysis into the account of the barriers to the development of class consciousness. Reich stressed the role of sexual repression in generating a servile populace. Through their work, psychic structure has become essential to a Marxist understanding of social life. While, in Gramsci's phrase, the dynamic of the mode of production may "set the questions"— i.e., define the major options and create certain basic tendencies and instabilities—what Reich called "mass psychology" will determine how those questions are answered.

What then does the working class need to know and to do? Marx's notion that radicalism flows unproblematically from economic depressions and industrialization was clearly mistaken. So was the Leninist/Stalinist distortion that "socialism equals soviets plus electrification." Lukács' argument that the key to class consciousness was for workers to see themselves as agents-treated-like-things is a good beginning. But how will this insight arise?

Reich's position, worked out in 1934 essay, "What is Class Consciousness?" (in Reich 1972), provides what may still be the best single treatment of this question. Reacting to the failures of the German Socialist and Communist parties in combating the rise of Nazism, Reich asserts that traditional Marxists simply had no understanding of class consciousness. To awaken this consciousness, he argues, we must begin with the assumption that capitalist society cannot satisfy the basic human needs of its members and that no social order that requires the frustration of instincts can lead to human happiness. Therefore, a fundamental dissatisfaction will always be present, at least in latent form. Radical politics must kindle this latent dissatisfaction into a revolutionary class consciousness. This consciousness need not include sophisticated theory or lifelong dedication, which are features of the consciousness of the leaders of the movement. Rather, it centers on fulfilling personal and family needs of everyday life: sexuality, leisure, immediate human relationships, housing, as well as the experience of work. Political organizing is aimed at uncovering workers' resentment about and resistance to problems in these areas of their lives, and to awakening the realization that their needs will not be satisfied under capitalism. Since the conditions of everyday life vary with different groups (men, women, adolescents, etc.), the revolutionary must attend closely to people's specific experiences rather than dissolve those experiences into the truisms of orthodox Marxist theory. Political organizing, in turn, does not aim at blind obedience or a lot of votes. Class consciousness is an awareness by the oppressed of what their real needs are, of how capitalist society poses insuperable psychic and institutional barrier to their fulfillment, and that only unity among the oppressed can overturn the system. Without class consciousness, the masses will be psychologically tied to an oppressive society—whether that society be dominated by capitalists or party bureaucrats. Only people fully in touch with their own needs and interests can be counted on to resist both capitalist exploitation and communist domination.

Only efforts to develop *this* kind of class consciousness really justifies any left-wing group's claim to leadership.

In the half century that has passed since Reich, Western Marxists have deepened and expanded his position, but its general parameters remain key. Note first that while Marx centered his economic and political theory on the concept of exploitation, that concept is now joined by the broader notions of domination and oppression. Although Marx recognized the existence of oppressions not specifically economic, he believed that when class domination ended they would simply pass away. Western Marxists, by contrast, have seen self-proclaimed "socialists" manifest or ignore bureaucratic privilege, sexism, nationalism, ethnic chauvinism, homophobia, and racism. If we are to find the resistance to the current social order in everyday life, as Reich suggests, we must be aware of this full range of oppression: in work relations, to be sure, but also in regard to gender, race, ethnicity, or physical condition. The devaluation of minority cultures, harassment and humiliation for racial difference, and threats of violence by a majority have all become serious political issues alongside more traditional economic concerns. Additionally, left critics see authoritarianism, sexual repression, and intellectual elitism as cultural and psychological aspects of domination that obstruct the development of class consciousness. They will also duplicate the oppressive elements of the present society in any purportedly radical political movement.

Further, the concept of oppression needs broadening because the widespread affluence of the West after World War II has made it unlikely that the proletariat will be radicalized simply to win greater wealth. As Marcuse argued in *A Essay on Liberation* (1969), the continually increasing standard of living has tied people to the system. When people's selves are shaped to a hierarchical, falsely "democratic," endlessly materialistic society, they cannot reject the system of domination without rejecting their own needs and values. In fact, however, the glitter of advanced capitalism is really poisonous:

> The entire realm of competitive performances and standardized fun, all the symbols of status, prestige, power, of advertised virility and charm, of commercialized beauty—this entire realm kills in its citizens the very disposition, the organs, for the alternative: freedom without exploitation. (Marcuse 1969: 17)

Where, Marcuse asks, are the social resources for the development of needs which would contradict the social order? Not in the working class, which has been pacified with high consumption . Rather, artists, students, racial minorities, the unemployed—these constitute the margin and the potential negation of the existing system.[5] On the basis of this negation, we can envisage a fundamentally different society. This would include the economic transformations of traditional socialism, but also a sensuous celebration of sexuality and aesthetic life, a use of technology which sees production and consumption as means rather than ends, and an educational system which cultivates self-confidence and independence of thought. The result would be dramatically different human beings:

men and women who have the good conscience of being human, tender, sensuous, who are no longer ashamed of themselves. . . . The imagination of such men and women would fashion their reason and tend to make the process of reproduction a process of creation. (Marcuse 1969: 21)

With economic exploitation included in—but no longer the center of—"oppression," the notion that the industrial working class is necessarily the leading revolutionary group has pretty much been abandoned. Writers like André Gorz and Marcuse have since the 1960s suggested that the political goal is not to organize a homogeneous working class around a unified set of proletarian demands. Rather, socialists face the much more complex task of organizing coalitions of different oppressed groups against the common enemies of capitalist economic power, the capitalist state, and embedded antagonisms among the oppressed themselves.

While Marcuse was searching for a resource to implement a new set of values, a mass political movement was being born which would find some of those "new values" existing immediately within the society which Marcuse and other Marxists had tried, but failed, to comprehend as a totality. What they had missed was something directly before them but which, like gravity or air, they had taken for granted or ignored—their mothers, wives, and daughters; i.e., the presence, experience, and capacities of women in patriarchal society.

# 6

## SOCIALIST-FEMINISM AND
## THE POLITICS
## OF DIFFERENCE

Starting in the late 1950s and continuing for two decades, much of the western world was shaken by a veritable explosion of radical political activity. In the U.S., this activity began with the civil rights movement as blacks demanded the rights and freedoms which our cold-war government trumpeted as the essence of the American way of life. Later, peace activists protested the threat of nuclear destruction. By the mid and late 1960s, millions of Americans had demonstrated against the Vietnam War.

Out of these movements a general climate of political, cultural, and social radicalism emerged. Authorities and traditions in every sphere of life were described as agents of repression, intellectually criticized, and politically challenged. Professors and doctors, government officials and psychiatrists, scientists and educators—all faced rebels who denied their competence, objectivity, and good intentions. It was this "New Left" that brought a living Marxism into post-World War II American intellectual and political life. While the mass movements of that time had subsided by the late 1970s, fundamental disagreements over foreign policy, race relations, education, health care, the value of traditional western culture, and our troubled relationship to the environment still permeate America and Europe.

The women's liberation movement emerged during this period. A complex amalgam of theory, political action, spiritual rebirth, and collective self-discovery, feminism continues to challenge many of the basic presuppositions of modern society. My focus here will be twofold: first, to explore the creative interplay between feminism and Marxism that created socialist-feminism; second, to chart some political implications of feminism for contemporary liberation struggles of people of color, lesbians and gay men, ethnic minorities—all the movements that can be summed up in the phrase "the politics of difference."

If socialist-feminism[1] has one major origin, it is among the activist women of the civil rights, anti-war, and student movements. (Evans 1980) Struggling alongside men for a variety of "politically correct" causes, these women gradually realized that they too were victims of oppression. As Marge Piercy complained: "The movement is supposed to be for human liberation: how come the condition of women inside it is no better than outside?" (Peircy 1970: 421) That "condition," women observed, included rampant inequality throughout a movement for social justice. Women were generally excluded from positions of power or leadership and had to do a vastly disproportionate amount of boring, repetitive labor while men made policy and headlines.

But there was something unique about women's situation: unlike relations between blacks and whites, workers and capitalists, Vietnamese and American, women's "oppressors" were their friends, lovers, comrades, fathers, and husbands. Women suffered not only from extra work or economic hardship. There was also something wrong in their most personal relationships, and this wrongness was internalized by women in the most basic ways they felt about themselves.

In responding to this unique situation, women joined an analysis of their social condition with collective reflection on their personal experience. They realized, in short, that "the personal is political." As a result, feminists had a double task: first, they had to *extend* previously existing critiques of injustice and exploitation from workers or racial minorities to women. How, they would ask, was the oppression of women materialized in the economy, politics, culture, and the family? Second, feminists had to define "politics"—i.e., group struggles for power and justice—as encompassing more than governments, factories, offices, and political parties. They saw that what was usually dismissed as "private"—sexual relations, small group interactions, and family life—embodied systematic and institutionally supported domination and exploitation. This perspective furthered the Western Marxist emphasis on class consciousness, the complexity of oppression, and new models of revolutionary change. In socialist-feminism, Marxism continued to be reborn.

## WOMEN'S OPPRESSION

Traditional Marxism had viewed the experience and interests of women in *reductionist* terms. It claimed that women's oppression was essentially a consequence of the class relations constituted by the mode of production. "The whole of human servitude," Marx had written, "is involved in the relation of the worker to production, and every relation of servitude is but a modification and consequence of this relation." (Marx 1964: 118) In other words, the oppression women experience *as women* is a product of the system that oppresses workers *as workers*. Women's inequality results from the structure of private property and will be ended by socialism.

Socialist-feminists offered strong criticisms of this view. To begin with, consider that Engels had in fact written that a properly "materialist" outlook focused on the simultaneous reproduction both of people and of things. (Engels 1977: 71–72) Yet Engels, Marx, and the tradition as a whole—with a few exceptions—had focused on the latter and ignored the former.[2] Marxism almost always focused on *production*: collective mastery of the material world or creative activity by a single self. Sexuality, child rearing, emotional relationships, and family life were at best treated as consequences of the relations of production. The theory could not recognize the importance of—and the exploitation involved in—culturally female activities between people rather than between people and things, such as caring for the elderly or mothering small children. And since Marxism did not take specifically female activities seriously, it could not address the specific political interests of women.

Western Marxism had its own limitations, of which I will mention only two. Lukács' concept of class consciousness, based entirely on the experience of wage labor, ignores how consciousness is necessarily shaped by family life as well as "commodification" at the workplace. Gramsci believed proletarian hegemony would find a political vehicle in workers' councils; that is, democratic self-management at the workplace. He ignored the fact that women, dominated by husbands in the home, are not likely to receive equal treatment from them in factories. (Feldberg 1981) In general, he could not see that the gender-divided proletariat is not just a victim of hegemony. In fact, male workers exercise hegemony (over women) while they are also subject to it (from capitalists).

To understand the oppression of women, socialist-feminist thinkers had to go far beyond the resources of both traditional and Western Marxist theory.[3] This task was advanced by the exploration of what was called the "sex/gender system." Like the mode of production, the sex/gender system was present in every society, since every society organized the biological facts of sexual difference into a gender system of child care, socialization, sexuality, and adult gender roles. (Rubin 1975) Just as the structure of the mode of production divided society into classes with opposing interests, so the sex/gender system created genders linked by oppression and domination.

Feminists of "radical" rather than socialist orientation had argued that male domination was an undifferentiated and nearly eternal rule of human history, and that this "patriarchy" was the key fact of social life. Socialist-feminists saw patriarchy as manifested in complex and variable social structures, taking fundamentally different forms in different historical periods. Changes in the ideology of women's inequality, the sexual division of labor, and the structure of the family had various causes, the most important of which was the mode of production. The theoretical task, then, was to see how the mode of production and the sex/gender system had influenced each other in the past, and how their contemporary interaction might make possible the liberation of women and other dominated groups. Socialist-feminists also argued that if patriarchy was not understood in its relation to other social forces, there was no hope for overcoming it.[4] What reason was there for men to give up control over women? How could women, powerless for centuries, overturn their oppression? These changes were possible only if social forces outside the sex/gender system could destabilize it.

Socialist-feminist analysis begins with the attempt to understand the family, both internally and in terms of its complex relations with the rest of the social order.

In pre-modern societies, gender distinctions were not made on the basis of who worked for wages and who did housework and child care. Very few people received wages, and both men and women engaged in productive labor centered in the home. Since they had distinct and recognized arenas of productive labor in traditional societies, women in some ways were accorded greater respect before industrial modernization. Moreover, the family unit was larger, more inclusive, less shaped by intense emotional attachments, and more directly open to the surrounding community. There were, however, differences between women and men in power, status, and type of labor. These differences were justified by religion and tradition and reflected in all major social institutions (especially the state and the church).

With the rise of capitalist industrialization, the modern family shaped gender in radically new ways. It did so as the economic and emotional complement to the public world of paid labor and democratic politics. Through industrialization, urbanization, and mass culture, the modern family detached itself from the community setting. As production and labor became commodified, the homebound wife seemed to inhabit a "private" sphere, and thus "femininity" could be defined as radically different from the public world of work, money, and power. Workers struggled for a "family wage" so that the price of labor would include support of a homebound wife. Within the family, moneymaking and authority belonged to men; child care, housework, and providing emotional closeness were up to women. An enormous weight was placed on emotional attachments in the nuclear family; men and women were to be emotionally intimate, parents and children were to develop family love. And women were supposed to make this all work.

> Within the family women are carrying the preposterous contradiction of love in a loveless world. They are providing capitalism with the human relations it cannot maintain in the world of men's work. (Rowbotham 1973: 77)

Thus, women became responsible for what some theorists have called "sex-affective labor." This labor includes quantifiable amounts of unpaid use values and services produced in housework and child care. (Banks and governments actually compute the economic value of work done in the home.) Additionally, studies have shown that whether or not they work for wages, women throughout America, Europe, Russia, and Japan work between fifteen and forty more hours per week than their husbands. (Hartmann 1981) Sex-affective labor also includes less quantifiable emotional work: taking the major responsibility in personal relations, dealing with people's feelings, or serving as the interpersonal "switchboard" for men who cannot reveal themselves or sustain relationships without women's help.[5] Women are not paid for sex-affective labor, and it earns them little respect and no social power. In performing it, women produce "services" for men in a relation of unequal exchange. Men enjoy the emotionally intimate family at comparatively little physical or emotional cost. They have children without having to get up at night to diaper babies; holiday meals without inviting relatives, shopping, cooking, or cleaning; and someone to care for their emotional needs without having to make themselves personally vulnerable. Groomed to satisfy men's needs and restricted in the public realm, women develop a host of eating disorders, exhausting psychological "symptoms," and psychosomatic complaints. Their frequent recourse to psychotherapy signals a basic truth: oppression is depressing. (Greenspan 1983) When they resist their oppression, they may be subject to rape or battering.

> There is a women's place, a sector, which is inhabited by women of all classes and races, and it is defined . . . by function: . . . the service of men and men's interests as men define them. (Frye 1983: 9)

To support male exploitation of sex-affective labor, an enormous cultural apparatus enforces gender roles and creates personality types. In the media, religion, culture, and educational systems, children learn and adults are reminded of the "essential" differences between men and women. Stereotypes of male rationality, competence, violence, and independence complement images of female emotionality, victimization, and dependence. Female skills of intimate communication, empathy, and nurturing are ignored or devalued, and the labor of child rearing is relegated to inconsequential status.

## MALE DOMINATION IN THE PUBLIC WORLD

Patriarchy is not confined to the family. In very concrete ways, the sex/gender system shapes women's participation in the realm of paid labor as well.

Recent structural changes in the economy have placed fundamental strains on the sex/gender system. Forty percent of the American workforce is female, and a high percentage of women—even those with young children—hold some kind of paid job. Yet women still earn from one-half to four-fifths of what men earn, get unequal pay for the same work, are concentrated in the worst paid jobs, and are much more likely to work part-time.

These statistics reveal that women enter the workforce as distinctively *female* workers. Jobs are frequently defined as exclusively or mainly female: secretaries, nurses, "salesgirls," "cleaning ladies," domestic servants, elementary school teachers, and clerical workers are routinely women. Notice how each category calls to mind a male superior: female nurses, teachers, and secretaries, for example, "require" male doctors, principals, and executives. These segregated occupations tend to replicate many of the nurturing and care-giving functions women play in the home.

Salaries and union protection for female jobs are typically significantly lower than those for "male" jobs. When women move into a job category (e.g., when they became clerical workers in the late nineteenth century), that area is devalued and the pay drops. Both men and women have tended to view women's paid labor as subsidiary to their work in the home.

As long as women bear the brunt of domestic labor, their participation in paid labor will continue to be less than men's. If women are subordinate in the home, they are unlikely to organize successfully for equality with their husbands and fathers. Similarly, without access to jobs, income, and social power, women remain largely dependent on individual men or male-controlled social institutions and are thus largely confined to unequal positions within the family.[6]

While there are real interests for men in the oppression of women, we cannot understand that oppression if we only consider male interests. The basic structures of modern life, after all, are not just the product of an undifferentiated "masculinity." They are also shaped by the development and needs of capitalism. Clearly, capitalism as a mode of production has several real material interests in the oppression of women. The male-dominated nuclear family is a highly mobile unit for an economy which needs to shift its labor force to changing areas of investment. The nuclear family also tends to create people who think of themselves primarily as individuals rather than as members of communities or classes. This self-understanding makes political organizing and mass radical movements extremely difficult. Having women do the household and emotional labor necessary to "reproduce" male laborers and raise new ones cheapens the reproduction of workers—and thus the cost of labor for capitalists. Women's inferior social status also allows capitalists to pay them less and treat them worse than men. Additionally, the atomized nuclear family is necessarily a high-consumption family, providing an ever-growing market for consumer goods. Finally, the power men enjoy over women makes up in a psychic sense for the powerlessness they experience on the job. After a day of demanding and at times degrading paid labor, a man may exercise power at home while he is catered to by his wife. At the same time, the authoritarian, non-egalitarian relationships within the home perfectly prepare children for a public world defined by hierarchy, competition, and unequal power.

## THE LIBERATION OF WOMEN

As I argued in Chapter 1 in explaining the basic claims of historical materialism, certain aspects of capitalist development undermine as well as reinforce the modern sex/gender system. Early capitalist ideologies of freedom and equality were eventually claimed by women for themselves. With women doing paid labor—even sex-segregated and poorly paid labor—it becomes increasingly difficult to sustain a cultural vision of women's essential inferiority. With the rise of state involvement in the economy and social life and the penetration of the home by mass culture, much of the formation of gender now occurs outside the immediate family relationship.

These structural conflicts created the possibility of feminism in general and socialist-feminism in particular. In understanding the contemporary battleground of gender, the socialist-feminist analysis both challenges and enlarges Marxist theory. While it continues to focus on the mode of production, it recognizes that the twin dynamics of patriarchy and capitalism form a unified system of oppression.[7]

In this system, men benefit in material, psychological, and cultural ways from the oppression of women. Their control over women's labor and lives is expressed in both collective and directly personal relations. It is embodied in the way women may be excluded from positions of power, culturally devalued, or oppressed by the system at large; by the lack of equality and respect in most heterosexual relationships; and by the reality and threat of rape and battering.

Since the oppression of women occurs throughout connected but distinct spheres of social life, women's liberation must be won in the family as well as the factory, by changing cultural values as well as by making new laws. Each of these spheres of life supports the others, and none will be finally made non-sexist until the others are. Along with equality in the public sphere, socialist-feminists have stressed that it is essential to reorganize the family. Men need to take an equal share in child rearing and to take equal responsibility for emotional intimacy. Through day-care and the socialization of housework, government and community support can undermine the family's isolation. Female reproductive freedom includes the rights to self-defined sexuality, birth control, and abortion.

The feminist vision also includes recognition of some of the distinct, culturally-based, characteristics of the way women think and relate: special gifts of women in moral reasoning, the acquisition of knowledge, and the capacity to nurture.[8] Understanding and honoring these gifts needs to replace their previous cultural devaluation. As a corollary, it is necessary to see how social policy and institutions are shaped by *male* interests and styles of interactions—as well as by the interests of capitalists and the money-oriented culture of commodities. Macho military policies, excessive competition, and extreme difficulty in emotional connection and empathy are not just abstractly "modern." They are essential to contemporary masculinity and to social domination as well.

In contrast to liberal feminists, however, socialist-feminists have argued that women's liberation requires the end of capitalism. "Equality for women" cannot be won simply by extending to women an equal right to be either capitalists or exploited workers. As the dramatic increase in female poverty of the last decade shows, women are tremendously vulnerable to the capitalist system, partly because of their structural inequality with men.

As distinct from radical feminists, socialist-feminists assert the necessity and possibility of alliances between women and men. The same system which marginalizes and degrades women does so—albeit in different ways—to most men. Black men, workers, unemployed husbands, fathers in the military—all these are subject to hierarchy, exploitation, and humiliation. As rape and battering keep women "in their place," so men are forced to function in a masculine world of domination and cruelty. Therefore, men too have an interest in creating a world in which communication and cooperation replace violence and domination. Such a world is unlikely to be created unless men and women are able to make some common cause across the gulf of gender difference.

Yet because male workers and capitalists share some interests in dominating women, the traditional Marxist goal of a unified, politically homogeneous, working-class movement to end all forms of domination has to be discarded. Realizing that "the workers" are really "male and female workers," feminists demanded separate, autonomous organizations to represent their particular interests. Any policy or program might well affect women and men differently and has to be analyzed and evaluated by groups capable of understanding and respecting women's needs. Because almost all previous leftist leaders were men, they tended to unthinkingly repeat the culturally male personal styles of competitiveness, aggression, and attachment to personal power. Without a feminist consciousness spread among men as well as women, these characteristics will shape any radical political movement.

Perhaps most profoundly, socialist-feminists have provided new models of revolutionary change and of the relation between personal identity and political beliefs. The movement has stressed that truly revolutionary possibilities can arise when people come to understand their oppression personally. The male tradition defined radicalization in terms of comparatively impersonal commitment to abstract, universal principles of justice. Furthering the traditional analysis, socialist-feminists have stressed the process of *self-discovery*. "The vast mass of human beings have always been mainly invisible to themselves. . . . Every mass political movement of the oppressed necessarily brings its own vision of itself into sight." (Rowbotham 1973: 27) As the early process of consciousness-raising showed, this process involves connecting one's personal problems to the social situation of the group. Given the nature of women's particularly personal oppression, it also includes serious self-examination of how women have internalized their oppressors' ways of thinking. While workers and other dominated groups had always faced this problem, the intimacy of male-female relations and the universal devaluation of women in culture made this a particularly crucial factor.

These writers also focused attention on the personal connection between radicals and the theories they espouse.[9] Both traditional and Western Marxist theorists avoided personal self-reflection, seeming to believe that their ideas, as opposed to those of the masses, come from "pure thought." (Rowbotham, Segal, and Wainwright 1979: 115) They reproduced the culturally male posture of the objective, impersonal, universal Voice of Reason. In fact, however, human beings—including theorists—have political views partly because of personal experiences of work, sexuality, family, gender, class, and race. The single, authoritative Voice of Reason is really just one more Voice of Authority.

This last insight suggests that just as radical political *organizations* need to recognize political differences between women and men, so political *theorists* must give up the fantasy of a single, objective, totalizing theory. In this way, feminism continues the dismantling of the positivist model of knowledge embedded in traditional Marxism. We no longer seek a single, comprehensive point of view, but instead see radical theories as expressing the self-discovery of different subjects and groups. *The political task is coalition rather than unity. The theoretical task is communication rather than monolithic truth.* People will unite on the basis of cooperation and empathy rather than because they have found the single, correct party line. The "revolution" will be made by particular, fallible, limited people, not by The Truth incarnated in the Revolutionary Vanguard.

## THE POLITICS OF DIFFERENCE

The above discussion has taken for granted that one can speak mono-lithically of "women" and "men", and that "women" and "men" have discrete social situations and political interests. This supposition extends, but also continues, the Marxist discussion of "workers," who all (supposedly) share a common situation and interest.

These suppositions have been seriously questioned by the emergence of a "politics of difference": the recognition, brought home by new social movements of women, people of color, gays/lesbians, Jews, and others, of the diverse experiences and interests of oppressed groups.[10] As the women's movement had challenged the Marxist notion of a unified working class, so women of color made comparable criticisms of all forms of white-oriented feminism. (Hooks 1982) The cultural images and practical life situations of black women, they argued, were simply not the same as those of white women. Black women had not been kept out of the workforce to exist as (supposedly) pampered and protected prize possessions of men. Black women had never been thought too frail to do demanding physical labor. Black women could not easily benefit from a liberal feminist stress on "choices for women" in the absence of simultaneous challenges to racism and class power. These facts implied that there were fundamental problems in feminist theory and practice. Men had spoken for women in the history of the socialist movement, concealing hidden inequalities and domination. So white women had often spoken for black women, ignoring the differences that basic structures of racism made in lives of whites and blacks. (Conversely, the various strategies for black liberation also suffered from patriarchy. Male domination had been accepted in the civil rights and black power movements of the '50s and '60s.)[11]

Out of the politics of difference and the new social movements, an innovative framework for understanding radical politics takes shape. While capitalist relations of production remain central to our society, the old Marxist notion of a society in which only two classes are of ultimate political significance has proved inadequate. In fact, when people confront the powers that be, they tend to do so not as members of a unified working class but as part of socially differentiated groups. All "workers" and their dependents may be in the working class from the standpoint of economic theory—but from the standpoint of diverse life experiences, cultural values, income level, and connections to the rest of society, they differ widely.[12] Consider, for instance, the different emotional experiences of a man and woman walking past a group of lunch-hour construction workers, blacks and whites hearing slave-holder George Washington described as the "father of our country," or Jews and Christians watching a president light the "national" Christmas tree. In each case a different sense of personal identity, social safety, and group interest will probably arise. And as feminism showed, radical politics emerge precisely from these very personal facts about us; i.e., from these fragmented and overlapping personal and communal identities. Recognizing this fact, contemporary forms of socialist organizing do not look for a Leninist "vanguard party" to represent a Marxist "universal class." Rather, they seek forms of coalition politics, a "rainbow" of different colors, immediate agendas, and sensitivities.

Sadly, however, the same personal experiences that give rise to radical political action often divide the groups that must cooperate for such action to succeed. We find racism among white feminists, sexism and homophobia in anti-racist struggles, or a predominantly white ecology movement which ignores the needs of the black ghetto.

This pattern is repeated often in the history of American radicalism.[13] During two periods in which the radical currents ran high—1900–12 and 1929–39—American leftists typically claimed to be part of *the* movement representing *the* working class. Under the influence of both traditional Marxism and Marxism-Leninism, the Socialist Party (SP) (1900–14) and the Communist Party (CP) (1923–40) often ignored the interests of groups with whom they had little contact. The SP, acting on a program and perspective much like that of Second International, represented the interests of white, native-born, or Western European immigrant male craft workers. They carried into the Party the racism, sexism, and nativism that divided American workers. Regarding sexism, one female SP member pointed out that:

Our menfolks, like ourselves, still have the capitalist mind, and they may theorize, read Marx and Bebel, yet when it comes right down to practice, they feel that the only place for women is in the home. . . . Women . . . also . . . feel like criminals if they dare venture outside their traditional sphere. (Buhle 1983: 132)

The CP was much more self-conscious about the need to include women along with men, blacks along with whites, industrial along with craft workers. Yet it suffered from the typical Leninist mistake of seeing itself as the vanguard, and was slavishly devoted to the Marxist-Leninist "experts" in Moscow. The result was that it simply could not tolerate the slightest political disagreement on the part of otherwise generally sympathetic radicals. The Party tried to rule any group with which it came in contact and castigated any articulate political person who expressed even minor reservations. It tried to impose a false unity on left politics, a unity based in the notion that its own "scientific" approach guaranteed the correctness of its position.

> Some people have the idea that a [member of the Young Communist League] is politically minded, that nothing outside of politics means anything. Gosh no. . . . We go to shows, parties, dances and all that. In short . . . members are no different from other people except that we believe in dialectical materialism as the solution to all problems. (Liebman 1979: 493)

Acting out of this belief, American communists were as hierarchical, intolerant, and controlling as the capitalists they wanted to overthrow. The party embodied what feminists have accurately described as culturally male values: attachment to authority, rejection of difference, inability to compromise, and absolutist thinking in which truth can only belong to one side.

The New Left of the 1960s and early 1970s was less conditioned by a Marxist strategy tied to the working class. The political and cultural conservatism of most industrial workers, especially concerning issues of foreign policy and racism, made the split between the New Left and workers inevitable. But the New Left[14]—while newly conscious of certain forms of "difference"—often took an unnecessarily hostile attitude to workers, and towards anyone else alienated from its life-style. A certain leftist arrogance pervaded the movement, which dissipated when it failed to root itself in continuing forms of community.

## CONCLUSION

Western Marxists rejected the domination implicit in positivist Marxism. The most creative and engaged contemporary Marxists and socialist-feminists reject the domination contained in the notion of a single, homogeneous revolutionary subject or point of view. The left is trying to integrate this perspective into a movement that can challenge all forms of social injustice. They believe that radicals need to understand differences, communicate across histories of pain and struggle, and ally in the pursuit of common political goals. These efforts must be undertaken in a context of mutual respect and empathy; and despite fundamental differences of outlook, experience, and theoretical perspective.[15] If Marxism is to stay alive, this must be its general political orientation. The creative, liberatory perspective which runs from the best of Marx though Luxemburg, Western Marxism, and socialist-feminism leads to a political present in which socialist politics should be characterized by theoretical breadth and openness, political modesty, and personal self-awareness.

# IV

## PRESENT AND FUTURE

# 7

## MARXISM AND
## CONTEMPORARY CAPITALISM

Part IV focuses on three themes, all roughly connected to the present status of—and current debates within—Marxist theory. In this chapter, I will present some of the ways Marxists have analyzed post-World War II capitalism. The richness of these contemporary applications of Marxist theory indicates why—despite my many criticisms of Marxism up to this point—I still believe we need it to understand and overcome the basic failings of our society. In Chapter 8, I argue against otherwise radical social theories for their abandonment of still-useful Marxist insights. The book concludes with an account of some of the inescapable limitations of even the most humane and modernized forms of Marxism.

It is necessary to situate this discussion by briefly summarizing my own conception of the contemporary theoretical and political status of Marxism; that is, of what it means to be a Marxist today.

1. Third World self-proclaimed socialist/communist movements have not created socialist societies. While at times increasing the standard of living and equalizing the distribution of wealth, they have also tended to totalitarianism, frequent failures of economic development, and aggressive foreign policies. It is hard to say how much these failures stem from internal weaknesses and how much from the relentless opposition of world capitalism, especially the U.S. In any case, neither the methods nor the achievements of these revolutions are proper models for Marxists facing the very different social conditions of the U.S. or Western Europe.

2. While there are single-issue movements of considerable importance throughout the West, there is no mass, or even sizable, movement which challenges the combined power of the state and the large corporations. Socialist visions and Marxist theory are on the margins of contemporary political life.

3. As we will see in this chapter, the central role of the state in contemporary economic life means there will in all likelihood not be any decisive economic breakdown of capitalism in the coming decades.

4. Given the central role of state power in social and political life, any vision of directly contesting for state power—i.e., *any vision of violent revolution* in the classic sense—is now a fantasy.

5. Marxist theory must take into account the fundamental importance of socialization and social differentiation as determinants of our capacity for liberating social change.

6. Hopefully, Marxists will join in *political* opposition to all forms of domination and injustice. Their *theoretical* task is to relate consistently the different forms of oppression to each other, and to connect historical change and the possibilities of human liberation to the continuing importance of the mode of production and class power. The practical goal of both theory and political organizing, in turn, is to awaken people's capacity for self-knowledge, collective activity, and social understanding—not to organize the masses into battalions led by revolutionary experts. The sad history of communism and the many failures of the left in the West should teach all who call themselves Marxists

that they can only speak *to*—and never *for*—the oppressed, and that they had better do as much listening as talking.

## THE EVOLUTION OF CAPITALISM

Marx's analysis of capitalist development was correct within the limits of one historical period. There *were* ever-larger business cycles, pronounced tendencies towards concentration and monopolization, the intensive and extensive spread of capitalism, and dramatic technological progress. Working-class political movements did grow, and a variety of forms of class struggle occurred.

In the present, concentrated wealth remains in private hands and basic economic decisions are directed toward creating private wealth. Most people have to work for wages (or are dependent on someone who does) and have little control over their own work or the economy as a whole. While lessened in degree, business cycles still occur, and class power still deeply influences virtually all significant political and cultural institutions.

Beginning in the last decades of the nineteenth century and continuing to the present, however, capitalist society began a series of profound alterations. In what follows, we will see how Marxist theorists have transformed their theory to make it adequate to this transformed society.

Two concepts will help us in this task. "Transformative maintenance" occurs when the self-generated obstacles to capitalist development are overcome by social changes that preserve the essential power of the capitalist class. Marx, we may remember, believed that capitalist accumulation would generate impenetrable barriers to further development in the form of economic crises. Instead, the evolution of capitalism has been marked not by collapse but by transformative maintenance.

The second concept is "displacement of class struggle." This occurs when the central tension of capitalism—between the owning and the laboring classes—is displaced by conflict between other groups. For example, instead of seeking higher wages, people may demand lower taxes or more benefits from the government; or coalitions of state employees and welfare recipients may be pitted against taxpayers and private employees; or economic and social problems may be viewed as racial rather than class issues.

On the most abstract level, Marx's claims about capitalism remain true: there continues to be considerable tension between social production and private ownership, expressed in economic instability, waste, war, and alienation. However, these general economic and social contradictions have not given rise to political challenges to the system as a whole. It has been the task of Marxist theory to try to explain why.

## MONOPOLY CAPITAL

The theory elaborated in Paul Baran and Paul Sweezy's *Monopoly Capital* (1966) remains a landmark contribution to post-World War II Marxist political economy. The authors described the fundamental difference between the highly competitive capitalism of Marx's time and the form which has dominated much of the twentieth century.

As we saw in Chapter 3, the rise of monopoly capital was one of the social changes that provoked Bernstein's revisionism. Yet while theorists of that period, including the political opposites of Bernstein and Lenin, were aware of the tendency towards monopolization, no developed theory emerged until *Monopoly Capital*. Marxists observed the concrete changes but stuck to the original expectation of inevitable economic crisis. The degree of transformative maintenance contained in the transition to monopoly capitalism was generally not recognized.

While the term "monopoly" is central to this theory, its basic claims center rather on the notion of "oligopoly." The main point is that the most important sectors of the economy—including transportation, energy, banking, and steel—are dominated by a small number of enormous firms. This essential structural change had major consequences for the relations among capitalists and between capitalists and workers.

Most important, capitalists no longer competed through lowering prices. As we saw in Chapter 1, there is in capitalism a fundamental intra-capitalist rivalry for profit. One of the central mechanisms of this rivalry is the progressive lowering of prices, a lowering made possible by reducing the cost or the amount of labor and mechanizing and expanding production. In the late nineteenth century, a constant round of price wars in basic industries contributed to a steady erosion of the rate of profit. A long-drawn-out economic slump (from approximately 1873 to 1896) resulted. From this period on, there developed a basic tendency towards centralization and concentration, the essential characteristics of monopoly capital. As a result, the dominant corporations came to accept relatively stable shares of the market and colluded with each other to set common prices or to agree that a giant firm in their particular field would typically be the "price leader." Given the enormous size of leading firms, competition from new firms became generally impossible. For example, while in the 1920s there were more than twenty-five automobile companies, the full maturity of the industry left America with three. That number has remained stable for thirty years.[1] We can see the same tendency accelerated in the computer industry. The initial plethora of hardware manufacturers has given way to fewer, larger firms in less than a decade.

Baran and Sweezy saw monopoly capital not only dominate the American economy but the world economy as well. Large corporations penetrated the Third World for raw materials and labor and organized local economies to meet U. S. corporate rather than domestic needs. The result was economic stagnation or "underdevelopment" in Third World economies. (This theme is developed in a following section.)

If competitive capitalism faces a tendency for profit to fall due to overinvestment or underconsumption, monopoly capital, argued Baran and Sweezy, faces the problem of the "unabsorbable surplus." Briefly stated, their claim is that giant firms make giant profits. They compete with each other by reducing the costs of production, but their monopoly status allows them to keep prices stable or to pass cost increases on to consumers via market-wide price hikes. Goods get cheaper to make—but they do not become cheaper to buy. They do become much more expensive to *sell*, since more and more resources go into advertising. Baran and Sweezy (1966) quote a detailed study of the car industry which estimated that in the 1960s, nearly 25% of the retail price of a car paid for its advertising. Again, this cost tends to be passed directly on to the consumer.

With ever-growing profits, a problem of the "absorption" of the surplus arises. The profits can for a while be invested in ever-greater productive capacity, but eventually society cannot consume what is being produced. Profits erode, investment declines, and the pace of economic development slows down. Instead of the dramatic economic crashes of earlier capitalism (such as the severe, world-wide depression of the 1930s), we get inflation (price hikes) combined with stagnation, or stagflation, as it was described in the 1970s.

Another consequence of monopoly capitalist super-profits is the "social peace" which calmed labor unrest from the late 1940s through the 1970s. As writers such as James O'Connor (1973) and Richard Edwards (1979) observe, monopoly capitalism creates a "dual labor market." Instead of a uniformly exploited working class, workers are divided into segments. In the "primary sector" of monopoly firms workers won—after bitter struggle, in most cases—union representation, comparatively high wages, and decent working conditions. In the non-monopoly "secondary" sectors of the economy, low wages, few benefits, and lack of unions, education, skills, and job security are the rule. Since monopoly firms dominate the economy, they can control the prices they pay to their non-monopoly suppliers. Facing a lesser profit margin, these non-monopoly suppliers must pay lower wages. In fact, the secondary sector is marked by some of the conditions of early, competitive capitalism: high competition and constant attempts to squeeze every last drop of surplus value out of the workforce.

The dual labor market is sustained by the social divisions which displace class struggle onto racial, ethnic, or gender antagonism. Until recently, primary workers were chiefly white and male. Women, racial minorities, and recent Third World immigrants continue to be highly overrepresented in the secondary market. Racist craft unions and sexist treatment of women in industrial unions have made it pretty much impossible for a united working class to challenge the rich and powerful. This racial and gender labor segmentation shows how functional racism and sexism can be for capitalism. (Reich 1980)

## POLITICIZED CAPITALISM

Another crucial feature of post-World War II capitalism is the dramatically increased role of the state in economic life. In Baran and Sweezy's model, it is state expenditures which help soak up the otherwise unabsorbable surplus. Military spending purchases commodities which no one uses and which can be called for indefinitely. The varieties of welfare payments go to people who otherwise could not afford to buy anything. Further, the social peace which characterizes capital-labor relations in the monopoly sector rests upon government protection of workers in everything from state-mandated unemployment insurance and social security to protection for safe working conditions.

Historically, even the most free market or laissez-faire forms of competitive capitalism—those of nineteenth-century America and England—were aided by state action to support particular industries, physically control the working class, and militarily conquer foreign markets and sources of raw materials. Now, however, the state is a decisive participant in and organizer of the accumulation process. This change creates a politicized economy and makes contemporary capitalism fundamentally different from earlier forms. State policies and self-conscious political struggles now play a large role in determining how the economy proceeds. The pace of investment and the price of labor and constant capital are partly the results of political processes, planning, political struggle, and compromise. Politically conscious groups interact with a state which not only functions in the interest of the system as a whole but *whose actions take that system as a whole as their object*. As Manuel Castells puts it:

> The state has become the center of the process of accumulation and realization in advanced capitalism. Without the state the process could be neither expanded nor reproduced. (Castells 1980: 130)

The development of politicized capitalism has important implications for Marxist theory. In the under-consumptionist models of economic crisis described in Chapter 1, for instance, downturns occurred when workers could not buy what they produced. With state involvement in the economy, however, workers now not only receive wages from their employer, but they also receive a "social wage"; for example, welfare payments, unemployment benefits, social security, veterans' benefits, Medicaid, government-sponsored work programs, state education, parks, and public support for the arts. The social wage significantly increases the capacity for working-class consumption and lessens the severity of the business cycle. Unemployment has a much smaller effect on demand when unemployed workers receive half (or more) of their wages for six months. The perennially unemployed constitute a source of consumption even though they receive no wages at all.

The state also cheapens the means of production and labor power and thus helps boost the rate of profit. It takes on some of the costs of production, for instance, by paying for scientific and technical research (and thus integrating the university into the corporate and military system). Such research is often a source of higher productivity, yet it is paid for not just by the industries which profit from them, but by society as a whole. State funds also cheapen the costs of labor. Engineers or technicians train at state universities, workers travel to work on state-financed transit systems, and some medical care is socialized. In all these cases, we see government expenditures complementing money wages, thus cheapening the cost of labor to the employer.

The state also provides the necessary infrastructure for the consumption of certain key commodities. The automobile industry would have been impossible without state-built roads. The U.S. nuclear power industry required that government assume financial liability in case of catastrophic accidents.[2]

Additionally, the government oversees the entire credit system and affects interest rates by controlling the money supply. Credit cushions or bolsters what might sometimes be stagnant consumer demand. Government support of home mortgages has been essential to the housing industry. For corporations, large-scale borrowing aids in technological development and overseas investment. In certain crucial cases—Chrysler and Lockheed are two of the best known—the state guaranteed loans to large corporations which might otherwise have gone broke. When the government rescued Chrysler, its investors and workers were saved from bankruptcy and unemployment. This was not a success in the free market but a political victory.[3]

In all these ways capitalist "rationality" came to be intertwined with the rationality of political struggle and political planning. Therefore, the social future of a society centered on a capitalist economy cannot be known from an analysis of the structure of the economy *as opposed* to politics—for in many respects the two have fused. Since political life reflects people's changing and unpredictable sense of their own interests and capacity to struggle for them, we must abandon any but the most vague and general sense of "laws" of capitalist development; for example, that there will be economic instability and class struggle. If there ever were more detailed and particular laws, they can exist no longer.[4] A corresponding change can be found in the way most Marxist economists write. Instead of claiming that political forces are created by the economic system, they show how political action is built in to economic life itself.

## THE FISCAL CRISIS OF THE STATE AND LEGITIMATION CRISIS

At the same time, however, theorists have pointed out that state involvement has changed the form of capitalist instabilities, not eliminated them. In particular, the very mechanisms which led to U.S. economic growth and world hegemony in the two decades following World War II created serious problems for the '70s and '80s. The overuse of credit led to inflation. The government-guaranteed social wage led to a falling rate of profit due to high corporate taxes. Monopoly protection from competition in key industries led to an overall decline of U.S. productivity compared to Germany and Japan. The export of U.S. capital to Europe after World War II helped generate competitors to the U.S. Paying for a military to enforce imperialism drained resources from the national economy. Socializing constant capital and the reproduction of labor power led to a perennial fiscal crisis of national and local governments.

In short, every solution created a new difficulty. While these difficulties in no way guarantee any particular political development, we can at least be confident that problems will arise. To this considerably weakened extent, the "laws" of capitalism remain.

James O'Connor (1973) explored the new problem areas of capitalism by focusing on how the state is torn between legitimation and accumulation; that is, between organizing the economy to support capitalist profits and convincing the population at large that this is a just and fair social system. Trying to meet both these goals leads to a recurrent "fiscal crisis" of the state. The over-utilization of state funds for welfare programs, the defense industry, and the pacification of insurgent groups makes deficit financing the rule. Huge debt payments and periodic restructuring of social programs afflict political life at the city, state, and national levels. Since it provides the social wage and manages the economy, the state—rather than the corporation—therefore becomes the focus of political struggle.[5]

Bowles and Gintis (1982) analyze the interaction of political and economic forces in shaping and resolving social crises. In their view the social conflicts, economic downturns, and fiscal crises of the state over the last decades have resulted from the manner in which *rights of persons* have become determining social principles alongside the *rights of property*. Production and distribution are no longer solely the result of the search for profit. They also reflect attempts to meet what are taken to be people's rights to a decent level of consumption. With this development, the previously much more separate realms of economics and politics have become so intermingled that we cannot speak of either one being dependent on the other.

Yet because state support of accumulation has begun to undermine itself, this system is not stable. The political power acquired by the working class and reflected in state action interferes with the necessary conditions of capitalist accumulation. Since World War II, U.S. capitalism has benefited from a "capital-labor accord" in which labor received high wages, limited power, and social security while left tendencies were purged and union membership was restricted to a minority of the working class. Worker consumption rose as a percentage of national income, a consumption made possible much more by the social wage than by wages from employers. Corporations, in turn, received higher profits but continued to face the possibility of renewed worker militancy. The state supplied an ever-increasing social wage to pacify the underemployed.

While this arrangement worked for a time, the capital-labor accord also posed a major barrier to the familiar resolution of the downturns in the capitalist business cycle. For instance, the traditional response of capitalism to over-investment is a recession in which unemployment and falling demand lower the cost of constant capital and wages. However, after decades of the capital-labor accord, it is much more difficult to face the political consequences of high unemployment or a fall in the standard of living. It was politically possible to enforce the 1982 recession only after the U.S. population had faced years of ravaging inflation. On the other hand, while lowering wages may reduce inflation and improve the position of the price of U.S. goods on the world market, too much of a recession means a slowdown in modernizing investment and a weakening of U.S. productivity vis-à-vis other capitalist nations. (Williams 1981) If the social wage stays high despite a falling rate of profit, other fundamental changes in the behavior of a capitalist economy may follow. Permanent inflation results when corporations know that price increases will not substantially lower consumption. Expecting inflation, unions tend not to moderate wage demands in the face of adverse economic conditions. In general, the accord weakens the capacity of U.S. capital to discipline labor.

Bowles and Gintis conclude that a return to an expansion in capitalist accumulation requires a restructuring of the institutional arrangements of liberal, democratic, capitalist society. This restructuring could take a variety of forms: increases in the use of labor from the Third World, modernization of U.S. production, or lower living standards through a decline in the social wage and greater use of non-unionized labor. The state may disengage from the accumulation process, letting the more familiar cycle take its course, or it may increase its role, both becoming more responsive to the needs of the working class and taking greater responsibility for making capitalist investment and production "rational." State disengagement, combined with unprecedented fiscal deficits and the globalization of capital (see below) characterized the Reagan years. We may pay the price for this reduced state role with an old-fashioned recession in the 1990s.

We should note how Bowles and Gintis' analysis concludes with the possibility of diametrically opposed structural changes. The state will have a greater—or lesser—role in the process of accumulation. The working class' standard of living will rise or fall. We will see increased rationalization of investment combined with increased welfare or a lower standard of living combined with greater "freedom" for capitalists. The "structural rules" of capitalism have not become irrelevant in this analysis. Rather, those rules are acted on by political agents. Analysis of political dynamics must therefore become central to contemporary Marxist theory.

Jürgen Habermas' (1975) concept of "legitimation crisis" is helpful in understanding the political implications of these developments. He offers an account of radical social change that can amend the traditional Marxist expectation of an industrial working class uniformly radicalized by an uncontrolled capitalist economy.

Basing himself on the kind of economic considerations we have discussed already, Habermas argues that state intervention and the rationalization of technical development make a "purely" economic crisis highly unlikely. Likewise, the inefficiencies and failures of state administration will provoke a crisis only if they are perceived by the population to result from political or economic class structure. Therefore, any "crisis" of advanced capitalist society will be found in the realm of "legitimation"; that is, the realm of public acceptance of the fairness and justice of the ruling institutions.

A legitimation "crisis" occurs when the social and cultural system produces people who do not "fit" into the existing forms of power and exploitation. Habermas believes that the structural contradictions between accumulation and legitimation can have this effect. The tensions between the proclaimed political principles of equality and justice and the reality of favoritism for the wealthy can provoke a critique of the system as a whole. State intervention, collective bargaining, and monopoly control demonstrate that society is shaped by collective and political forces, not just individual merit and an impartial "market."

This realization can lead to the politicization of all of social life. In the '60s, for instance, a variety of new values challenged the old bourgeois norms. The new social movements of that period were motivated not by the abstract rights of individualism and competition but by the demand for true equality of opportunity and participatory democracy.

Of course, the details of Habermas' analysis seem less compelling after a decade of deregulation, declining unionism, and political quietism. But the general rule holds: there now exists the ideological capacity to subject *all* of social life to political and moral evaluation. In the present, this challenge is rooted, for instance, in feminism and the ecology movement. The breakdown of traditional gender roles and the fundamental questioning of the values of consumption can seriously threaten the established order. There is also a sizable distrust of the claims made for male, scientific, and professional expertise. The canon of western culture has been criticized for its sexist and racist dimensions. Traditional medicine has been challenged by holistic medicine and alternative healers. The failures of our "leaders" to confront nuclear and environmental perils or provide successful models of health or happiness bring all forms of authority—including, but not limited to, the state—into question. This questioning, while essential to any radical movement, can also provoke more displacement of class struggle. Recent years have seen growing antagonisms between women and men; between those who (supposedly) must choose between a clean environment and jobs; and between those who support and those who reject the nuclear family, established religion, and conventional forms of authority and rationality. Perhaps most important, demands for racial justice have provoked a profound backlash among those white workers who would rather blame social and economic problems on minorities than on capitalism.

## "LONG WAVES" AND THE "SOCIAL STRUCTURES OF ACCUMULATION"

For contemporary Marxist theory, capitalism has no inevitable tendency to break down; rather, it develops through cycles of crisis and transformative maintenance. Some writers have understood this pattern aided by the helpful concepts of "long waves" and "social structures of accumulation." These concepts help put the recent changes analyzed above into historical perspective.

Long waves are (approximately) fifty-year cycles. Each wave contains a phase of expansion followed by a phase of stagnation or contraction and includes several of the shorter business cycles. Expansionary phases begin when technological innovation makes means of production cheaper or more efficient and social conditions give capital a clear upper hand over labor. The stagnant phase is caused by an exhaustion in investment outlets for the new forces of production and an upsurge in labor militancy and bargaining power.

In Ernest Mandel's (1978, 1980) account of long waves, capitalist post-war prosperity is rooted in technological and political developments which began in the mid 1930s. Innovations in the use of energy and machine production went hand in hand with the subduing of the European working class under fascism and the placating of the American working class by the New Deal. Modern productive techniques coincided with a rise in the rate of exploitation made possible by the defeat of European workers' organizations. Mandel describes the post-1960s decline of the U.S.-based capitalist world economy as the contraction phase of a long wave. This contraction occurred because of an exhaustion of the system's capacity to utilize the new forces of production and the increased political power of primary-sector labor stemming from the capital-labor accord.

The transition from one long wave to another is marked by an economic crisis. This crisis is more than simply an economic depression. It happens when difficulties in accumulation can only be remedied by fundamental transformations of some or all of what David Gordon (1982) has called the "social structures of accumulation." Gordon claims the general source of long waves is the periodic incompatibility between capitalist accumulation and the varied political and social frameworks which support that accumulation. Social structures of accumulation include religion and family life, forms of personality structure, and the geographical concentration of labor—all of the values, institutions, and practices which make profit and exploitation possible. Without a certain "fit" between these structures and the particular form taken by capitalism at any given time, long-term profit is impossible.

The resolution of any particular crisis of accumulation is determined to a great extent by the new form taken by the social structure of accumulation. Past resolutions have included the transition from competitive to monopoly capital, increased state involvement in the economy, the development of the nuclear family, and the spread of an ethic of consumption. As the new forms are created, accumulation accelerates with the transition from stagnation to expansion.

Eric Olin Wright (1979) provides an overall perspective on the history of capitalist development by showing that different periods in that history are marked by different kinds of economic crises. Each crisis is really a different transformation of the social structures of accumulation; or, to state it in my terminology, the end of each period is shaped by a different kind of transformative maintenance.

Wright divides the growth of capitalism into four stages. In each stage, accumulation is eventually blocked by existing arrangements of the relations and forces of production. In the last phase of intense competitive capitalism in the U.S. (1870–90), a falling rate of profit spurred the transition to monopoly capitalism. The consequent lessening of price competition helped sustain profits but led eventually to chronically lower demand; i.e., to the under-consumptionist crisis of the 1930s.

In the post World War II period, argues Wright, the under-consumption and stagnation tendencies of monopoly capitalism have been dealt with by the expansion of the state. However, the politicization of the economy has led to an unhealthy growth of unproductive state expenditures. This factor, combined with the increase in unproductive corporate expenditures (e.g., on marketing and advertising) leads to chronic state fiscal crisis and lagging productivity.

This entire process was also shaped by overseas economic connections. After World War II, the U.S. emerged as the leading capitalist power, and monopoly capital found investment outlets in a malleable, U.S.-dominated world. By the 1970s, however, the costs of dominating an empire drained the U.S. economy of its vitality. The Western European and Japanese economies rose from the ashes to create a U.S. trade deficit. The U.S. position in the Third World was threatened by a wide variety of anti-imperialist movements. Some raw material exporters organized around their own interests, and some Third World countries developed an indigenous capitalism which threatened to compete with the exports of the established capitalist nations.

The general lesson of the foregoing analysis is that different periods of capitalist development are marked by different types of economic and social crises. Each particular "fit" of economy and social structure requires a different form of transformative maintenance. For example, a developing capitalist society, drawing on labor reserves from a recently uprooted peasantry, will function differently than a late capitalist society in which the labor force possesses large, powerful, and disciplined unions or a socialist or labor political party.

To the extent that different long waves are defined by different social structures of accumulation, we should not expect to find the same mechanisms determining all phases of capitalist accumulation. With a series of historically specific and varying "fits" between accumulation and social structure, later phases will not repeat the patterns of earlier ones. While some form of instability will be present, we do not observe "laws" of capitalist development.

A clear political implication—in line with the discussion of the politics of difference in Chapter 6—is that the key groups constituting the "radical vanguard" will in all likelihood differ from period to period. Society-wide transformations required to usher in new social structures of accumulation typically require "the creation of a new political constituency to effect the necessary changes." (Gordon 1982: 242) The craft workers who sustained the Second International were in many places peripheral to the radical struggles of the 1930s. The peasant revolutionaries who resisted U.S. imperialism in Vietnam and made the Chinese Revolution were certainly not the industrial working class of traditional Marxist theory. The black-student-anti-war coalition of the 1960s was unforeseen by virtually all radical theorists, and the dynamics of the women's movement did not fit any pre-existing model. In all probability, the leading forces—and the slogans—of the next challenge to the ruling class will be a great surprise to those who fought the battles of the 1960s and 1970s.

## WORLD-SYSTEMS AND GLOBAL CAPITALISM

With a few exceptions, my discussion so far has focused on national economies within a context of U.S. hegemony. Two schools of Marxist theory show how this discussion must be expanded.

The "world-systems" framework grew out of the general perspective of monopoly capital theory, especially Paul Baran's *The Political Economy of Growth* (1957). Theorists began to emphasize the fact that capitalism had always existed not just in the local confrontations between capitalists and workers but also between geographically separate political units existing in unequal relations of power.

A bird's-eye view of this position provides the following analysis of capitalist development. During the sixteenth century, a fundamentally new social form came to dominate the world economy: a world-system. Centered in northern Europe but spreading first to the Americas and the Orient, and later to Africa, this capitalist world-system integrated many different political units into a whole marked by

> an expansion of the geographical size of the world in question, the development of variegated methods of labor control [i.e., wages, or slavery, or serfdom] for different products and different zones of the world-economy, and the creation of relatively strong state machineries in what would become the core-states of this capitalist world economy. (Wallerstein 1974a: 37–8)

The "core" states of northwestern Europe specialized in capital-intensive agriculture and the export of manufactured goods. The "periphery" (then Eastern Europe and Latin America, later expanded to Asia and Africa) provided agricultural raw materials and bullion and coerced labor through serfdom, slavery, or (eventually) political dictatorship. The key to the entire system was the creation of *world-wide trading patterns* that locked different geographical areas into different economic roles. These roles determined how labor was controlled in each area, what kind of products were traded, and who reaped advantages from the exchange. Given this complicated interlocking there are, claims Immanual Wallerstein (1974a, 1974b, 1980), no capitalist *nations*. There is only one unique, evolving *world-system of capitalism*. Local relations between classes may include slavery, serfdom, or wage labor. But as long as the local economy is part of a world-wide trading system, Wallerstein sees it as part of the capitalist system.

Analysis of this system has found a succession of dominating core nations whose power stemmed from higher levels of productivity, advanced social infrastructures, military power, and superiority in trade relations. At different times the imperialist center exports goods or capital, seeks large markets, or employs cheap labor. Historically, the core nations have destroyed local production and distorted the local economy round production for export. (Baran 1957, Magdoff 1969, Mandel 1980, Sklar 1980) From the world-systems perspective, temporary fluctuations of the core's superiority co-exist with a long-term continuity in its overall power. The basic hierarchy of core and periphery and the relation of unequal exchange will remain.

The world-systems model[6] makes two decisive contributions to contemporary Marxist theory. First, it effectively challenges the claim by liberal capitalist development theorists that Third World poverty arises from failures to duplicate western society. In fact, western development and Third World underdevelopment cannot be separated. The international division of labor between the rich (core) and poor (periphery) is a permanent and necessary feature of capitalism. Without the cheaper raw materials, coerced labor, and stolen bullion and land of the Third World, northwestern Europe could not have taken off into the industrial revolution. Without the distortion of their economies by colonialism and imperialism, the Third World would be considerably better off.

Second, world-systems theory challenges the traditional Marxist belief that capitalism, as unpleasant as its spread might be in the short run, will eventually develop all the nations it penetrates. Marxists had thought that capitalism would homogenize the world, just as it would diminish differences of race and gender within any one country. In opposition to this model, the world-system theorists described the spread and maintenance of *inequality* which accompanied the spread of capitalism. They also developed the Leninist notion of a "labor aristocracy" whose wages reflected both monopoly super-profits and the imperialist wealth derived from superior technological development and military power. In the modern world this led to another displacement of class struggle: from within the developed economies to between the developed and the underdeveloped worlds.[7] This displacement can be seen in working-class political support for America's aggressive, interventionist, and imperialist foreign policy.

Another perspective on the world capitalist system, described by the phrase "global capitalism," takes issue with many parts of both the world-system perspective and the monopoly capitalism model. As developed by Ross and Trachte (1990), this perspective identifies some of the key elements of capitalism's most recent round of transformative maintenance. Against monopoly capital theory, Ross and Trachte see not an absence of price competition among *national* oligopolies but, rather, intense *international* competition among multi-national corporations. These corporations may be based in America, Europe, Japan, or even developing capitalist centers such as Taiwan, Thailand, or Brazil. New technologies of transportation and communication make it possible to break up production into different sites. Instead of social peace, high wages, and effective political power for primary-sector labor, previously dominant unions have seen a loss of good jobs and a weakening of organized labor. From a world-system dominated by a few core nations, there has emerged a world of trans-national or multinational corporations that are less and less defined by ties to particular countries. Also, rather than thinking of American and Western European capitalism as permanently underdeveloping the Third World, this perspective sees the spread of centers of capitalist development throughout the globe.

In short, while the theoretical models of monopoly capital and world-systems theory are accurate for the post-war decades up to the early 1970s, another round of transformative maintenance has occurred. This transformation is itself a product of the structural contradictions of earlier forms of capitalism. For example, in response to the high cost of labor in the monopoly sector, capital has migrated abroad in search of lower labor costs. Equally important, it uses the *threat* of such mobility to curtail wages and benefits—and evade such costly regulations as pollution controls—at home. The capitalist state had responded to the economic crisis and labor militancy of the 1930s by developing a certain amount of autonomy from direct capitalist control. Now, however, capital's capacity to move operations throughout the globe tilts social power back towards the corporate elite. For workers, deteriorating wages and the loss of primary-sector jobs once again threaten to homogenize the American workforce. The last decade has shown a persistent decline in working-class standards of living in the U.S., matched by the continued concentration of wealth at the top of the economic ladder. Finally, contrary to world-systems theorists, portions of the Third World are developing at a rapid rate, competing with the First World production centers that heretofore had wielded unquestioned dominance. Independent centers of economic power can now be found in Brazil, Thailand, Singapore, and Korea. Clearly, there is no "center" to be found in the U.S., as Japan and Western Europe, with their higher productivity, have outstripped America in many, if not most, areas of competition.

While their own authors are not always clear on this matter, both the world-systems and global capitalism models further our under-standing of the interdependence of politics and economics. For these models, economic development is a function of international relations between global capital, nation states, and the culturally diffuse popula-tions of the world. In this system, state action is essential to trade, credit, development policy, taxation, research, and military support. And state action, in turn, reflects the shifting and unforeseeable balance of political forces and norms of legitimation. While the major actors may still be motivated by class interests, we do not know what social effects their actions will have. Marx could tell us what social effects the closed system of nineteenth-century competitive capitalism would have. And he did. With the politicization and globalization of capital-ism, no Marxist theorist can do that now.

## CONCLUSION

The flaws of socialist movements should not obscure Marxist theory's continuing contributions. For one thing, some key features of the original capitalist structure remain: concentration of wealth, periodic phases of economic instability, and structural opposition of interests between the two dominant classes. Marx's fundamental intuition that capitalism would frustrate human capacities and alienate us from our own powers remains valid. We still live in a society that is enormously rich in things yet terribly poor in spirit. The plagues of our society betray a sickness of heart that is all the more painful in a social world of vast material wealth. These key principles define the essence of a far from outmoded Marxism.

Further, as capitalism developed, so did Marxism. There is a clear line of evolution from Marx's original writings to Western Marxism, socialist-feminism, and contemporary radical theories of politics, economics, and culture. Along the way, Marxism has—one hopes—become more modest. Its arrogant confidence about the future has been replaced by more circumspect analysis of the present situation. Likewise, the failures or limited victories of the political movements it has influenced have generally eliminated any sense that Marxism corners the market on paths to human liberation. Yet the perspectives described in the last three chapters show that any comprehensive attempt to understand and overcome the social problems of the present world must contain—though need not and should not be limited to—elements of Marxist analysis.

# 8

## MARXISM AND SOME
## RADICAL CRITICS

This chapter describes, in a fairly technical and detailed way, some negative consequences of too readily discarding basic Marxist insights. The discussion is intended to enable the reader to experience something of the flavor of contemporary debates in Marxist and radical social theory.

The widely read and well-respected authors examined here are all deeply critical of capitalist society. But they tend to dissolve the *specific* features of capitalist class power into more *abstract and general* concepts of political, ideological, or psychological domination or into the demands of a classless technological rationality. As we shall see, these theoretical strategies seriously weaken their attempts to construct radical social theories. The point of this discussion is to show that while Marxism has evolved, it has neither been completely refuted by its own internal weaknesses nor rendered irrelevant by social change and the failures of the left. Reborn considerably less ambitious than in its first incarnation, it is alive and kicking even now. What Marxism can tell us, we still need to know.

## ANTHONY GIDDENS

In place of Marxism, Anthony Giddens' *A Contemporary Critique of Historical Materialism* (1981) offers a "theory of structuration." For Giddens, social life is a dialectic not of productivity and exploitation but of power and control. In this theory, human action and interaction, in relations of "transformation" and "mediation," are socially primary. "Transformation" refers to the fact that people, unlike machines or nature, are guided by intentions and beliefs. "Mediation" describes the way human interaction extends across space and time through ongoing institutions and technologies. Giddens believes that all human interaction involves the communication of meaning, ways of justifying values, and the operation of power. Therefore, social life necessarily involves signification, legitimation, and "domination"—with the last term understood as both power over people and power over things.

> In the theory of structuration, transformation/mediation relations, as embodied in concrete social practices and definite forms of society, take the place of the concept of "labour" as traditionally invoked in many versions of "historical materialism." (Giddens 1981: 53)

Giddens rejects the basic claims of historical materialism for two reasons. First, the mode of production is not always the key to explaining social structure. Second, historical changes only sometimes express a tension between forces and relations of production and are often the product of either a transitory crisis or encounters with other societies. To claim that the mode of production is always socially primary, thinks Giddens, is mistakenly to extend the characteristics of capitalism to non-capitalist societies. Primitive societies tend to be structured by an "existential contradiction" between human beings and nature (Giddens 1981: 236). In pre-capitalist societies there is no drive to transform the forces of production nor is exploitation part of production itself. Exploitation is not primarily "economic" but a product of physical coercion and entrenched values. More sophisticated but still pre-modern societies are shaped by conflicts between the agricultural producers and more centrally organized city dwellers who exploit them. Only in capitalist society is economic activity as such the basic social contradiction; i.e., the basic source of social change.

Giddens accepts much of Marx's analysis of capitalism, but he believes an unjustified "evolutionism" kept Marx from seeing that capitalism's contradictions could be resolved without a socialist revolution. Also, Marx's stress on labor as essential to human identity obscures the importance of a general—not class-based—ecological crisis. For Giddens, an adequate theory of capitalism must take into account not just economic relations, but also the accumulation of information about social processes and persons ("storage and surveillance") and the development of a uniform "managed space" not dependent on town/country divisions.

While promising a great deal—and utilizing some of the insights we have already discussed—much of this position repeats earlier theories. When Giddens describes the advent of class society as an increase in "time-space-distantiation" (i.e., an increase in the temporal and physical space across which humans can relate to each other), he is really saying little more than that such characteristically modern phenomena as banks and telephones increase our ability to communicate abstractly and across long distances. Marx made this observation in the 1840s. Stressing storage and surveillance in the capitalist city is very similar to sociologist Max Weber's much earlier notion of bureaucratic rationalization, since bureaucrats must acquire detailed knowledge about the social processes they manage. To argue that workers resist commodification, and thus that "structure is also object," is a repetition of Lukács' arguments concerning the proletarian response to reification.

More importantly, Giddens' generalizations about social primacy are confused. He claims, for instance, that authorization (politics) takes priority over allocation (economics) in pre-capitalist, class-divided societies. This claim falsely presumes that in such societies this distinction is as clear as that between the economy and the state in competitive capitalism. Actually, the power to command and the power to exploit are fused in pre-capitalist societies. Similarly, the development of feudalism and the transition to capitalism were decisively shaped by the class conflicts between lord and peasant. Without a Marxist perspective on these conflicts, Giddens has no theory of the breakdown of feudalism. He can only lamely appeal to generalizations about the importance of military force in expropriation and to the city/countryside tension. Yet peasant rebellions (dismissed by Giddens as "sporadic and rare" [Giddens 1981: 163]) were actually pre-conditions of capitalism. These rebellions focused on the quantity of surplus the lords and/or the state could expropriate. If such actions do not qualify as struggles concerning social labor, as economic struggles over allocation, it is hard to know what would. The priority of class conflict returns.[1]

Similarly, Giddens frequently stresses the importance of direct violence in social life, especially in pre-capitalist societies. Yet if that violence is not understood as part of a struggle over "allocative resources," it becomes largely inexplicable. Relying on military force rather than technological development is one "fact" about the feudal mode of production. In the twentieth century, imperialist wars cannot be understood without reference to economic interests in capitalist society. Again, a class analysis remains fundamental to understanding social life.

Giddens' attempt to replace class conflict rooted in the mode of production with a "dialectic of control," in which human agents engage in more general "power relations" of dependence and autonomy, is not successful. Struggle in both class-divided and "class" (i.e., capitalist) societies cannot be fully understood without concepts drawn from Marx's basic model of direct producer and expropriator. It is also

hard to use Giddens' account to understand the particular history and
structure of gender, racial, and national conflicts, when all of these have
been shaped by class antagonism and capitalist economic development.
Lacking an historical account of such conflicts, Giddens' cannot justify
his attribution of social primacy to transformation and mediation.[2]
Without an historical justification of the centrality of his categories,
Giddens' apparatus remains at the level of description, not theory.
Power and control do not unfold abstractly, as he supposes, but within
the concrete dynamic of class exploitation.

## STANLEY ARONOWITZ

Stanley Aronowitz's *The Crisis in Historical Materialism* (1981) emerges
from the dilemmas of leftist political practice, especially those that
stem from traditional Marxism's attempt to identify a revolutionary
class and a strategy for revolutionary change. Aronowitz's response is
to reject much of Marx's analysis of the political effects of capitalist
development. The rationalization of technical change, he claims, makes
the labor theory of value inapplicable. The industrial proletariat is
being dismantled by changes in the structure of production. Material
affluence and a managed economy make economic demands only a
small part of radical political motivation. Therefore, confidence in the
revolutionary vocation of the working class is no longer justified. It is
not the conflict between capitalists and workers which is central, but
resistance to any and all forms of domination. Therefore, human
liberation requires a loose confederation of different oppressed groups
in anticipation of a future society of self-managed workplaces and
communities.

Further, capitalism is not the underlying source of other forms of
domination, as traditional Marxism asserted. Rather, there are a number of related, overlapping but also distinct social and economic hierarchies. These hierarchies, including those of race and sex, are

> *rooted in the domination that social and economic hierarchies have attempted to*
> *inflict upon nature, including human nature. . . .* "woman" is linked with the

uncontrollable in nature. She becomes the "dark side" of universal human nature insofar as she is identified by men with the irrational, emotional, physical, sexual feelings which are displaced as the otherness of socially constituted "rationality." (Aronowitz 1981: 98, my emphasis)

Marxism faces other problems. Adopting a quasi-scientific confidence that revolution will occur, it inevitably ignores the moral basis of the varied forms of radical political activity. Bound by an "economic logocentricity" (Aronowitz 1981: 127), its political agenda is limited to the struggle of the working class against capitalism. Yet political movements concerned with ecology, women's liberation, and racial equality, argues Aronowitz, arise in resistance not just to class inequality, but to many different forms of repression. Accepting the domination of nature as essential to human freedom, Marxism has little to offer the full range of struggles against oppression.

Today the creative impulse in social theory comes from outside Marxism. It is lodged in feminism, ecology, theories of new nationalism often linked to racial freedom, and in liberation theologies trying to appropriate the social analysis of Marxism for a new morality based upon secular movements against capitalist oppression. (Aronowitz 1981: 133)

Aronowitz does at times connect his general notion of domination to accounts of struggles over wealth and political power. But he stresses that if the principle of domination as such is not recognized as the central category of social life, it will be repeated in supposedly radical organizations and socialist nations.

This position grows out of the new social movements and the experience of the authoritarian tendencies of Marxist organizations. In it, Aronowitz raises valuable questions for Marxist political practice, especially challenging Marxism's understanding of our relation to nature. Further, his basic political orientation properly emphasizes the consequences of the politics of difference. Unfortunately, however, his overall perspective suffers from many of the same problems as Giddens'. Aronowitz has separated himself too far from the concrete effects of class interests and power. This separation causes his position to vacillate among a political idealism in which he constantly appeals to what people "must" or "should" do, a disjointed theory which finds social primacy nowhere and is caught between ahistorical generalizations and temporary trends, and a reliance on the Marxist categories he claims to go beyond.

Since issues of political strategy are central for Aronowitz, let us begin with the first of these stands. Aronowitz foresees an alliance among politically autonomous groups which will be "genuinely oppositional to the prevailing social and political order, as well as challenging the hegemony of capital." (Aronowitz 1981: 127). Yet given his argument for the autonomy of groups such as women, the non-white underclass, and ecologists, we have little reason to expect these groups to ally with each other. Recent political history shows it is possible to struggle for women's equality without being anti-capitalist, to be concerned with the domination of nature but not of people, or to seek racial autonomy and be sexist. Perhaps Aronowitz's generalizations about domination are correct. But he gives no reason for believing that disparate groups will be guided by them. Trying to discard Marxism's traditional focus on the mode of production, he seems to retain its notion of a unified interest motivating a revolutionary group. Since he cannot root such an unified interest in the structure of capitalism, he attempts to do so in "domination." Unfortunately, his analysis does not provide any connection between this abstract concept and the concrete social experience and political movements of particular dominated groups.

Relying so heavily on the often vague abstraction of domination, Aronowitz's analysis alternates between ahistorical generalizations and temporary social trends. This lack of historical sense is shown, for instance, in his claim that women's oppression is rooted in their being equated to the "uncontrollable in nature." This claim treats an historically specific conceptual system as being true in all societies. Yet not every sex/gender system equated women and nature. Moreover, traditional societies marked by a reverence for nature may be more sexist than technological societies.[3]

Without directly acknowledging the real—even if limited—primacy of the economy, Aronowitz is tied to temporary developments when he analyzes the interests motivating political change. For instance, he sees an economic underclass created by racism, sexism, and a secondary labor market of low-paying, non-unionized, small-firm jobs. This underclass possesses specific political interests separate from the predominantly white, male, unionized and high-wage working class. However, these groupings may shift when a significant number of the white male workers lose their jobs or when blacks in a particular community achieve significantly higher living standards because they are able to take advantage of temporary labor shortages. The major forces responsible for such shifts stem from capitalism (e.g., the advent of global capitalism described in Chapter 7). Aronowitz's rejection of Marxism leaves him unable to account for the way both working class and underclass are subject to the same capitalist logic: the need to improve technology, the replacement of labor with machines, the business cycle, the control over the labor process, the flight of capital from highly unionized areas. Political differences, especially in regard to state programs, may divide white workers and the underclass. Yet the basic social structure remains common for both. That is why a Marxist approach focusing on economic structures is still essential to any strategy for liberating these groups.

Finally, when Aronowitz does attempt to provide some historical explanation, his theory invariably turns to more or less traditional Marxism. For instance, he explains "racial hatred" as an effect of the "unevenness and segmentation of American capitalist development."[4] (Aronowitz 1981: 94) Also:

> Labor market segmentation theory *explains* how the distinctions within the working classes become wider owing to the formation of sectors in the American economy that have a differentiated relation to the international social and technical division of labor. (92, my emphasis)

Finally, science and technology insist on their autonomy *not* from social purposes but from those that *subsume* it under capitalist domination. (56) Perhaps capitalism is really socially primary after all!

As we have seen, then, Aronowitz seeks a coalition of disparate groups, which have no seeming motivation for forming the coalition.

Yet while he denies the central role of capitalism in his general theoretical statements, he maintains that reliance in particular contexts.

> Capitalism is the structure-in-dominance in the historical dialectic of multilayered reality. But this dominance merely signifies that the submerged differences . . . must refer to the dominant reality as a boundary, not the operative principles of their functioning. (Aronowitz 1981: 72)

But can we so neatly separate "operative" principles and "boundary," as if having capitalism as a boundary will not seriously affect the internal principles of all other forms of domination? No Marxist ever claimed that every oppressive institution or ideology functioned in exactly the same way—that the church or the school, for instance, were exactly like the corporation. They said, rather, that we could not understand the effects or histories of churches, schools, etc., without understanding their relation to class power and technological development. Once this point is accepted we are, like it or not, back to some form of centrality of class analysis, to some form of social primacy for the mode of production; in short, we are back to Marxism.

My own view[5] is that economic class, socialization processes, and political life possess different, but equally important, forms of social primacy. The economy sets our society's possibilities. Socialization processes make the population psychically compatible with class domination. Political structures and struggles express the unity or fragmentation of social groups as they seek to manage or change society. We ignore the continuing, albeit limited, primacy of capitalism at our peril.

## NANCY CHODOROW

Nancy Chodorow's contribution to critical social theory focuses on the universal fact that the care of infants and small children ("mothering") is done by women (1978, 1979).[6] In outline, her influential perspective claims that male power and sexist ideology stem from a psychology determined by the experience of exclusively female mothering. Female mothering makes the individuation essential to ego development fundamentally different for boys and girls. The daughter's psychological identity is based in her view of herself as like her mother. Sons, by contrast, become persons by becoming *unlike* their mothers; for them, individuation and separation go together. Male development, therefore, requires rigid ego boundaries and a critical sense of "difference" from others. Since women's separation is less complete, they need and are capable of much greater affective closeness than men. These needs and capacities reproduce women as sex-affective laborers, while men control the public realm. Additionally, the fact than men can only "mature" by escaping their mother's love and power contributes to male misogyny.

The work of Chodorow (and other "mothering" theorists) makes a critical contribution to our understanding of how gender is reproduced and how it connects to other forms of domination. The gendered subjects of class society learn the rules of domination and submission, the alternatives of rational competence or emotional closeness. Later, the powers of the capitalist, the foreman, the party bureaucrat, the general, the bishop, and the professor reinforce the models of human relations learned in the home. Chodorow's theory also helps explain why men, who dominate the working class, find authoritarian and hierarchical capitalist societies compatible with their own personality structures. Moreover, the different personalities of men and women lead to a sex/gender system and a sexual division of labor that create a conflict of interests within oppressed groups, and women's attachment to mothering restricts their participation in the public sphere.

However, mothering theory fails if it seeks to replace the social primacy of class with that of mothering.[7] While there is an understandable attraction to positing early childhood experiences as crucial in the development of any particular individual, this form of explanation fails for society as a whole. Children's lives are molded by an already existing social organization. Identifying with or separating from a female mothering figure is significant only in a society where gender distinctions carry great weight. Closeness and distance, individuation and separation, are part of a system of power and valuation. They are not inevitable parts of a universal, purely individual, psychology.

Theoretically, women's emotional closeness could lead to social power based in female bonding, with competitive and isolated men subjected to the organized power of women.[8] This possibility is not realized because men have a variety of forms of power throughout the social world. It is not women's relational styles which guarantee them less social power. It is the gendered system of social power which makes women's relational styles less "valuable" than men's. Women's mothering is not the source or reproducer of patriarchy, it is one of patriarchy's aspects.

Equally important, this perspective tends to depict mothering as historically unchanging. Yet history reveals important differences in the mothering relation. In feudal Europe, high infant mortality and the practice of sending children to work in other homes from age seven on led to mother–child relations radically different from those that exist today. Similarly, male personality styles have varied throughout time. While male power and female mothering co-exist in tribal, feudal, capitalist, Western, Oriental, black, white, Christian, and Jewish cultures, men are not uniformly emotionally detached, competitive, and instrumental in all of them.[9]

Further, by positing mothering as a socially primary universal, the mothering theorists cannot tell us *why* anything should undermine it. If we wish to explain how mothering has changed in the past and could change in the future, we cannot simply appeal to the personality structures produced by mothering, for these would seem to be able to continue indefinitely. Chodorow acknowledges that family structure has changed in the last several centuries, and at times appeals to capitalism as the cause of that change. Yet she also wishes to use mothering as an explanation of some of the most basic features of capitalism: fetishism of commodities, militarism, and the excessive rationalization of technological thought. But this explanation does not square with the facts. Women have *always* mothered. How then did ancient Greece escape a fetishism of commodities or India generate an anti-rationalist mysticism? If women's mothering only produces these cultural characteristics in modern, industrial societies, something other than a psychology acquired in early childhood must be at work.

Similarly, mothering theory suggests that women confine themselves to domestic labor because of the emotional effects of female mothering. This claim ignores the fact under capitalism women have been shuttled in and out of the labor force to serve the interests of capitalists, the state, male-dominated labor unions, and their own husbands. Women entered industrial unions during World War II and were removed when their husbands returned from the war. "Rosie the Riveter" making planes in a defense plant became Doris Day making breakfast in the kitchen. In the late nineteenth century, women began to staff clerical and service occupations, thus cheapening wages in those areas. All these varied uses of women coexisted with the constancy of female mothering. In fact, an adequate explanation of changes in mothering, gender, and women's public position requires an understanding of the dynamics of class: class conflict and technological developments leading to cultural and political changes; hyper-inflation driving women into the workforce; the advent of new family forms and cultural styles to accommodate transformative maintenance and new social structures of accumulation.[10] In short, we cannot understand gender without the basic elements of Marxist theory. These elements, of course, must be themselves fully shaped by a feminist analysis and recognize relations between class and gender domination in both the macro social structures as well as the micro encounters of the nuclear family.

## G. A. COHEN

In his highly respected and enormously influential [11] *Karl Marx's Theory of History: A Defence* (1978), G. A. Cohen intended to present the basic ideas of Marx in a form clarified by the analytical techniques of contemporary philosophy. Cohen believed he was both representing Marx accurately and presenting an essentially correct theory of history. Actually, he by-passed central Marxist insights about the role of class relations in social life. This mistake is not only at odds with the best of Marx's own writings; it also passes off some of the general features of a positivist perspective on political life as an up-to-date Marxism.

Cohen resurrected a traditional version of Marxism. The basic thesis of this position is that there is a universal human drive to expand our control of nature by developing the forces of production. Clearly distinguishable from the forces of production, social relations of production evolve in order to promote the development of the forces. "Social change *consists* of change in social relations of production. But its *function* is to promote changes in material relations and productive forces." (Cohen 1978: 167) This universal tendency towards technological development may be inhibited or resisted at times, but it will prevail. People express their natural rationality by using their intelligence to improve their material conditions. As a result, productive relations are altered in order to facilitate growth in the powers of productive forces. And they are altered in the best way possible for that end. "We say that the relations [of production] which obtain at a given time are the relations most suitable for the forces to develop at that time, given the level they have reached at that time." (Cohen 1978: 171)

Cohen cites many quotations where Marx more or less explicitly makes a categorical distinction between the forces and relations of production and accords explanatory primacy to the former. The notion that an unstoppable drive to develop forces of production animates all of history *can* be found in Marx. Yet contrasting statements can also be found, and I will begin by discussing two of them before turning to Marx's actual analysis of historical change.

Cohen's position rests on the distinction between the forces and relations of production. If this distinction is not always clear, then no case can be made for the primacy of the former. Yet Marx's commitment to this distinction is made questionable by the following passage from *The German Ideology:*.

The production of life . . . appears as a double relationship: on the one hand as a natural, on the other as a social relationship. . . . It follows from this that a certain mode of production, or industrial stage, is always combined with a certain mode of co-operation, or social stage, and this mode of co-operation is itself a "productive force." Further, that the multitude of productive forces accessible to men determines the nature of society. . . . (Marx and Engels 1947: 18)

It is unfortunate that Cohen did not examine this passage in detail. For here Marx is relating the forces and relations of production "dialectically." They can be distinguished in thought but not in reality; i.e., they always occur simultaneously. Thus the dialectical elements, the "industrial" and the "social" stages, are "always combined"; and the totality, the "production of life," appears "as a double relationship." Yet the "social stage" is itself a "productive force." And changes in either significantly affect the other. The way in which they combine in reality tends towards instability, and the resolution of any particular incompatibility tends to give rise to new ones. Most important, while in particular instances we might find an incompatibility or contradiction between the two resolved "in favor" of one rather than the other, no consistent pattern of priority exists.

For Cohen's position, there must exist in Marx a rigid separation between society—which comprises an economic structure and non-economic institutions and practices—and the forces of production. Yet if the passage quoted above is to be taken seriously, Marx does not always maintain such a distinction. And at times he asserts that the general determinant of social life is not technological development but the interaction between productive forces and social relations in a mode of production.[12] Consider this statement:

> The specific economic form, in which unpaid surplus-labour is pumped out of direct producers, determines the relationship of rulers and ruled, as it grows directly out of production itself and, in turn, reacts upon it as a determining element. Upon this, however, is founded the entire formation of the economic community which grows up out of production relations themselves, thereby simultaneously its specific political form. It is always the direct relationship of the owners of the conditions of production to the direct producers—a relation always naturally corresponding to a definite stage in the development of the methods of labour and thereby its social productivity—which reveals the innermost secret, the hidden basis of the entire social structure. . . . (Marx 1967 III: 791)

A number of complex relations are suggested in this compressed statement:

1. The specific economic form of the expropriation of surplus-labour determines the relationship between rulers and ruled.
2. The relationship between rulers and ruled grows directly out of production itself and reacts upon it as a determining element.
3. The formation of the economic community grows up out of production relations.
4. The direct relation between owners and producers reveals the basis of the social structure.
5. The direct relations correspond to a definite state in the development of the methods of labour.

It might be suggested that 2 and 5 reflect Cohen's theses of the primacy of the productive forces. Yet this is true only if they are taken in isolation from the rest of the passage. There is no suggestion of causal priority in either statement. For 2 really just asserts that political relations are founded in the direct social relations of the expropriation of a surplus. And 5 makes no suggestion of primacy. Rather, it only echoes the point made over and over in Marx (and explicitly in the passage from *The German Ideology* just quoted) that relations of production and forces of production (here "methods of labour") must always exist in a "correspondence"—they necessarily co-exist. Numbers 1, 3, and 4, by contrast, support an interpretation of Marx in which the dialectical unity of forces and relations of production is the key to explaining social structure and historical change. For in 1, 3, and 4, we find a class relation of expropriation considered as basic to the "social structure"—and not itself viewed as the product of some other forces. Furthermore, this passage occurs in a context in which Marx is distinguishing feudal ground-rent from expropriation in slave, plantation, and oriental societies. In this discussion he characterized these societies not by the level of development of *productive forces*, but by the social relations they use in extracting surplus labor. He argues, for instance, that the specific social relations involved in ground-rent motivate increased productivity. While the producers can write off the time they spend working for the lord:

The productivity of the remaining days of the week, which are at the disposal of the direct producer himself, is a variable magnitude, which must develop in the course of his experience, just as the new wants he acquires, and just as the expansion of the market for his product and the increasing assurance with which he disposes of this portion of his labour-power. (Marx 1967 III: 794)

Thus, while labour-rent may be "based upon the imperfect development of all social productive powers" (793), its particular *social relations* contain a spur to development not found in societies with similar technological development. Social relations, not technology, determine historical change.

Cohen discusses the use of "correspond" in Marx's methodological generalizations (Cohen 1978: 146–8). He claims that while the term may indicate co-determination, Marx always generalized by asserting that relations correspond with forces, and never the reverse. (138) In response, it can be said that Marx's particular historical studies are never as simplistic as his generalizations. Why then did he over-generalize? I can offer two highly speculative reasons. First, throughout his life he faced Hegelian idealism and consequently over-stressed the "material" aspects of life to compensate for the way the Hegelian tradition ignored it. Second, his claim is as much or more prescriptive as it is descriptive. The generalizations about the bursting of social relations are meant less as a summing up of the historical record and much more as a political imperative to the European working class. The political message behind the historical generalization is, simply, that the management of production in particular and society in general need no longer be left to capitalists. The statements on which Cohen places so much emphasis, on this reading, are meant as a stimulus to political action, not as a definitive theory.

We have here two opposing interpretations. Cohen believes that for Marx, there is a rigid distinction between forces and relations of production and that the development of the forces is the motor of historical change. I have argued that for Marx, forces and relations are dialectically connected.[13] Given the ambiguity of Marx's writings, no definitive case can be made for either position. One test, however, is to see how Marx actually analyzed particular cases of historical change. I will examine his account of how pre-capitalist societies are destabilized and how he explained the origins of capitalism. These accounts do not match Cohen's interpretation.

In the *Grundrisse,* Marx describes three social formations based in agricultural production and landed property. Production in these communities aims at the "sustenance of the individual proprietor and of his family, as well as of the total community." (Marx 1973: 472) In contrast to the capitalist entrepreneur, "The individual is placed in such conditions of earning his living as to make not the acquiring of wealth his object, but self sustenance, his own reproduction as a member of the community. . . ." (476) In these communities, however, reproduction has three essential features. First, the conditions of labor appear as natural conditions, not as human products. Second, despite this appearance the relation between individual laborer and conditions of production is "instantly mediated" by the "presence of the individual as member of a commune." Third, determination of this social whole is neither solely by the objective conditions of labor nor solely by the structure of the community; rather, it is reciprocal.

> His relation to the objective conditions of labour is mediated through his presence as member of the commune; at the same time, the real presence of the commune is determined by the specific form of the individual's property in the objective conditions of his labour. (Marx 1973: 486)

In short, the objective conditions of labor (which appear to be natural but are "human products"), the individual laborer, and the community stand in co-determining relations to each other. The primacy of the forces of production is nowhere to be found.

Marx claims that the goal of these communities is stable self-reproduction. Nevertheless, "production itself" (Marx 1973: 486) necessarily ends up making social stability impossible. Does this confirm Cohen's interpretation? Not if we examine Marx's examples of *how* production undermines these communities. He lists population growth, warfare, slavery, concentration of land possession, exchange, and the money system. (486–7) No one factor, or characteristic tension between factors, is the key.

These passages are part of a long section in which Marx is discussing the emergence of free wage labor. Since this emergence is one of the two pre-conditions for the creation of capitalism (the other being the accumulation of wealth), it is of central importance in Marx's theory. In explaining this transformation—both in the *Grundrisse* and in Volume I of *Capital*—Marx never relies on simplified general formulas attributing primacy to the development of the productive forces.

Though he does say that the social relations of capitalism require a certain level of development of the productive forces, he never lays such an emphasis on that development as he does on accumulated wealth and "free" labor. Nor does he anywhere in his detailed histories explain historical changes as simple results of a universal drive to higher productivity. Typically, he will list a chain of reactions. These chains might start with a technological innovation, the growth of a particular social relation, or an interaction between separate communities (e.g., trade or conquest). And they include human development of "new powers and ideas, new modes of intercourse, new needs and new language." (Marx 1973: 494)

In this section of the *Grundrisse*, there does occur the kind of statement Cohen is fond of quoting. Marx claims that alienating laborers from the conditions of production always involves replacing use value by exchange value. Relations transformed in this process "were possible only with a definite degree of the development of the material . . . forces of production." (Marx 1973: 502) But this statement is no contradiction to the position I have been suggesting. For even as certain social relations require certain material forces of production, so particular material forces of production are created by the demands of social relations and not their own inherent, natural properties.

> Urban labour itself *had created means of production* for which the guilds became just as confining as were the old relations of landownership to an improved agriculture, which was in part itself *a consequence* of the larger market for agricultural products in the cities. . . . (Marx 1973: 508, my emphasis)

Only if we focus on the first half of this passage and ignore the second can we fail to see how Marx's historical explanations rely on a variety of factors.

In his account of "primitive accumulation" in Volume I of *Capital,* Marx notes that the triumph of industrial capitalism "appears" as a victory over feudal privilege and the "fetters" which guilds placed on the "free development of production." In reality, however, capitalists succeeded only "by making use of events of which they themselves were wholly innocent." "The expropriation of the agricultural producer, of the peasant, from the soil, is the basis of the whole business." (Marx 1967 I: 715–6) Marx then describes in compressed detail the factors which led to the creation of the proletariat in England. Among other factors, he cites as crucial the growth of Flemish wool manufacturers, which led to a rise in the price of wool in England and thus provided a motivation for evicting peasants from their traditional land. Now Cohen interprets (Cohen 1978: 176) this claim as confirming his view. Yet it is doubtful that Marx believes that the foundation of primitive accumulation is a technical change in Flemish wool manufacture. He knows he must ask: where does the English rural capitalist come from who would want to or could respond to changes in Flemish demands? (Marx 1967 I: 742) For the English peasantry, this transition is not from lower to higher productivity, but from a subsistence agriculture (for them) to a profit making one (for someone else). The Flemish textile manufacturer had an interest in getting English wool, but under what conditions did anyone in England have an interest in providing them with it? Marx's answer is that the "capitalist farmer" evolves through a variety of factors. These include employment of wage labor, an agricultural revolution, the usurpation of common lands, and a transformation of prices in the sixteenth century which benefited farmers by lowering the cost of rent and labor relative to agricultural products. (Marx 1967 I: 742–4, 812–3) On Cohen's reading of Marx, all these factors themselves would have to be products of the historical drive to unfetter forces of production. (Cohen 1978: 176–8) As we have seen, Marx's account is much more complex and varied than Cohen thinks.[14]

This is confirmed by the *Communist Manifesto*'s more compressed account of the transition from feudalism to capitalism. Marx does make the statement (cited by Cohen) that "the feudal relations of property became no longer compatible with the already developed productive forces; they became so many fetters . . . they were burst asunder." (Marx and Engels 1954: 20) Yet this statement may be seen as a powerful descriptive summary of one aspect of the transition rather than as an explanation of it. For when we turn to his detailed account, he lists the following factors: the emigration of serfs to towns to become burghers and the way colonization, discovery, and an increase in exchange and commodities gave "to industry, an impulse never before known." (15) If feudal social relations had to be replaced to match the increased capacities of its productive forces, those productive forces had no internal developmental impluse themselves. Rather, after the events just mentioned, "The feudal system of industry, under which industrial production was monopolized by closed guilds, now no longer sufficed for the growing wants of the markets." (16) Later, manufacturing was replaced by steam power to keep pace with the "ever growing" markets. Again, there is no simple formula—relations change to increase productive forces—which can explain a concrete historical circumstance.

Whether or not it is Marx's, the historical materialism developed by Cohen is inadequate. Social relations may be transformed to meet the demands of higher productivity, and human history obviously does show, in the long run, a dramatic increase in productive power. Yet it is also the case that increases in productivity stem not only from human interests in combating scarcity, but also from the manner in which scarcity is faced by a particular class structure. As a consequence, human history reveals both the development of productive powers and periods of stagnation and decline. And while some social relations will be changed to accord with technical innovation, technical innovation is often shaped by those relations—or left unused for centuries because limitations in the existing social relations provide no basis for a social transformation.[15]

Cohen understands class struggle as a sort of competition to develop the forces of production, with class rule achieved by that class "whose rule best meets the demands of production." (Cohen 1978: 292) Yet, contrary to Cohen, developing productive forces is only one of the many resources in the arena of class struggle. Physical force, psychological or ideological manipulation, and political organization are omitted on his view—or are seen as ultimately reducible to developing the forces of production. This approach cannot account for the continued power of socialization to create mass acceptance of highly inefficient forms of class rule, or the way the political power of a (more or less) unified ruling class can overcome a working class divided by race, nationality, and sex.

Similarly, many observers have shown that capitalist technologies are not created for productivity alone. The American automobile could be a much more efficient form of transportation if its goal were transportation and not profit. The current form taken by energy consumption is geared to intensive investment by centrally-controlled, multinational corporations, rather than ecological sanity or decentralized control. Under different social conditions, technologies for renewable energy sources and conservation would have been developed. Scientific research itself is based in the needs of those who control the funding for that research. This means that the investigation of basic physical processes is directed to areas conducive to salable commodities.[16]

For Cohen, *class interests* based in capitalist economic structure serve a universal *human interest* in greater productive power. Yet the point is that the forces of production created by this economic interest bear its stamp in both their quantitative dimension (capitalism makes more of them) and their qualitative dimension (their form, content, and direction). Cohen pretty much ignores the many ways in which productive forces are not developed by and do not reflect a universal drive to increase power but rather partial interests based in class relations.

This belief that productive forces are "natural" powers to which social relations must inevitably conform reflects the "technocratic ideology" we have focused on a number of times already. In Cohen's version, scientific and technological advances are represented as independent of the social structures in which they are created. A myth of scientific and technical neutrality masks the class interests contained in technology itself. In this myth, the expansion of knowledge and technique imposes certain imperatives on society. These forces are thus represented not only as objective structures external to human interests but as having "interests" of their own. Apologists of the current order use these interests to justify the rule of managers and technical experts. As in Stalinism, class consciousness and political self-organization can then be relegated to a secondary role.

For Cohen, our interest in technological development would be responsible for the transition to a new social order. Thus, he writes:

> Production relations reflect the character of the productive forces, a character which makes a certain type of structure propitious for their further development. We denied that this formulation removed class struggle from the centre of history, saying instead that it was a chief means whereby the forces assert themselves over the relations. . . . *That class tends to prevail whose rule would best meet the demands of production.* (Cohen 1978: 292, my emphasis)

The "demands" and "assertions" of the productive forces—along with a universal human rationality—are at the center of Cohen's historical materialism. For him, these factors are distinct from either the interests of a traditional Marxist "working class" or the loose coalition of oppressed groups sought by much of the contemporary Left. It is an abstracted human rationality which enables "societies or economic units" to be "self-maintaining and self-advancing." (Cohen 1978: 264) It is the "demands" of the forces of production which lead that rationality to bring into existence new social relations.

> But why should the fact that the relations restrict the forces foretell their doom, if not because *it is irrational* to persist with them given the price in lost opportunity of further inroads against scarcity? (Cohen 1978: 159, my emphasis)

If my argument is correct, however, such an absolute and disinterested sense of "the irrational" (or rational) has no place in fundamental historical explanation. Reason is not universal, but situated; especially, it is situated by collective relations to production, distribution, ownership, labor, and social power. Cohen has made class interests subsidiary to the forces of production. His functional explanations require that history be made by agents in pursuit of goals. But since class is secondary to technology, he therefore has to suggest that technology has "interests." But the only interests in technology are the ones which stem from the various human relationships of class, gender, race, nationality, etc., which define the power relations of a given society. Since the identity of these social agents is determined by the concrete and characteristic tensions of their particular social order, historical change does not reflect the pursuit of some trans-historical goal. This point repeats the arguments from earlier chapters that both reason and interest are historically and personally situated. In his most authentic voice, this was realized by Marx. It is a mistake to make "later history the goal of earlier history" (Marx and Engels 1947: 38) or to think that "social phases" realize "in their logical sequence the impersonal reason of humanity." (Marx 1963: 11)

## POST-MODERNISM AND DECONSTRUCTION

It is necessary to say something—even though in a brief and perhaps superficial way—about the recently prominent developments in philosophy, social theory, and literary theory known roughly as post-modernism and deconstruction. These trends originated with a number of French thinkers, most significantly Michel Foucault and Jacques Derrida. Richard Rorty is their most noteworthy American spokesperson.[17]

Marxism, a number of writers from these traditions have suggested,[18] shares certain crucial failings with the rest of the Western philosophical tradition. Most critically, it seeks to be a "master discourse": the sole theory, or only descriptive vocabulary of social life, the single way to make sense of history and shape the future. This pretension is a form of domination, and must eventually be expressed in the totalitarian politics of Stalinism. Actually, deconstructionists argue, there can be no "master discourse." Human life is constituted by an endless play of "signification and difference." It resembles a language, which can function only because words are different from each other. In much the same way that particular concepts fit into a general system of potentially infinite expressions by being distinct from each other, human beings can function as bearers of consciousness

*humans respond + interpret differently*

because they have different interpretations of, responses to, and ways of making meanings out of life. There is no final, objective, or ultimately adequate system of interpretation. Like texts, reality is not a knowable, given entity or system that can be revealed by science, knowledge, or theory. It is simply a continual play of possible interpretations. The claim to definitive knowledge of *any text*, to the authoritative interpretation, is actually a strategy in a system of power relationships. Claiming definitive knowledge—whether this is the "knowledge" of positivist science, bourgeois sociology, or Marxism— is always an attempt to control or exclude rival forms of interpretation. Marxist discourse is as susceptible to this failing as any other; perhaps more so because it, as opposed to other philosophies, has been self-consciously identified with state power.

*There is no concrete reality achievable thru science*

*all attempts at control*

Just as there is no final theory, or given reality, so the "subject"— a unified, knowable, discrete self residing at the heart of each person's identity—is also a fiction. This notion is another fantasy of Western thought. Personal identity is as variable, shifting, and plastic as any text. As there can be no final reading of the world, or of a book, so there can be no final reading of a person. We simply interpret, endlessly, between the limits of birth and death. There is no "inner truth" to persons, books, or the world. All of these, in fact, are "textual." Human beings and language, knowledge and interpretation cannot be finally distinguished.

*endlessly searching for inner truth*

In place of the pretensions to absolute meaning and objective truth of all traditional modes of thought, including Marxism, writers such as Foucault and Derrida offer "genealogy" and "deconstruction." Genealogy describes the evolution and transformation of systems of concepts and the social institutions and practices in which they are embedded. It reveals how these systems serve the accumulation of power rather than providing an objective or rational account of the world. This power, according to Foucault, is not the property of any particular group or class, but simply a "field" of relations which changes shape over time. The "deconstruction" of a theory shows how its positive valuation of some cluster of qualities always necessitates the rejection of "otherness and difference." Despite this rejection, the theory's positively valued concepts are shown to depend upon and utilize that which

*Genealogy = evolution of systems of concepts + instit + practices; serve accumul-ation of power, not accounting cul*

*Deconstruction shows how acceptance of some cul qual leads to rejecting other differences*

they seek to exclude. They are thus "deconstructed." For instance, the pretense of traditional philosophy to absolute rationality—as opposed to emotion—is shown to be motivated by the very emotionality it seeks to deny or repress.

These doctrines are the most recent move in the long collapse of positivism and in the decline of "Enlightenment" notions of objective, rational knowledge held by unitary, self-subsistent, reflective, emotionally and physically detached subjects. In this respect, post-modernism and deconstruction are not opposed to—but allied with—Marxism. At least, they are allied with the form of Marxist theory which originated in the 1920s in a rejection of Stalinism. As we saw in Chapter 5, this Marxism avowed a connection of theory and practice, a denial of pseudo-scientific detachment, and a commitment to a particular set of social interests.

Of course, Marxist theorists may have a difficult time with some of Foucault's general assessments of the nature of power; for instance, that it is not the property of any group. They may also want to ask him how he connects his claim that "knowledge" and "truth" are essentially forms of power to his supposed attempt to provide true histories of social practices. Yet Marxists should appreciate the way Foucault's brilliant genealogies of medicine, social science, and criminal disciplinary practices reveal the social domination bound up in those modern institutions and ideologies. Similarly, Marxist theory can benefit from deconstruction's skeptical interrogations of pseudo-objectivity and theoretical completeness. And pretentious Marxists should be reminded by deconstruction that there are valid non-Marxist frameworks for making sense of human life. A spiritual understanding (see Chapter 9) and an aesthetic response, to name but two, really have little place in Marxism, yet must be allowed to exist comfortably beside it.

There are also, however, basic limitations to post-modernist thinking. The most important lies with its central theoretical metaphor: the use of concepts of language, the text, and interpretation as models for social relations, the physical world, and selfhood. Conceiving of reality and personal identity as endlessly interpretable texts ignores the crucial structural *differences* between texts and other parts of the world. Texts, for one thing, are not only systems of meaning capable of interpretation. They are also physical artifacts which are produced, exchanged, and owned under particular social relations. Before we can read a text, we must have access to it—by owning it, borrowing it from a library, etc. Before we can interpret it, we must learn to read; that is, we must be shaped by a particular set of educational and socialization processes. Before we can join the endless play of varying descriptions which Rorty claims is all that philosophy amounts to (rather than any objective "mirroring of nature"), we must have a building in which to have this long conversation. This building will be owned by someone rather than someone else, and only certain people will be allowed into it.

In short, the *metaphorical* extension of reading, talking, and interpreting into the rest of human life ignores the *material contexts* of actual reading, talking, and interpreting. Deconstruction especially seems to be a kind of idealism: the infinity of interpretation floats in space, unconnected to socially situated human beings. Deconstructionists usually avoid addressing how class or gender privilege—situated in material relations and not just wrong ideas—determines how and what interpretations are made. Facing this social reality, they would have to *distinguish* between social relations and textual interpretation, and *privilege* the former over the latter. But since for them, all of reality is textual, all of reality gets flattened out into one big "book"—of which no chapters are more important than any others. And of course it is true that for books, one chapter does not "cause" anything in the rest of the text. In actuality, however, the book is produced by an author—and the author is produced by a set of social relations.

The notion of authorship is, however, also denied by deconstruction, since it is for them part of the fiction of the subject. This position has its own problems. Of course, critiques of the Cartesian or Platonic concepts of the self have revealed crippling limitations to claims that the self is unified, essentially unconnected to other people, distinct from the body, only peripherally burdened with emotions, and individually capable of universally valid knowledge. Attacks on this notion have come from a variety of sources, not just post-modernism: Marxism itself, Pragmatism, Existentialism, forms of sociology, and feminism. But human beings remain subjects, persons, and in some contexts individuals for all that. One need only reflect on the actual practice of deconstructionist theorists: they write personally authored papers, stand at lecterns in crowded convention halls defending their views, author books with their names on the covers and, presumably, collect their personal royalty checks—all for theories which proclaim the death of the subject![19] Can we doubt that behind every post-modernist there lies an existing human being with hopes, fears, and the desire for recognition?

Politically and ethically, the post-modernist rejection of subjectivity veers towards the abandonment of personal and collective responsibility. And this perspective may in fact reflect the fact that many post-modernists were involved in the rise and fall of radical politics during their youth. Whatever its origin, however, there is a fundamental error here. It is forgotten that interpretations, theoretical positions, or concepts are not made final or objective simply by being "justified" in a pretentious and dominating "master discourse." Interpretations are made ultimate by our personal and collective willingness to act on them, to change history forever in their name; by our willingness to die—and perhaps kill—for what we believe. It is in our ability and need to act that our essential subjectivity resides. In just this sense every person and every community necessarily authors his/her/its own master discourse, and each person and community contributes to humanity's process of self-creation. It is the enduring importance of a Marxist perspective to show the centrality of this process, and to insist on the way inequalities and exploitation in social relations of production make it less conscious, controllable, and fulfilling than it might be. As long as human beings live in a class society, such a "discourse" will be indispensable.

# 9

# MARXISM AND SPIRITUALITY

There are certain limitations which Marxism—no matter how transformed, modernized, or joined with other perspectives (Marxist-feminism, black Marxism, etc.)—simply cannot overcome.[1] Of these limitations I will explore here how left movements in general, and Marxism and socialist-feminism in particular, are incomplete without some of the resources and insights of spirituality.[2] Unlike earlier chapters, the tentative argument that follows is less of a commentary on Marxism's past than an attempt to shape its future.

As will become clear in the course of the discussion, the sense of "spirituality" I am using is broader than any particular theology, set of rituals, or institution. It is, rather, a synthesis of teachings which can be found in a wide variety of traditions, traditions that have often—but not always—existed as minority currents within organized religions. Even as a synthesis, what I am describing is a somewhat selective—and perhaps idealized—version of spirituality. It is an optimal picture of what spirituality is and can be. While idealized, however, this image *can* be found within past traditions and in the teachings and actions of many people in the contemporary world.[3]

## RADICAL POLITICS AND THE EGO

Radical political perspectives promote models of a society characterized by equal rights, a just distribution of goods and opportunities, non-oppressive social relations, and personal freedom. These models correctly identify some of the root causes of human suffering in hierarchy, exploitation, and oppression. However, these models also face a fundamental difficulty. To put it simply: most radical political activity seems to aim at satisfying the conventional social self, what I will call here the "ego."

The radical vision seems to say: if people want to consume, we will offer them a higher, more equitably distributed standard of living. If we are powerless now, we will achieve power through revolution. If we are culturally degraded through racism or ethnocentrism, we will have our traditions given respect. If work has become drudgery, we will reorganize the factory or the office to share responsibilities and expand creative opportunities. If social decisions are made against our interests, we will open the processes of political power. If sexual repression leads to false consciousness and violence, we will release the floodgates of desire and sexual fulfillment.

All this, it is presumed, will make us happy. Or, at least, even if there continue to be conflicts of interest after the institutional overthrow of capitalism, racism, sexism, etc., these are essentially the only *kinds* of things we need to change in order to create lasting happiness. And, in fact, it can hardly be doubted that such changes *would* remove a tremendous amount of suffering and provide some real satisfaction.

Yet because the Marxist tradition pre-supposes—with little or no argument—that human fulfillment results from the proper arrangement of social relations and consumption, its model ignores a basic dimension of human experience. The problem arises from some unstated—and unexamined—premises: If we are given enough bread and justice, we will be satisfied and not want more. We will no longer be driven by greed, insecurity, envy, boredom, or the fear of death. We will conquer—or eliminate—any core sense of shame or guilt. We will accept ourselves and others. Having achieved equality, we will not seek superiority. Being offended, we will not seek revenge. Having so much, we will not want more. In short, once external injustice is ended, internal misery will dwindle, perhaps to the vanishing point.

I think these suppositions are false. The ego—as presently historically and socially constructed—is not so easily pacified. Consider whether the financially well-off, well-respected, non-oppressed people in our own society show a calm, balanced, and loving temperament or a fundamental acceptance of their lives. Do they seem deeply satisfied? Hardly. White, well-educated, well-off men—no less than the rest of us—provide stark examples of greed, personal dissatisfaction, escapism, and self-hatred expressed in addictions and the abuse of women and children. The rich, powerful, and prestigious have much more pleasure, security, and comfort than the rest of us. Yet they are poor models of lasting happiness.

To understand why this is so, let us examine the ego.

By "ego" I mean the contemporary experience and practice of selfhood, a selfhood structured by "Individualism" and "Possession/Accomplishment."

*Individualism* is a sense of self-identity based in exclusion from and opposition to others. Individualism may apply literally to the particular person, or it may attach to the person's group (religion, nation, ethnicity, gender), nuclear family, or close personal relationships.

Individualism is made up of competitiveness, exclusion of others, continual desire for self-enhancement and self-protection, hostility to difference, emotional over-dependence on a few relationships, and difficulties in achieving intimacy. As individuals, people are alienated from their surroundings and dependent on only their own actions for self-fulfillment. Trust is given only to the individual self (or single cathected other, or restricted group) for care and love. What is good for the self is to be achieved by the self, in competition with, or at least separate from, other individual selves, dyads, or groups. In its most extreme male version, individualism is the capitalist entrepreneur or the cowboy hero riding off into the sunset. In another form, it is also found in the housewife who is emotionally bound to a sexist relationship with her husband.

The second fundamental dimension of the ego is that of *accomplishment/possession*. The self, separated from and in opposition to others by the structures of individualism, is here accorded value only in terms of doing and possessing. The person has no value simply by virtue of human identity. Rather, the ego feels itself as essentially lacking, needing over and over to prove its worth. To overcome this inadequacy we seek to drown our misery in the measurable phenomena of wealth, consumption, or achievement. Possession/accomplishment is an essential part of the culture of mass consumerism, the culture which so effectively co-opted working-class radicalism of the 1930s.[4] It is also part of the drive to succeed which permeates middle- and upper-class work and leisure, from the unnecessary workaholism of professionals and executives to the hordes of (supposedly) recreational joggers who consult their complex chronographs to see if they are running fast enough to be considered to be having a good day. The attachment to accomplishment can also be found in Marx's original belief that human beings are most fulfilled through creative activity. Marx never asked— nor have very many of his followers—*why human beings are not of value or cannot be fulfilled by being rather than doing*; why, that is, we must objectify ourselves in creative labor in order to realize ourselves.

The ego, structured by these two principles, is endemic to our age.[5] It takes different forms in men and women, in different classes, races, and ethnic groups. But it is there, I believe, in virtually all of us; and it is, along with the oppressive structures of social relations, a source of profound unhappiness.

The ego, after all, constantly seeks external support to guarantee its sense of self-worth, a sense which can never be achieved because a sense of inadequacy is built into the ego from the start. Therefore, genuine happiness is always elusive. If I am not enough, or of enough worth, without possessing and accomplishing, then anything I own or do can only give me the most temporary of pleasures. My attachment to having and doing will organize my life like an addiction. Any temporary gratification—this "A" on my report card or that professional success, this new gadget or that "well-earned" vacation—will pacify the ego for a very short time. How long does the pleasure at the new car last? How lasting is our satisfaction at placing that essay in the prestigious journal? Why do we live a life from which we need to "escape" in one way or another? What do we prove—and avoid—by being so busy all the time?

As an individual, furthermore, it is extremely difficult for me to trust others to help me out of this dependence on doing and having. Others are, after all, essentially different from, opposed to, and in competition with me. Because I feel myself as so essentially unconnected, so essentially separate, I must rely on myself alone. Conversely, because I place so much stock in what I can own and consume, produce and take credit for, my sense of connection to others is attenuated. For if what I have and do must serve to overcome my fundamental sense of emptiness and alienation, then having and doing cannot connect me to others but only further my isolation from them.

This dismal picture suggests—as a host of spiritual traditions (and some humanistic psychologies) have agreed—that satisfying the ego may simply be impossible. Buddhism, for example, begins with the simple claim that desire is the root of suffering; and that the constant round of seeking to possess or control inevitably becomes an unstoppable, unsatisfiable cycle of wanting and having, wanting more and not getting, getting and becoming bored or dissatisfied, missing that which we had but have no longer, fearing the loss of what we have, resenting that we don't have as much as want or didn't get it sooner or won't have it longer, or that we get less of it than other people. The attempt to impose our will on an essentially uncontrollable reality makes it impossible to get lasting fulfillment.[6]

If we were to stop living for accomplishment/possession, what else could we live *for*? If we do not see ourselves essentially as individuals, what are we?

Spiritual traditions share—in a very broad sense—a common answer to this question. They assert that identifying with and understanding ourselves in terms of our social role, possessions, physical body, pleasures or pains, and individual achievements is a grave error. Our true identity is rooted in a source of strength, value, and contentment which is more lasting, powerful, and benign than anything that can be purchased, measured, or evaluated; in short, than anything which can be possessed or accomplished.

This spiritual perspective has no vengeful Divine Father who will punish a lack of faith, nor is there the promise that delayed gratification waits in some other world. There is instead the simple claim that only with the discovery of a sense of selfhood beyond the ego can we become released from the ego's compulsions and inevitable disappointments. This ego itself is not to be completely eliminated but integrated into a more comprehensive personal identity, one based in connections to others beyond the individual self and in sources of value beyond what we own or produce. We do not quit our jobs or surrender our zip codes, blending into some faceless, personality-less tapioca pudding of bliss. Just as our body continues to feel pain if pressured in certain ways, so our sense of self-identity continues. The difference, however, is that now we have some distance from and perspective on the ego and its foibles.

Does this sense of personal identity beyond ego require belief in spiritual or "cosmic" forces? Is it (you should pardon the expression) religious? If it is, many people may reject the notion altogether. Faith in God or in spiritual realities is often hard to come by. Moreover, such faith is all too often purchased at the expense of *denial*—unconscious avoidance of the manifest horrors of human experience from concentration camps to violence against women, from the ravages of racism to the epidemic of child abuse. Traditional religion and pop spirituality frequently ignore social injustice, and radicals have rightly rejected their politically conservative and sexist tendencies. Too many spiritual traditions also enshrine hierarchy and power within their own organizations.

But we can no more fully understand spirituality if we focus on its lowest manifestations than we can fully understand Marxism if we only look at Stalinism. The model of spirituality I am developing must be understood as distinct from dogmatic religious attachments to particular rituals, creeds, or organizations. After all, if we truly believe that we are more than our social ego, religious persecutions and holy wars become impossible. From this perspective, the concrete form of spiritual practice or belief is a means to self-transformation, not a way of deciding whom to hate. Further, an authentic spirituality cannot ignore social suffering. The more powerful, enduring, and credible spiritual messages do not counsel denial but openness to the truth, not the rosy security of a blissful avoidance, but a committed involvement with others.

What the Marxist tradition can learn from this mode of spirituality is that selfhood can transcend the bounds of ego; or, rather, that the normal, and certainly necessary, ego can be enfolded in another mode of being. This less limited selfhood may stem from a "God" or simply from a basic human capacity to exist in a larger and happier way than the conventional social ego does.

This identity is marked first by self-acceptance: a deep sense that further possession or accomplishment will not enhance us and is not of essential importance. The ego's basic dissatisfaction with itself and life is pacified; and its frenetic, desperate search for a meaning outside itself can stop. This self-acceptance might be signaled by the familiar phrase that we are all "children of God." We do not have to embrace some traditional creed to appreciate this statement's pragmatic effect. The metaphor of a shared and cosmic Origin helps sooth our insecurities, quiet our doubts as to our essential worth as persons, and diminish our tendencies to reject difference and seek hierarchy.

A spiritual perspective also undermines individualism. Many of the central personal virtues of a spiritual life—compassion, mercy, empathy, love—can all lead to constructive and healing bonds with others. These bonds are based in a rejection of individualism and a recognition of underlying commonality despite differences in social situation.[7] As our attachment to possession/accomplishment diminishes, we can be significantly more *open* to others. We can also get some distance on our social role, and thus may be less likely to "just do our job" when that job might involve the oppression of others. As spirituality can get us to examine the confused workings of our own minds, it can also prompt us to ask if the way we earn a living or relate to others socially is consonant with spiritual development.

Descriptions of the content and goal of spiritual life are alien and confusing to many people. We may find it hard to imagine that a life not circumscribed by the ego is possible—or worth living. If we are not driven by wants and needs, what will get us out of bed in the morning? Without the passions of love and hate, how will we relate to other people? If we are really so connected to others, won't our sense of self get lost?

The response is that our human reality is more than the ego, and that we have available to us other sources of energy, compassion, and creativity. Some will call this source God, or Christ, or the Tao. Others simply observe that people are at their best when they connect to others in a non-dominating, non-egoistical way, and when they do not desperately cling to getting what they want out of their actions. The manic energy of desire, once removed, need not give way to passivity or depression. Rather, the ego's cycle of drudgery, drivenness, and collapse—often accompanied by alcoholism, drug abuse, compulsive eating, or mindless escapism—can be replaced by the joy of engaging fully with all the tasks that life sets before us. Those tasks are no longer experienced as badges of our worth, proofs of "success" or "failure," or chores to be suffered in exchange for future gratification.

These spiritual gifts can transform our relations to other people. Our capacity for compassion flourishes, because our growing lack of fear of our own pain makes us more open to that felt by others. Drawing on a trans-personal source of love, our compulsive need for ego reinforcement lessens. Knowing that all people are connected to the essential Truth of life, we are not threatened by difference, intimidated by power, or contemptuous of the less fortunate.

This transcendence of the normal social ego can be found in the lives of devoted revolutionaries no less than of spiritual teachers. We are all capable of it. And it is something most of us who are neither radical heroes nor "gurus" have known—if only briefly—in our own lives. We have, that is, experienced moments of unconditional serenity and compassion. We have found that some seemingly inescapable and painful situation could be redeemed only if we faced it with acceptance and love.

The ego is not only the source of a tremendous amount of individual suffering. Because it is spontaneously led to competition, hierarchy, selfishness, and institutionalized domination and exploitation, it is also incompatible with the goals of a socialist, feminist, liberated society. People who identify with individualism will not cooperate in either radical politics or the collective control of social life. People who identify with doing and having will drive social life towards higher and higher levels of consumption, binding society to an ecologically destructive form of life. People wracked by ego make megalomaniacal political leaders or passive, dogmatic followers.

Yet we find little of substance in the Marxist tradition—or in very much of secular socialist-feminism—to analyze and critique the ego. There are rejections of bourgeois individualism in theory and political life, but (see the next section) these rejections connect to models of group identity based in self-righteous anger, victimhood, and vengeance. There are (in Marcuse, for instance) brief appeals to an aesthetic "new sensibility" which should be oriented towards play and beauty rather than work, control, and power. But this concept has been largely undeveloped. When communists talked of the "new socialist man," they typically focused on self-sacrifice rather than self-transcendence. The sexual revolution of Reich and other Freudian Marxists stressed sensual gratification. The Frankfurt School generally was interested in the socially critical power of suppressed desire, not in questioning the structure of desire itself. While certain forms of cultural feminism lead in this direction, the perspective I am developing here goes beyond the bounds of both Marxism and its continuation in socialist-feminism. We may think of Gandhi and Martin Luther King, of feminist spirituality, of the peace movement, of deep ecology, but not very much of the Western socialist tradition.

It might be replied that spiritual concerns (as used to be said about those of women) will be dealt with "after the revolution." When class, gender, and racial domination have been overcome, there will be time enough to deal with the more esoteric, utopian, and (some might say) flaky goal of transcending the ego.[8] It might also be suggested that the essentially psychological problems of individualism and possession/accomplishment are simply consequences of capitalism in particular or modern class domination in general. Once a radical social transformation is achieved, psychological liberation is *bound* to follow.

It *is* surely the case that the inner ego and the outer society condition each other. Yet it will not do to put off the spiritual shift until the social one is accomplished, because overcoming the ego is a *basic part*, not just a *consequence*, of liberating societal change. How are we to overcome the distortions of individualism embedded in social structures (e.g., the institutionalized selfishness of capitalism) if we do not address their presence in each person's ego as well as in institutions? How are we to unite as an effective "revolutionary" force if we are driven by individualism or attached to possessions and personal accomplishment? How are we to guard against the re-appearance of domination and exploitation within new social forms if we do not address the full range of their present causes—those based in the ego as well as those flowing from the structures of power and property? The lessons of feminism concerning the political importance of personal life are operative here: self-transformation and the collective effort to alter the public world are interdependent.

A host of small, everyday, particular practices in schools, factories, offices, armies, hospitals, bureaucracies, etc., create the ego in the ego-centered self. Similarly, a variety of political *and* spiritual practices—from consensus decision making to being self-conscious about racism, from learning to appreciate what we have to learning to get a distance on our anger—can help create a new sense of subjectivity and the possibility of a new society. As food co-ops, consciousness-raising groups, and progressive schools may give us a small hint of what socialism could be like, so spiritual practices can help teach us about a life in which the ego has its proper—and limited—place.

As Rosa Luxemburg said about political reforms, however, there is no guarantee that any particular spiritual practice will be used to further human liberation rather than simply for escaping from current misery. Thus, I am not suggesting that spiritual perspectives *replace* the radical tradition. Rather, although my focus here is necessarily on what Marxism can learn from spirituality, I believe these two ways of understanding and acting need to enhance each other. (For instance, while spirituality can help us appreciate what we have instead of always wanting more, we still need to think about whether our possessions are held at someone else's expense. And we have to wonder about the plight of those who have very little.)

To see in more detail what radicals might learn from spirituality, I will now extend the discussion to two central political questions: What consciousness is to be expressed in radical political change? Can Marxism help us confront the environmental crisis?

## SUFFERING, ANGER, AND RADICAL POLITICS

How are the oppressed mobilized for radical political activity? Leftist political theories have generally taken for granted that suffering caused by social oppression can be made conscious by some form of political organizing. This consciousness should hopefully issue in righteous anger at oppression and political awareness that leads to action in defense of the group, rebellion, and perhaps ultimately revolution. The links in the chain of political change are thus suffering-anger-revolt.

In more particular terms, *Marxist theory* claims that workers suffer from exploitation, cycles of unemployment and restricted production, alienated labor, and relative poverty. This suffering is a necessary condition for organizing workers into a self-conscious revolutionary force. When an awareness of the nature and causes of their pain blossoms into political action and combines with the working classes' vast numerical superiority and essential role in industrial production, we have the basis for social revolution.

*Feminism* builds on many Marxist insights, but it adds a strong emphasis on the everyday experiences of personal life. When women directly and honestly share their individual pain, they see that their particular situations reveal a common oppression. In this way consciousness raising politicizes suffering, transforming self-blame, depression, addictive behavior, and compulsive self-humiliation into empowering anger at male domination. This anger over past and present

suffering is, supposedly, the basis for constructive action and ultimately the liberation of women from their social subordination—
especially the intimate oppression characteristic of male-female sexual/
romantic relations.

The uses of suffering and anger in Marxism and feminism are
repeated in the *new social movements*: racial struggles, gay and lesbian
liberation, ethnic liberation movements of all kinds, etc. These movements represent groups that have been depicted as not fully human.
Consequently, oppressors have felt justified in taking lands, destroying
cultures, exploiting labor, humiliating, excluding, and limiting their
victims. As in the case of feminism, the response has often been to
become aware of the collective character of suffering and to respond
with anger. Franz Fanon (1968) provided the most extreme example of
this response when he claimed that only violence could bring colonized
peoples to a full psycho-social identity.

Along with this theoretical stress on suffering and anger, we find
meetings, books, pamphlets, arguments, shouts, confrontations—all
the times when members of oppressed groups voice their anger about
their pain. Many men have been taken aback by a woman's anger over
some past or present sexism. Many times radicals have gathered for a
rally, a march, or a meeting and felt the rush of adrenalin that comes
with the power of our rage: blacks at whites; women at men; those on
the left against the Reagans and Rockefellers and Bushes of the world;
and Jews, remembering a Holocaust, at the entire, enormous, threaten-
ing non-Jewish world.

As widespread as they have been, can it be that in some ways these
models of the radicalizing process actually obstruct the good of the
group and the collective project of human emancipation?

To paraphrase Gandhi, an awareness of collective suffering and
the anger that typically flows from that awareness are better than
passivity, self-blame, isolation, or drowning your sorrows. They are
much better than believing the lies that are told about oppressed people,
and they can be an essential part of overcoming the politically crippling
effects of oppression.

But they have their limits. And these limits, I believe, are often
unexplored.

To begin with, the Marxist expectation of proletariat immiseration has been frustrated. State-managed economies and mass culture have improved workers' living standards and assuaged alienation by consumerism, media spectacle, alcohol and drugs, and nationalism.[9] Even more important, however, in some ways the oppression which causes their suffering also ties workers' to the system. The degradation of work and culture has made even moderately successful movements of the oppressed extremely rare. For some time now, the consumer society has bound its victims with plastic chains forged of credit cards. Further, psychological awareness of suffering in and of itself does not necessarily lead to collective political rebellion. More often, it leads to self-blame—as in "my life as a worker is a result of my failure to take advantage of the freedoms of our society." Or an awareness of suffering leads to a desire to escape—through more toys, more drugs, more TV. Or the suffering is projected outward as hatred of those who seem different.

In short, models of revolution based on angry uprisings to overcome material suffering and injustice have meant very little in the last seventy years. The idea of "revolution" in any traditional sense has been irrelevant in the advanced industrial countries.[10]

The more subjectively-oriented models of feminism and the new social movements also face critical problems, beginning with the effects of identifying with powerlessness. Too much of a personal identification with suffering leads to a victim psychology: we define ourselves as the one wronged by fate or the world, by our older brother or our abusive father, by the rich, the white, or the male. The more we identify with our suffering and get in touch with our oppression, the more we may come to see our lives only as a series of things we never had or didn't get a chance to try for, of experiences lost, pleasures lacked, advantages which others had and we did not. What follows is often self-pity and hostility, not collective political action; scenarios from Nietzsche (a life of bitter resentment) rather than Marx (a life of revolution).

Further, as we blend our individual personhood into a group defined by suffering, we can become mesmerized by a history of injustice. Consider, for instance, some images from black and Jewish history, images which transfix us with horror, shame, despair, or paralyzing fear. Think of the slave ships and the concentration camps which destroyed millions, of isolation while the world looks on uncaring. And think, if you are a parent, what it means to tell your child: "This is the legacy of your blackness or Jewishness. This is what the world did to your ancestors." Think of some eight year old who will now come to know that, "They can murder you, your family, your friends, your village. Put you in chains. Destroy your world."

Such a legacy is often a poor source of positive group identity. Thus, rather than "revolution," one response to all this is to flee, to become the self-hating, assimilationist Jew or the Uncle Tom black who sees all the power on the side of whiteness. If group identity means suffering, leave the group.[11] Join the other team or at least move to the sidelines. If you cannot, you must carry in your heart that terrifying knowledge of how dangerous it is to be you.

Or you may get angry. And of course this is the preferred political response. And a much better response it is, if the only alternative is fear and self-hatred. "Never forgive, never forget," Jews are taught to say about the Holocaust. "Black power, black rage, black pride." "Sisterhood is powerful . . . Rising up angry . . . All power to the people." This anger, we are told, will fuel our power, self-respect, and resistance to oppression. And so it does.

But what *else* does it do?[12]

Well, a certain kind of aggressive, unreflective, self-righteous anger simply becomes an entrenched habit of mind, a basic, pervasive, and potentially limiting viewpoint. If victimization defines our fate, then we constantly seek to understand situations as defined by oppressor and oppressed. Such a framework is appropriate for some situations but hardly for all of them.

Since this politicized anger has a real tendency towards self-righteousness, it can have, for instance, a disastrous effect on political life. To begin with, if I am right, then someone else must be wrong. Thinking in these terms contributes to a compulsive attachment to disagreement and conflict. Part of my identification with my rage is also a permanent sense of being treated unfairly. I therefore will be unable to stop seeking retribution. If I cling to my bitterness, I can likewise become suspicious. In every situation there lurks the threat of disrespect, violence, or exploitation. The more I look for these, the more I will see them—whether they are there or not. Worst of all, the more pervasive this anger is, the more it extends far beyond the people who actually oppress me. It finds handy targets in members of my own group whom I don't like or who disagree with me and members of other groups who frighten me, don't like me, or who seem, for the moment at least, to have it a little better than I do. The result is people trying to see who is most oppressed, whose anger is most justified, whose "credentials" of suffering are most authentic. These behaviors have permeated the left. When they are present, solidarity simply evaporates.

To take one example: it is partly an identification with suffering and the anger that accompanies it that makes so many Jews intent on stressing not only the limitless horror, but also the uniqueness of the Holocaust.[13] As necessary and inevitable as sorrow and rage at the Holocaust are, they have at times made us less than sensitive to the sufferings of others. This problem is at least one element of the endless Middle East conflict. By the same token, Palestinians have shown an endless attachment to *their* misery as well. The lost olive groves, the never-to-be forgotten little house in Haifa—as if no one ever had to give up a home before, as if this loss of Palestine had to define their reality for a thousand years.

I mention the Israeli-Palestinian conflict because it affects me personally, but this analysis fits other conflicts as well. The forever angry person, bonded to his or her group's history of suffering, is not very good at negotiating or compromising. The past reality is always present in the room. The sorrow and the fury make all demands absolute, every threat overwhelming, any concession a betrayal of your murdered brothers and sisters. Conversely, if your group is a collection of righteously angry victims, it is very hard to see its own tendencies towards violence or domination. When they manifest themselves, they must be denied, for they contradict the homogeneous image of virtuous suffering.

Groups that define themselves by victimization and rage are also not very good at cooperating. Is it any wonder that the Left, trying so hard to mobilize anger out of misery, is so ineffective at creating lasting coalitions? But without these, there is no hope for radical politics. The magical, scientific Leninist party is not going to lead us all to socialist salvation. The liberal-welfare state is dominated by monopoly capitalism, state bureaucrats, and an occasional special interest. What hope is there for deep and lasting social change except in that elusive rainbow coalition of groups that have a lot of different things to be angry about: racism, sexism, anti-Semitism, poverty, and all the rest? But if it is anger which mobilizes each color of the rainbow, how will it hold together? If our suffering makes us who we are, how are we to see the reality of other histories, especially when those histories may lead to different strategies, values, or interests? In fact, if all I can see is a world of victimizers, I will never have the courage or calmness to make peace with allies, or the ability to distinguish friends from enemies. These considerations apply not just to the obviously victimized, but also to those who work on their behalf. Sometimes it is the white, male, middle-class radical whose anger is the most relentless!

I am not saying that we should repress our justified anger or expect radicals to be saints. The point is that politicized anger must be evaluated by the way it fits into the ongoing processes of particular lives and group relations. A healthy, rebellious "anger" is not identical with a posturing or driven self-righteousness or with bitterness, internalized anger, displaced anger, fury, helpless rage, tantrum, or frenzy. Each of these terms suggests a different particular experience and a different way that the immediate spasm of feeling is integrated into an ongoing personal and group life history. While anger may be useful and at times necessary, it need not be glorified as the hallmark of revolutionary correctness. It should be subject to critical scrutiny and joined with other values.

It is not hard to see the relation between what I have called the ego and this analysis of the effects of anger in the politics of social change. This victim anger remains stuck in a form of individualism. It cannot know its own strengths and needs without hatred of others. It cannot feel its pain without blame. It cannot seek what it deserves without continual rage.

I do not think that the recognition of and resistance to oppression have to remain forever wedded to this response. It is possible for radical political activity not only to prompt anger and recognize suffering but also to be guided by images of compassion and love.

By compassion I mean a literal "feeling with" the Other, a feeling that is both an emotional and an intellectual process in which I see the Other's pain as I see my own. This process begins when I can imagine that others have feelings just as I do; when my bond to my own pain is not so great that it keeps me from connecting to that felt by others. It means that I suspend the evaluative comparison—is the Holocaust worse than slavery? Is the exile of Palestinians matched by the exile of Jews from Arab countries? Do blacks suffer more than Puerto Ricans or Cambodians?—in favor of the embracing realization that all who are human suffer. If I have that realization, I can acknowledge my own suffering—face it, feel it, know it—without using it to isolate myself from others who have been victims. If suffering is part of the human condition, and not something I and my group have special title to, I no longer need a special redress—just the decent and humane treatment that all people deserve. My suffering can become a ground of connection to others, a basis of solidarity, for I can recognize that their pain is as real to them as mine is to me. While pleasures and possessions usually addict us to wanting more, our sorrow can liberate us to compassion; in our individual suffering we can truly know the whole world. Yet this knowledge arises only if we use compassion to move beyond the ego's individualism, bridging the gaps between Jews and blacks in this country, or between survivors of the Holocaust and Palestinian refugees, between men and women, or between all the diverse groups of different income, education, and prestige who must unite if capitalism is to be overthrown.

This process requires a compassionate *intellectual imagination* and a dispassionate *self-examination*. When we identify with our suffering and anger, it is quite difficult to understand the Other or honestly evaluate ourselves. If we are essentially victims in a world of enemies, why should we think ourselves into our oppressors' minds? Only if we realize the universality of suffering, that it has come to us all, can we begin to understand why other people do what they do. Even the ruling class has its miseries. These do not excuse its behavior or justify its privileges. The point is simply that we need not see oppressors as completely Other than ourselves in order to resist them.

In this realization, we can dispassionately reflect on our own short-comings, the ways in which we have been not only the objects of injustice but also its agents. Realizing how we have thoughtlessly, carelessly, or coldly created or ignored suffering can help us think ourselves *out of victimhood*, out of self-righteous anger, out of the isolation of the oppressed. We begin to see the little slaveholder in ourselves, the tiny reflection of the Nazi in our own souls. No ethnic group of "victims," after all, is without its oppression of women, its own internal hierarchy of wealth and privilege, or its homophobia. Every group victimized by oppression is liable to seek victories at the expense of another group: witness alliances between black and white men in pursuit of a suffrage that ignored the rights of both black and white women.

Understanding ourselves and others is the ground of a productive—rather than a passive—forgiveness. In this spirit we admit that we—the world's biggest victims—have actually caused suffering to others. By examining our own acts and reconstructing the thoughts and feelings that led to them, we learn to reconstruct the causes of what other people do. And suddenly, they seem less incomprehensible or different. They seem much more like us.

None of this means that we abandon our dreams of justice and our struggle for a better world or that we excuse oppression of any kind. Nor does it mean that we forget about what our group has suffered. If we have not studied that suffering, felt it in reality or imagination, and been decisively moved by it, we can understand neither ourselves nor the world—nor do very much to change either for the better. Our suffering is essential to our strengths and weaknesses, jokes and sadness, art and music—and to the stories we tell our children.

Similarly, our anger may well remain. And at times we may even seek to arouse it among those crippled by self-hatred, passivity, or denial. Yet we can still ask: Who is our ideal? Who are our teachers? Is the model revolutionary Lenin or Gandhi? Andrea Dworkin or Susan Griffin? Malcolm X or Martin Luther King? Those whose dominant political message is rage or love, hatred or compassion? As we try to construct our radical communities and discourses, what virtues gain our respect and what human weaknesses require understanding? It is in this sense that a journey from suffering and anger to compassion and love is possible.

This journey can mean, to use a Marxist phrase, that we move from the realm of necessity to the realm of freedom. We liberate our subjectivity from the pain of the past not by denying but by moving through and beyond it. This passage takes us in the direction of political effectiveness and group political empowerment in the most positive sense. In compassion there is no self-hatred, self-blame, or tacit acceptance of degradation. In universal love and forgiveness there is no tolerance of militarism or violent nationalism or exploitation, no acceptance of racism or ethnocentrism or misogyny. Once we take off the strangling vise of anger, we should breathe easier and see clearer. The more truly loving we are, the more we may understand and work with other people, compromise, and negotiate. Ideally, the spiritual values of compassion and love, joined with the analytic power, concrete vision, and determination of the radical political traditions of Western Marxism, socialist-feminism, racial liberation, and environmental concern can create a powerful force for progressive political change.[14]

Of course, this will not be easy. If we are immersed in the day-to-day pain of the struggle against oppression, it is very hard not to give way to despair or rage. If we engage in the soothing pursuits of spiritual life, it is hard not to become attached to the experiences of bliss which those practices can provide. If my analysis is correct, however, neither path can succeed without the other. As politics without spirituality is stuck in rage and conflict, so spirituality which seeks bliss at the expense of social involvement is just another form of the ego.[15]

## MARXISM, NATURE, AND THE LIMITATIONS OF THE EGO

Contemporary civilization is poisoning the earth and unbalancing the complex and fragile web of life.[16]

Is Marxism adequate to this ecological crisis?

Clearly, no understanding of the environmental threat is possible without some elements of Marxist theory. Concepts such as alienation, fetishism of commodities, commodification, and rationalization—developed in both traditional and Western Marxism—pinpoint with great accuracy some of the basic features of the crisis, including:

—the way humanity's own power and activity are destroying human life (alienation).

—the way patterns of human production and consumption seem to have a life of their own, uncontrollable by the human subjects who engage in them (fetishism).

—the way tremendously sophisticated technical processes exist in a social framework which is irrational to the border of insanity (rationalization).

—the way the natural entities which are essential to complex ecosystems are reduced to objects whose only meaning is their value in the marketplace (commodification).

More generally, the Marxist and neo-Marxist analysis of the dynamic of capitalist development provides something of an economic explanation for the crisis. Competitive capitalism tends to rapid and uncontrolled expansion, destroys community though urbanization, and turns traditional forms of agriculture into the factory farm. Monopoly capital requires mass consumption. Imperialism integrates the Third World into export-driven modernized agricultural production. These are essential elements in the crisis and have been extensively analyzed by Marxism.

Further, Marx and Engels did write in many places about the destructive effect of capitalism on the natural world. At times, they even suggested that there was a basic connection between humanity and nature. (McMurty 1978: 229–31 and Parsons 1977)

More radically, and in fragmented and undeveloped claims, Western Marxists Horkheimer, Adorno, and Marcuse claimed that there are distortions not just in the uses of western science and technology, but in their content. Despite the success of modern science, its model of nature as something which exists only to be mastered by human beings is deeply flawed. For instance, seeing nature as an object of mastery inevitably leads to seeing human beings in the same light. The manipulation of human beings—in factories and wars, hospitals and concentration camps—becomes integrated into "scientific" practice. The more we are emancipated from the power of nature, the more we are enslaved—both socially and psychically—by the system which produces that "emancipation."[17] This result "denounces the rationality of the rational society as obsolete." (Horkheimer and Adorno 1974: 38–9)

Marcuse (1972) further suggested that a transformed science would result if we sought the liberation of nature instead of its domination. Such a liberation is

the recovery of the life-enhancing forces in nature, the sensuous aesthetic qualities which are foreign to a life wasted in unending competitive performances: they suggest new qualities of *freedom*. (60–1)

This project is rejected by capitalism, because capitalism takes it as given that nature "is there for the sake of domination." But:

A free society may well have a very different *a priori* and a different object; the development of the scientific concepts may be grounded in an experience of nature as a totality of life to be protected and "cultivated," and technology would apply this science to the reconstruction of the environment of life. (61)

Recently, Marxist economist James O'Connor (1988) has argued that capitalism is undermining the ecological conditions of its own survival. Consequently, corporations must allow for increased political restrictions, thus giving more power to the state and the community to monitor the ecological effects of capitalist production. For O'Connor's "ecological Marxism," the agencies of social change no longer center on the traditional working class, but necessarily include groups trying to save the environment.

Despite these contributions, however, we must recognize that Marxism has not systematically investigated the relation between humanity's treatment of nature and treatment of other people. Marx and

Engels' comments on ecology were peripheral to their work (as might be expected for people living before the crisis took shape). Many leftist critics have found Marxist theory and socialist practice to be conspicuously lacking in regard to the environment. Not Marxism, but radical feminism, ecofeminism, and environmental perspectives have exposed the links between science, capitalism, male domination, and the ecological crisis.[18]

More important for my purposes here, a fully adequate understanding of and response to the ecological crisis requires a critique of the ego and a model of human life which moves beyond it.

It is very well to see the roots of modern consumerism in the needs of monopoly capital, but *how are we to escape the cul-de-sac of dependence on consumption if we do not begin to identify with something other than possession?* If we are bound to capitalism because of our selfhood, where are the resources—conceptual, practical, ideological—to free us? To a great extent, Marxist theory takes the ego for granted. For all its faith in the "social individual" and in collective ownership, it often tacitly accepts the individualistic model of selfhood formulated by eighteenth-century liberalism. Thus, Marxist political practice has little recourse but to put off changing the ego until "after the revolution." Socialist parties, Left caucuses in the democratic parties, etc., usually call for increasing government transfer programs, higher wages, more services, more things. In that way, the Left practices a politics of *entitlement*—with that concept defined by income and social status (e.g., education or career opportunities). A program based on *less* consumption has almost never been possible for Marxists or socialists, precisely because such a program cuts into the usual leftist commitment to fully satisfy the ego. Yet any serious revolutionary movement—and any serious post-revolutionary government—that respects the environment will need to drastically alter and limit existing patterns of consumption. If a mass movement does not put forward models of living based in acceptance and gratitude—rather than greed and dependence on objects—such limitation will be impossible.

Further, it has always been essential to Marxism to see human history as based in collective struggle and antagonism. Yet while class domination is part of the ecological crisis, it is only a part. The ultraviolet rays which penetrate the hole in the ozone layer, the epidemic of cancers, the foul air, the toxic wastes which arise in a wide variety of neighborhoods—all these are potential sources of a solidarity that can bridge differences in gender, race, nationality, and perhaps even (to some extent) class. Along with class consciousness, there is needed a *global* consciousness. In such a perspective connection is not based only on short-term political goals, but on a more extended sense of partnership with the web of life as a whole. Global consciousness is not possible for an individualistic ego. It requires a capacity for communion with the Other as well as with the deepest reaches of the Self, and is not forthcoming from a radical political perspective based in conflict and antagonism. Nor is it fully compatible with the Marxist idealization of action, transformation, and objectification. Watching, waiting, communing, opening, empathizing—these are not capacities which are taken seriously in radical politics generally or Marxism in particular. Feeling a spirit of life in us—as opposed to making the world conform to our image of what it "should" be—is not something Marxists have ever felt comfortable with. Yet if we do not cultivate these capacities, ecological action will be a series of temporary, and probably not very effective, reforms. A global consciousness, based in openness to the present, sensitivity to others and to the environment, and awareness of the self's physical, emotional, and political condition would begin to allow us to intuitively understand what is or is not an ecologically sound form of life.

## HISTORICAL MATERIALISM AND CONTEMPORARY SPIRITUALITY

It was part of Marx's genius to try to ground his vision of a better world in a theory of how historical development would make that vision a reality. This historical materialist principle should extend to my claims about integrating a spiritual consciousness with radical politics. Accordingly, I will now sketch some contemporary social tendencies that make the prospect of a living and vital spiritual form of life more than simply an engaging fantasy.

*First*, there is the widespread collapse of the belief that the endless growth of science and technology will create a happier and more just world. The bright images of technology, professionalism, and masculine control have been somewhat tarnished of late. In our century bureaucracy has become a tool for genocide, our sophisticated gadgets are owned by a population wracked by drug abuse and random violence, our most brilliant scientists are devoted to the creation of weapons, and our entire civilization is toxic for nature. And all the self-proclaimed experts of "scientific" medicine, psychology, social planning, and politics fail to solve these ills.

Many people, therefore, seek forms of knowledge—and especially self-knowledge—that cannot be formulated in technical or scientific terms. They are using traditional and newly forged perspectives on body, mind, nature, and the universe to aid in solving personal and social problems. These perspectives are often spiritually oriented and challenge the basic structures of the ego.

*Second*, the social upheavals of the 1960s sparked a deep interest in spirituality in several ways. The use of psychedelic chemicals provided experiences of transcendent, non-ordinary forms of consciousness, forms which have been studied and practiced for thousands of years by many traditions. When the highs wore off, the simple limits of transcendental states derived from chemicals were revealed. It was then natural to try to find teachers to help us explore non-ordinary reality. Varieties of meditation, yoga, breath control, and guided visualization—to name only some—promised that we might integrate the uncontrollable but vital visions and insights of drug states into our daily lives in a healthy and ultimately much more rewarding way.

The feminist struggle for political equality and social freedom that began in the '60s led women to transform old religious ideas and institutions and create new ones. They have identified distortions and ʼnitations of male-dominated spirituality. Moving beyond critique, ʼnists have also constructed new models of religious community, ʼn, faith, and human relations.

ʼ, the environmental consciousness which first flowered in ʼged with spirituality when people began to question our ʼsumption that the earth is a "thing" devoid of inherent value. Spiritual ecologists started to imagine the possibility that the eco-sphere might need to be saved not just to protect human life, but because it had a worth in its own right. There was a corresponding interest in teachings from wicca ("witchcraft") and Native American traditions that view our relations with the natural world not as simple exploitation but as sacred exchange.

*Third*, our society of unparalleled wealth and quite considerable personal freedom is plagued by anxiety, depression, and addictions. In response, psychology and psychotherapy have aroused widespread popular interest. Yet while the "personal growth" model of humanist therapies helps break through the rigidities of conventional social roles, it frequently leaves the ego's individualism intact. Unlike secular psychology, spiritual approaches to emotional pain do not take the social ego for granted. Some people have turned to the Buddhist critique of attachment, yogic training in steadying the mind, or Sufi parables of engaged wisdom for help in moving beyond the ego's fruitless attempts at self-satisfaction.

*Fourth*, there is a pervasive dissatisfaction with our society's stress on consumerism and career success. We have so many "things"—yet we are so miserable. Instead of calm enjoyment and appreciation, we are gripped by ever-increasing desires only temporarily satiated by new acquisitions. The Christmas-time orgies of consumption leave a lingering sense of emptiness. The obsessions with success in career and wealth never seem to be placated, no matter how much we try to gratify them. This suffering directs us towards spiritual perspectives which deny that material possessions or social success can bring happiness, explain this failure, and offer another model of human fulfillment.

*Fifth*, a growing number of political radicals, while retaining their social values, now see that a spiritually uninformed political movement may repeat the domination and aggression of the larger society. They have seen too many factional splits, too much pretentious self-righteousness and self-indulgent anger on the left. They have learned that conflicts between power elites and their victims co-exist with society-wide sicknesses of the heart and soul. A culture of violence, greed, and despair requires a revolutionary politics which combines the struggle for social justice with the peacefulness and love embodied in spiritual life, the Marxist or feminist analysis of social structures with the spiritual quest for self-knowledge.

Also, as a generation of radicals moves into middle age, we find that a purely social or political vision is inadequate to some of life's most rewarding and difficult experiences. Political ideologies do poorly with pain which is not caused by injustice and with processes which need witnessing and acceptance rather than continual control. The birth and development of children, the death of parents, our own growing sense of mortality, the loss of friends, the pains of debilitating illnesses—such experiences are overwhelming if we do not approach them with the spiritual virtues of patience, mental and emotional clarity, and compassion for ourselves and others.

## CONCLUSION

As long as capitalism exists, claimed Jean-Paul Sartre, Marxism will continue to be the dominant philosophy of the age.

This statement is both true and false. It is true because the continued concentration of class economic power makes Marxist theory indispensable for understanding socially caused pain. Marxism provides a necessary perspective from which to understand some of the actions and effects of corporate and governmental policy and power and their relations to other dimensions of oppression. The self-knowledge and compassion of a spiritual perspective must be joined to a historical materialist and feminist understanding of ownership, politics, and ideology. If it is not, even a well-intentioned spirituality is likely to degenerate into an escape from reality rather than a transformed relation to it.

Yet Sartre's claim is also false. As I think this book has shown, the complex changes in social life since Marx make it impossible to rest solely within the Marxist tradition. A liberating social theory—and social movement—will have to transcend the Marxist tradition even as it preserves that tradition's best insights and most humane goals.

# NOTES

## CHAPTER 1
## MARXISM: THE ORIGINAL THEORY

1. I am simply ignoring the thorny question of the relation of Marx to Friedrich Engels, his longtime collaborator. To justify claims about what Marx believed, I will use works he wrote solely or with Engels. Since Engels credits Marx with the most important theoretical discoveries of their joint work, this position seems justified.

2. "*Man* is not an abstract being, squatting outside the world. Man is *the human world*, the state, society. (Marx "Contribution to the Critique of Hegel's *Philosophy of Right: Introduction*," in Tucker 1972: 11).

3. His criticism of religion, for instance, was very much influenced by that of Ludwig Feuerbach.

4. At times, "mode of production" and "economy" are used interchangeably. In this usage, however, it should be remembered that only in capitalism is the economy institutionally separated from political life. In pre-capitalist societies (and in the Eastern bloc nations), political power and economic power tend to be intertwined or fused.

5. In fact, a tremendous amount of interpretation and commentary on Marx has just gone into finding a single, coherent explanation of his claim about the primacy of the mode of production. I will provide a somewhat more detailed study of this question in Chapter 8.

6. That is, in all but the most primitive, classless societies.

7. Also: "Man's ideas, views, conceptions, in one word man's consciousness, changes with every change in the condition of his material existence, in his social relations and in his social life." (52) See Gottlieb 1975.

8. The economic reasoning behind this claim will be explained in the next section.

9. A few of the many more detailed treatments, from a variety of viewpoints are: Sweezy 1942, Elster 1985, Mandel 1962, and Wolff 1984.

10. Marx (1967 I: 713–774) calls the creation of the primary classes of capitalism "primitive accumulation."

11. In competitive capitalism that is. Marx is presupposing non-monopoly, non-state control. The consequences for his theory of the historical change in these conditions will be discussed in Chapter 7.

12. Even if the scarce commodity can be gotten easily, this situation is so rare as to have little effect on the general working of the economy.

13. For varying accounts of the labor theory of value, see Elster 1985 and Woolf 1984.

14. For this underconsumptionist argument in detail, see Sweezy 1942: 102–86.

15. The rate of profit can remain high if the rate of exploitation grows faster than the organic composition of capital.

16. See his discussion of political changes in France, *The Eighteenth Brumaire of Louis Bonaparte*. Marxist theory of the state now has a considerable literature. There is an overview in Gottlieb 1987; see also Carnoy 1984.

17. As I have found in twenty years of teaching Marxism.

18. As it now is in a variety of workers' self-managed or collectively organized industrial enterprises.

## CHAPTER 2
## MARXISM: BASIC FLAWS

1. On a fictional level, this mentality is brilliantly described in Arthur Koestler's novel, *Darkness at Noon*.

2. Within the Marxist tradition itself, the term "vulgar Marxism" is sometimes used.

3. Bernstein (1978 and 1983) surveys many of the arguments here.

4. Marx (1967 I: 231–302) has an extended discussion of the struggle to limit the length of the working day: "The creation of a normal working-day is, therefore, the product of a protracted civil war, more or less dissembled, between the capitalist class and the working-class." (299)

5. See MacIntyre (1984). Some commentators have suggested that Marx's view is a secular version of the Judeo-Christian faith in the eventual coming of a Messiah who will usher in an age of complete human fulfillment.

6. We will examine some of the disastrous consequences of this form of Marxism in Chapters 3 and 4.

7. The journal *Monthly Review* and certain factions of the New Left stressed the political importance of Third World revolutionary movements. For the underdevelopment school, see Amin 1976, Frank 1967, and Wallerstein 1974b. Lenin used the phrase "aristocracy of labor" to refer to politically conservative English workers.

8. For Buchanan (1982), Marx does not appeal to morality to motivate workers, nor does he claim that the process of making a revolution is its own reward. While Buchanan's point is important, his approach suffers (as do many of the "analytical Marxist" school) from ignorance concerning both Western Marxist and feminist responses to these dilemmas. See discussions of Marx and morality in Arnold 1990, Peffer 1990, and Fisk 1989.

9. Habermas (1970: 81–122; 1973: 195–282; 1968: 43–60). Habermas may be overstating his case and mistakenly implying that for Marx there is always a rigid distinction between production and interaction. After all, Marx stressed that the mode of production encompassed both a social process and a natural-technical one.

10. The whole of human servitude is involved in the relation of the worker to production, and every relation of servitude is but a modification and consequence of this relation. Marx (1964: 118)

    At a certain stage of development, the material productive forces of society come into conflict with the existing relations of production. . . . From forms of development of the productive forces these relations turn into their fetters. Then begins an era of social revolution. (Marx 1970: 21)

11. It is perhaps not irrelevant that Marx, while being a devoted socialist, scholar, and activist, was extremely inconsiderate in his performance of his duties as husband

and father. His theoretical work committed his family to extreme poverty, which at times bordered on starvation. Also, intellectual adversaries often found him to be intolerant and domineering.

# CHAPTER 3
# SOCIAL-DEMOCRACY: THE PLAGUE
# OF POSITIVISM

1. Surveys of the period can be found in Joll 1966, Lichtheim 1965, and Kolakowski 1978.

2. Orthodox Marxism also ignored the following problem: after the revolution, in a centralized, even if "democratic" society, state bureaucrats tend to be cut off from the day-to-day experience of ordinary citizens, power centers seek to consolidate and expand their power, and governments generate revenues by expropriation as well as economic development.

3. The Austro-Marxist philosophers of this period sharply distinguished between science and ethics, taking Marxism as a specific kind of sociology and basing their ethical stance on Kant. See Bottomore and Goode 1978.

# CHAPTER FOUR
# SOVIET COMMUNISM: THE DEATH OF MARXISM

1. At the congress of Russian social-democracy in 1903, a split between Leninist and non-Leninist factions over the nature of party membership occurred. The Russian term "Bolshevik," meaning majority, applied to Lenin's faction. "Mensheviks," or "minority," were the other group. Virtually all the well-known leaders of Russian Marxian socialism went to the Mensheviks, leaving Lenin as the most powerful and respected voice and giving him a near monopoly of power and influence in his faction.

2. He justified the vanguard party but also, at times, criticized the Bolsheviks for lagging behind the masses. During the last year of his life, he struggled against the bureaucratic and totalitarian party machine he had created. While he sought rigid discipline in the party, his vision of socialism in *State and Revolution* emphasized the withering away of the state and the possibility of all administrative tasks being shared by the mass of the population. See Harding 1977, Carr 1964: 134–50, Lichtheim 325–80, Leonhard 1971: 47–94, Menashe 1973, Siranni 1975, and Cliff 1980.

3. As the Bolsheviks soon renamed themselves.

# NOTES

4. This encirclement and hostility continued—except for a brief alliance during World War II—until recently. It helped provide a continuing defense of internal tyranny.

5. In 1921, Lenin argued against self-described "representatives of the proletariat":

> What do you describe as proletariat? That class of labourers which is employed in large-scale industry. But where is [your] large-scale industry? What sort of proletariat is this? Where is your industry?

At the Party congress he 1922 he claimed:

> Since the war it is not at all working-class people but malingerers that have gone to the factories. And are our social and economic conditions at present such that genuine proletarians go to the factories? No. They should go, according to Marx. But Marx wrote not about Russia—he wrote about capitalism in general, capitalism as it has developed since the fifteenth century. All this has been correct for 600 years, but it is incorrect in present-day Russia.

A representative of the Workers' Opposition later argued:

> Vladimir Illich said yesterday that the proletariat as a class, in the Marxian sense, did not exist [in Russia]. Permit me to congratulate you on being the vanguard of a non-existing class. (Deutscher 1959: n. 14–5)

6. For the Comintern see Deutscher 1959, Borkenau 1962, and Gruber 1972.

7. There was some support from western trade unions to help end foreign intervention during the civil war. But no other successful revolutions occurred.

8. My interpretation of the Russian Revolution and Soviet Marxism is based on the sources listed in note 2 and the following: Deutscher 1959, 1963, 1965; Carr 1966 I–III; Lichtheim 1965; Trotsky 1970; Kingston-Mann 1983; Rowbotham 1974; and Marcuse 1958.

9. In Siranni 1975. The argument of this paragraph owes much to Siranni's trenchant critique.

10. Thus, the theoretical recovery from Leninism begins with a change in our understanding of class consciousness. This point is developed in Chapter 5.

11. Or as comedian Lenny Bruce remarked: "Russia is like one big phone company."

12. There may well be resources other than liberalism. Marcuse's claim is that none were activated in the Soviet Union.

13. For recent studies of this question, see Peffer 1990 and Arnold 1990.

14. This question is examined from different points of view in Koestler 1961, Trotsky 1961, and Merleau-Ponty 1969.

15. I am leaving aside the issue of the careerist, cynical, self-interested, power-hungry members of the Party. These plague virtually any organization which provides power to its members.

16. These comments resemble the anarchist critique, with its insistence that Marxism

always put too much faith in the centralized party or state. The Marxist reply is that successful revolutions and modernized societies are impossible without some central authority, but that this authority can be rendered benign with the elimination of economic classes. My point is that rendering authority benign requires certain kinds of basic personal transformations, and that to avoid the fate of communism these transformations must be at the heart of the Marxist program.

# CHAPTER FIVE
# WESTERN MARXISM: THE ROLE
# OF CONSCIOUSNESS

1. The term was first used in a Soviet critique of Karl Korsch and Georg Lukács—the earliest theorists of this group—in the early 1920s. For an overview, see Gottlieb 1989 and Klare and Howard 1974.

2. As I mentioned in Chapter 2, there are currently many deep criticisms of the positivist understanding of natural science.

3. This way of putting the issue owes much to Habermas 1968, 1973. It is can also be found in Marx's early statements of his goal. See virtually any of the pre-1847 writings.

4. Gramsci's concern here reflects his experience of the Second International's response to the outbreak of World War I and of the Italian Socialist Party's abandonment of militant workers in the Turin General Strike of 1920.

5. His emphasis on the marginal groups of capitalist society shows a dependence on a temporary surge of radical activity by students and racial minorities in the late 1960s and early 1970s. Confusing a temporary rising with a permanent vanguard status is a frequent Marxist error.

# CHAPTER SIX
# SOCIALIST FEMINISM AND THE POLITICS
# OF DIFFERENCE

1. Distinctions between liberal, radical, and socialist feminism are enlarged below, though they are often clumsy in any case. Radical and socialist feminists share a critique of capitalism, thus differing from liberals, who tend to accept the basic individualism of bourgeois democracy and simply want equality for women in that context. For a detailed discussion, see Jagger 1983.

2. For feminist criticisms of Engels, see Barret 1980 and Sacks 1974.

3. Of the very large socialist-feminist literature I would stress: Rowbotham 1973, Mitchell 1973, Ferguson 1989, Barret 1980, and Eisenstein 1979. A history of the movement can be found in Hansen and Philipson 1990.

4. For examples of radical feminism, see Firestone 1970 and Dworkin 1979. For socialist-feminist responses, see Hartmann 1989 and Ferguson 1989.

5. See Ferguson 1989 for the idea of sex-affective labor or the similar "labor of relatedness" in Greenspan 1983. Studies of the family from this perspective can be found in Gardiner 1979, Malos 1980, Poster 1980, and Nicholson 1986. See also Aries 1965 and Stone 1977.

6. Some relations between capitalism and the family are charted in Mitchell 1973, West 1978, Hartmann 1989 and 1981, and Rothman 1980.

7. Exactly how these two forces relate to each other, or whether they are not two systems but one combination of capitalism and patriarchy (or capitalism, patriarchy, and racism), is the subject of extended debate. See Young 1990, Ferguson 1989, Sargent 1981, Hansen and Philipson 1990, and Gottlieb 1987.

8. Gilligan 1983 initiated the discussion of female as opposed to male styles of moral reasoning. Belenky 1986 introduces the idea of specifically female ways of knowing. Ruddick 1989 describes particular characteristics of the thinking which mothers do in raising children and relates that thinking to peace politics.

9. As I mentioned in Chapter 5, one can find the beginnings of this approach in Wilhelm Reich. It was only with feminism that it received mass attention.

10. For the complexity of the issues here, see Young 1990, Laclau and Mouffe 1985, and Brittan and Maynard 1984.

11. Questions concerning relations among gender, race, ethnicity, class, etc., are addressed with great care in Spellman 1989. For a view of the commonalities of women's oppression, see Frye 1983.

12. Relations between class and other forms of domination are explored further in Chapter 8. A detailed examination of the relative importance and effects of different forms of oppression is the major subject of Gottlieb 1987.

13. The following brief remarks summarize the lengthy discussion in Gottlieb 1987.

14. Including myself.

15. This political perspective is reflected in contemporary left journals, including *Socialist Review* and *Radical America*. In Chapter 9, I will describe some ways in which Marxism is inadequate to this task.

# CHAPTER 7
# MARXISM AND CONTEMPORARY CAPITALISM

1. However, as we shall see below, under the "global capitalist" framework of the last fifteen years or so, foreign car manufacturers both sell and produce here.

2. The state's role in the economy is summarized in O'Connor 1973 and Gough 1975.

3. Mandel (1978, 1980) is excellent on the credit system. He points out that the system of both national and international credit poses certain real risks, from the defaulting of local governments to an international debt crisis. The Savings and Loan crisis may be only the first of its kind.

4. Not all of these developments are unique to contemporary capitalism. What is unique is the *degree* to which they shape economic structure and the way that structure is treated as a totality by contending political forces.

5. For detailed accounts of the the capitalist state, see Carnoy 1984 and Wolfe 1977.

6. As well as for the earlier versions based on the notions of "dependent development" and "unequal exchange." See Amin 1976, Emmanuel 1972, and Frank 1969.

7. See Gottlieb 1984a for some criticisms of the world-systems perspective.

# CHAPTER 8
# MARXISM AND SOME RADICAL CRITICS

1. When Giddens tries to explain these struggles by a division of labor between cities and countryside, he forgets the seasonal exchange of population between the two and the fact that a developed conflict of interest between city and countryside (rather than between some city dwellers and some agricultural laborers) is really found only in the comparatively unimportant attempt by guilds to monopolize petty commodity production. See Gottlieb 1984a.

2. Why are surveillance and the commodification of time (say) more essential than the sexual division of labor or the rise of mass culture? The limitations addressed here reappear in Giddens 1990.

3. In Rosaldo and Lamphere (1974), a wide variety of sex-role systems are described. Much socialist-feminist criticism of radical feminism is directed against the idea that there exists a universal and static form of female oppression.

4. This explanation badly distorts the way socially differentiated groups create their own separate social identities in response to a variety of life circumstances. See the discussion of race in Gottlieb 1987.

5. Argued for at length in Gottlieb 1987.

6. Other theorists in this tradition include Dinnerstein 1977 and Balbus 1982.

7. While mothering theorists are not always consistent in their statements about how important mothering is, the following are examples of clear statements giving it social primacy: Chodorow in Lorber 1981, Balbus 1982, and Dinnerstein 1977. My points here summarize the detailed treatment in Gottlieb 1984b.

8. See recent discussions of the more cooperative, less individualistic form of management among Japanese corporations in Ouchi 1981 and Athos and Pascale 1981.

9. On the history of the family, see Aries 1965, Oakley 1976, Poster 1980, and Tilly
and Scott 1978.

10. These patterns are traced in many places. Good sources include Brenner and Ramas
1984, Hartmann 1979, and Rothman 1980.

11. It was called by the editors of *New Left Review* "arguably the most important work
of Marxist philosophy to appear in the last decade." Cohen's position is shared by
many authors, including Wood 1981, McMurty 1976, and Shaw 1978. For these
reasons, it deserves detailed attention.

12. Richard Miller (1984) has developed the position (which I share) that the mode of
production, not developing the forces of production, is primary.

13. Rader 1982 and Miller 1984 (among others) argue against the rigid forces/relations
distinction. It is questionable in any case whether Marx's writing can be summarized
in one clear and consistent position.

14. When Cohen discusses this passage, he fails to explain how the importance of a
commercial opportunity fits with his doctrine of the primary role of the development
of the forces of production. Neither does he mention the many factors listed by
Marx that contributed to the process besides improvements in agricultural technique;
for example, the expropriation of church lands in the Reformation. Nor does he
give more than a passing nod to how Marx connects the genesis of capitalism to the
creation of a world market and to the wealth appropriated through colonialism. See
Frank (1979: 38–43) for a summary of Marx's position here.

15. Consider Braudel's generalization concerning the spread of technology from the
fourteenth to the nineteenth centuries:

> Every invention that presented itself had to wait for years or even centuries
> before being introduced into real life. . . . Technology is sometimes the possi-
> bility which men are not capable of attaining and fully utilizing, primarily for
> economic and social reasons . . . and at other times the ceiling which materially
> blocks their efforts. . . . The movement that overcomes the obstacles is never
> a simple *internal* development of technology . . . or certainly not before the
> eighteenth century. (Braudel 1973: 246)

In a study of "Technological Progress in the Industrial Revolution," Samuel Lilley
claims:

> The inventions of the early Industrial Revolution were *primarily* . . . responses
> to economic demands. Inventors did not act, nor did the social environment
> encourage them to act, unless the need was already clear. . . . The idea of
> invention as good in itself, as something that can be reasonably undertaken
> even when the need is doubtful—this idea is one that could only arise in a world
> that has passed through an industrial revolution and discovered . . . that new

techniques, in sufficiently affluent societies, create their own demands. (Lilley 1973: 213)

16. A variety of radical critiques of science support this view. See for instance Arditti 1980, as well as the general thrust of the Frankfurt School's critique of positivism.

17. Examples include Derrida 1982, Foucault 1975, and Rorty 1982.

18. Derrida himself has not attacked Marx in print, probably from a certain amount of critical sympathy with Marx's emancipatory, critical intent rather than because of adherence to very much of the content of traditional or even Western Marxist theory.

19. I owe part of the formulation of this point to Mario Moussa. It could be replied that Marxists own private property. But there is an extensive Marxist literature investigating the class position of theorists. No comparable post-modernist consciousness has emerged.

# CHAPTER 9
# MARXISM AND SPIRITUALITY

1. The supposition that *one* theory could answer all the questions of human existence expresses a longing for a complete authority. This pre-modern wish is found in the positivist glorification of natural science and the orthodox communist worship of Leninist revolutionary expertise.

2. Typically, there have been three kinds of relations between spiritual teachings and progressive, emancipatory politics: mutual criticism leading to rejection, the political use of religious ethics, and the religious use of leftist social analysis. My approach here charts a fourth course. While liberation theology has some affinities to what I am doing, it is too rooted in traditional Christianity and too oriented to the political and social conditions of Latin America to speak directly to the questions I am raising.

3. See Gottlieb 1990 for contemporary expressions of spirituality which exemplify the perspective developed here.

4. See my discussion of the Communist Party and the CIO in Gottlieb 1987.

5. The individualism of the modern ego has roots in the rise of the nuclear family, detachment from the community, increasing personal choices, undermining of religion and social tradition, and rise in material standard of living. How different it is from pre-modern selfhood is a question I cannot deal with here.

6. Goldstein and Kornfield 1987 offer an excellent exposition of Buddhism.

7. Ingram 1990 provides a survey of contemporary spiritual social activists, for whom spirituality and social concern are completely interdependent. See especially the discussion with Joanna Macy in that volume. We can also think of a variety of

political movements—especially the civil rights and peace movements in the U.S.—
which were positively shaped by spiritual perspectives.

8. The Left's present antipathy to spiritual consciousness or practice repeats a familiar
   phenomenon: leftists of every generation, armed with the memory of the particular
   slogans, battles, allies, and enemies of their activist youth, typically misconstrue the
   sources and structures of radicalism in a later generation. Marx's vision was formed
   by the battles of 1848 and 1871, and this perspective shaped social-democratic
   strategic thinking for decades. Much of the American Socialist Party was incapable
   of recognizing the power of Communist militancy, its appeal to immigrant groups,
   and the importance of allying with industrial unions. The Communist Party did not
   understand the New Left. We who came of age in the '60s may be manifesting a
   similar blindness now. Many of the ideas I am putting forth here do not derive
   from even the most sophisticated versions of Marxism, feminism, anti-racism, etc.
   Rather, they come from the present resurgence of spirituality. Connections can be
   forged between this resurgence and the Left. Already, the discourse of love, God,
   peace, and nature is at least as motivational in getting people to act on political issues
   as is the discourse of class, oppression, and revolution. From the religiously based
   sanctuary movement to spiritual trends in ecology and peace movements, there does
   exist the attempt to combine the two traditions.

9. Marx actually states both that workers will get poorer in absolute terms, and also
   that they will have less compared to the ruling class.

10. It may actually be more relevant to the overturning of the Eastern bloc. We have
    yet to see, however, where that will lead.

11. Consider the discussion of the attempt to escape working class identity in Sennet
    and Cobb 1973.

12. The following discussion benefited from very helpful comments by Virginia Warren
    and Douglas Allen.

13. The emphasis on Jewish experience in this chapter expresses my own history.

14. Exactly how this "spiritual socialism" might work in particular political contexts is
    a subject for future work.

15. I have focused on the tensions between the radical and the spiritual perspectives in
    Gottlieb 1991.

16. There is now an enormous literature describing these dismal facts. See, for example,
    Shiva 1989 and McKibben 1989.

17. The power of control over non-human nature and over other men . . . was con-
    nected to the "denial of nature" in man. . . . As soon as man discards his awareness
    that he himself is nature, all the aims for which he goes on living—social progress,
    the enhancement of all material and spiritual powers, even consciousness itself—are
    as nothing. . . . Man's mastery over himself, which is the basis of his self, is almost

without exception the destruction of the individual as subject. . . . (Horkheimer and Adorno in Wellmer 1974: 131)

18. See Balbus 1982, Aronowitz 1981, and Bookchin 1982 for ecological criticisms of Marxism. As has been widely documented, the environmental pollution in the Eastern bloc is now truly horrendous.

# BIBLIOGRAPHY

Amin, Samir. 1976. *Unequal Development*. New York: Monthly Review Press.

Arditti, Rita. 1979. *Science and Liberation*. Boston: South End Press.

Aries, Philip. 1965. *Centuries of Childhood: A Social History of Family Life*. New York: Vintage.

Arms, Suzanne. 1977. *Immaculate Deception*. New York: Bantam.

Arnold, N. Scott. 1990. *Marx's Radical Critique of Capitalist Society*. New York: Oxford University Press.

Aronowitz, Stanley. 1981. *The Crisis in Historical Materialism*. South Hadley, Mass.: Praeger.

Athos, A. G., and R. T. Pascale. 1981. *The Art of Japanese Management*. New York: Simon & Schuster.

Avineri, S., 1970. *The Social and Political Thought of Karl Marx*. Cambridge, U.K.: Cambridge University Press.

Bairoch, Paul. 1973. "Agriculture and the Industrial Revolution," in Cipolla.

Balbus, Isaac D. 1982. *Marxism and Domination*. Princeton, N.J.: Princeton University Press.

Baran, Paul. 1957. *The Political Economy of Growth*. New York: Monthly Review Press.

Baran, Paul, and Paul Sweezy. 1966. *Monopoly Capital*. New York: Monthly Review Press.

Barret, Michele. 1980. *Women's Oppression Today*. London: Verso.

Beechey, Veronica. 1978. "Women and Production: A Critical Analysis of Some Sociological Theories of Women's Work." In Kuhn and Volpe.

Belenky, M. F., M. Clinchy, N. R. Goldberger, J. M. Tarule. 1986. *Women's Ways of Knowing*. New York: Basic Books.

Bernstein, Richard J. 1978. *The Restructuring of Social and Political Theory*. Philadelphia: University of Pennsylvania Press.

Bernstein, Richard J. 1983. *Beyond Objectivism and Relativism: Science, Hermeneutics, and Praxis*. Philadelphia: University of Pennsylvania Press.

Bookchin, Murray. 1982. *The Ecology of Freedom*. Palo Alto, Calif.: Cheshire Books.

Borkenau, Franz. 1962. *World Communism*. Ann Arbor: University of Michigan Press.

Bottomore, T., and P. Goode, eds. 1978. *Austro-Marxism*. Oxford: Oxford University Press.

Bowles, Samuel, and Herbert Gintis. 1982. "The Crisis of Liberal Democratic Capitalism: The Case of the U.S." *Politics and Society* 2, no. 1.

Braudel, Fernand. 1973. *Capitalism and Material Life, 1400–1800*. New York: Harper & Row.

Brenner, Johann, and Maria Ramas. 1984. "Rethinking Women's Oppression." *New Left Review* no. 144 (March–April).

Brewer, Anthony. 1980. *Marxist Theories of Imperialism*. London: Routledge & Kegan Paul.

Brittan, Arthur, and Mary Maynard. 1984. *Sexism, Racism, and Oppression*. London: Basil Blackwell.

Buchanan, Allen, 1982. *Marx and Justice: The Radical Critique of Liberalism*. Totowa, N.J.: Rowman and Littlefield.

Buhle, Mari Jo. 1983. *Women and American Socialism, 1870–1920*. Urbana, Ill.: University of Illinois Press.

Carnoy, Martin. 1984. *The State and Political Theory*. Princeton, N.J.: Princeton University Press.

Carr, E. H. 1964. *Studies in Revolution*. New York: Grosset & Dunlap.

Carr, E. H. 1966. *The Bolshevik Revolution*, vols. 1–3. London: Pelican.

Castells, Manuel. 1980. *The Economic Crisis and American Society*. Princeton, N.J.: Princeton University Press.

Chodorow, Nancy. 1978. *The Reproduction of Mothering: Psychoanalysis and the Sociology of Gender*. Berkeley: University of California Press.

Chodorow, Nancy. 1979. "Feminism and Difference; Gender, Relation, and Difference in Psychoanalytic Perpective." *Socialist Review* no. 46 (July–August).

Cippolla, C., ed. 1973. *The Fontana History of Europe: The Industrial Revolution*. London: Fontana.

Cliff, Tony. 1980. *Lenin*, vols. 1–2, London: Pluto Press.

Cohen, G. A. 1978. *Karl Marx's Theory of History: A Defence*. Princeton, N.J.: Princeton University Press.

Cole, G. D. H. 1950–65. *History of Socialist Thought*, vols. 1–4. London. MacMillan.

Collard, Andree. 1989. *Rape of the Wild*. Bloomington, Ind.: Indiana University Press.

Colletti, Lucio. 1972. *From Rousseau to Lenin*. New York: Monthly Review Press.

Colletti, Lucio. 1975. "Introduction" to *Karl Marx the Early Writings,* edited by Q. Hoare. New York: Vintage.

Daniels, Robert Vincent. 1960. *A Documentary History of Communism*, vols. 1–2. New York: Vintage.

Daniels, Robert Vincent. 1969. *The Conscience of the Revolution*. New York: Simon & Schuster.

Derrida, Jacques. 1977. *Of Grammatology*. Baltimore, Md.: Johns Hopkins University Press.

Derrida, Jacques. 1982. *Margins of Philosophy*. Chicago: University of Chicago Press.

Deutscher, Isaac. 1959. *The Prophet Armed*. New York: Vintage.

Deutscher, Isaac. 1963. *The Prophet Unarmed*. New York: Vintage.

Deutscher, Isaac. 1965. *The Prophet Outcast*. New York: Vintage.

Dinnerstein, Dorothy. 1977. *The Mermaid and the Minotaur*. New York: Harper & Row.

Edwards, Richard. 1979. *Contested Terrain*. New York: Basic Books.

Eisenstein, Zillah, ed. 1979. *Capitalist Patriarchy and the Case for Socialist Feminism*. New York: Monthly Review Press.

Elster, Jon. 1985. *Making Sense of Marx*. Cambridge, U.K.: Cambridge University Press.

Emmanuel, Arghiri. 1972. *Unequal Exchange*. New York: Monthly Review Press.

Engels, Frederick. 1941. *Ludwig Feurbach*. New York: International Publishers.

Engels, Frederick. 1969. *Socialism: Utopian and Scientific*. New York: International Publishers.

Engels, Fredrick. 1977. *The Origin of the Family, Private Property, and the State.* New York: International Publishers.

Evans, Sara. 1980. *Personal Politics.* New York: Vintage.

Fanon, Franz. 1968. *The Wretched of the Earth.* New York: Grove Press.

Feldberg, Roslyn L. 1981. "Women, Self-Management and Socialism." *Socialist Review* no. 56 (March–April).

Ferguson, Ann. 1989. *Blood at the Root: Motherhood, Sexuality and Male Dominance.* London: Unwin Hyman.

Firestone, Shulamith. 1970. *The Dialectic of Sex.* New York: Bantam.

Fisk, Milton. 1989. *The State and Justice: An Essay in Political Theory.* New York: Cambridge University Press.

Fitzpatrick, Sheila. 1982. *The Russian Revolution, 1917–1932.* New York: Oxford University Press.

Foucault, Michel. 1975. *The Birth of the Clinic: an Archeology of Medical Perception.* New York: Vintage.

Frank, A. G. 1967. *Capitalism and Underdevelopment in Latin America.* New York: Monthly Review Press.

Frye, Marilyn. 1983. *The Politics of Reality.* Freedom, Calif.: Crossing Press.

Gardiner, Jean. 1979. "Women's Domestic Labor." In Eisenstein 1979.

Giddens, Anthony. 1979. *Central Problems in Social Theory.* Berkeley: University of California Press.

Giddens, Anthony. 1981. *A Contemporary Critique of Historical Materialism.* Berkeley: University of California Press.

Giddens, Anthony. 1990. *The Consequences of Modernity.* Stanford: Stanford University Press.

Gilligan, Carol. 1983. *In a Different Voice.* Cambridge, Mass.: Harvard University Press.

Goldstein, Joseph, and Jack Kornfield. 1987. *Seeking the Heart of Wisdom.* Boston: Shambala.

Gordon, David M., Richard Edwards, and Michael Reich. 1982. *Segmented Work, Divided Workers.* Cambridge, U.K.: Cambridge University Press.

Gorz, André. 1973. *Socialism and Revolution.* New York: Anchor.

Gottlieb, Roger S. 1975. "A Marxian Concept of Ideology." *Philosophical Forum* 6 no. 4 (Summer).

Gottlieb, Roger S. 1981. "The Contemproray Critical Theory of Jürgen Habermas." *Ethics* 91, no. 2 (January).

Gottlieb, Roger S. 1984a. "Feudalism and Historical Materialism: A Critique and a Synthesis." *Science and Society* 48, no. 1 (Spring).

Gottlieb, Roger S. 1984b. "Mothering and the Reproduction of Power." *Socialist Review* no. 77 (September–October).

Gottlieb, Roger S. 1985. "Forces of Production and Social Primacy." *Social Theory and Practice* 11, no. 1 (Spring).

Gottlieb, Roger S. 1987. *History and Subjectivity: The Transformation of Marxist Theory.* Philadelphia: Temple University Press.

Gottlieb, Roger S., ed. 1989. *An Anthology of Western Marxism: From Lukács and Gramsci to Socialist-Feminism.* New York: Oxford.

Gottlieb, Roger S. 1990. *A New Creation: America's Contemporary Spiritual Voices.* New York: Crossroad.

Gottlieb, Roger S. 1991. "Heaven and Earth: A Dialogue Between a Political Radical and a Spiritual Seeker." *The Sun: A Magazine of Ideas* No. 182 (January). Also in Gottlieb 1990.

Gough, Ian. 1975. "State Expenditure in Advanced Capitalism." *New Left Review* no. 92 (July–August).

Gramsci, Antonio. 1971. *Selections from the Prison Notebooks,* edited by Quentin Hoare and G. N. Smith. New York: International Publishers.

Grubner, Helmut, ed. 1972. *International Communism in the Era of Lenin.* New York: Anchor.

Habermas, Jürgen. 1968. *Knowledge and Human Interests.* Boston: Beacon Press.

Habermas, Jürgen. 1970. *Towards a Rational Society.* Boston: Beacon Press.

Habermas, Jürgen. 1973. *Theory and Practice.* Boston: Beacon Press.

Habermas, Jürgen. 1975. *Legitimation Crisis.* Boston: Beacon Press.

Hansen, Karen V., and Ilene J. Philipson. 1990. *Women, Class and the Feminist Imagination: A Socialist-Feminist Reader.* Philadelphia: Temple University Press.

Harding, Neil. 1977. *Lenin's Political Thought.* New York: Columbia University Press.

Hartmann, Heidi. 1981. "The Family as the Focus of Gender, Class, and Political Struggle: The Example of Housework." *Signs: a Journal of Women and Society* (Spring).

Hartmann, Heidi. 1989. "The Unhappy Marriage of Marxism and Feminism: Towards a More Progressive Union." In Gottlieb 1989.

Hartsock, Nancy. 1983. *Money, Sex, and Power: Towards a Feminist Historical Materialism.* New York: Longman.

Hooks, Bell. 1982. *Ain't I a Woman?* London: Pluto Press.

Horkheimer, Max. 1932. "Geschicte und Psychologie." *Zeitschrift für Sozialforschung* 1, nos. 1–2.

Horkheimer, Max. 1972. *Critical Theory.* New York: Seabury.

Horkheimer, Max. 1974. *Critique of Instrumental Reason.* New York: Seabury.

Horkheimer, Max, and Theodor Adorno. 1974. *Dialectic of Enlightenment*. New York: Seabury.

Howard, Dick, and Karl E. Klare, eds. 1972. *The Unknown Dimension: European Marxism Since Lenin*. New York: Basic Books.

Howe, Irving, ed. 1976. *Essential Works of Socialism*. New Haven: Yale University Press.

Ingram, Catherine. 1990. *In the Footsteps of Gandhi: Conversations with Spiritual Social Activists*. Berkeley: Parallax Press.

Jagger, Alison. 1983. *Feminist Politics and Human Nature*. Totowa, N.J.: Rowman and Allenheld.

Jessop, Bob. 1982. *The Capitalist State*. New York: New York University Press.

Johnpoll, Bernard K. 1967. *The Politics of Futility: The General Jewish Workers Bund of Poland, 1917–1943*. Ithaca, N.Y.: Cornell University Press.

Joll, James. 1966. *The Second International, 1889–1914*. New York: Harper & Row.

Kaustky, Karl. 1964. *The Dictatorship of the Proletariat*. Ann Arbor: University of Michigan Press.

Kingston-Mann, Esther. 1983. *Lenin and the Problem of Marxist Peasant Revolution*. New York: Oxford Univesity Press.

Koestler, Arthur. 1961. *Darkness at Noon*. New York: Signet.

Kolakowski, Leslek. 1978. *Main Currents of Marxism: The Golden Age*. Oxford: Oxford University Press.

Korsch, Karl. 1971. *Marxism and Philosophy*. New York: Monthly Review Press.

Kuhn, Annette, and AnnMarie Wolpe, eds. 1978. *Feminism and Materialism*. London: Routledge & Kegan Paul.

Laclau, Ernesto, and Chantal Mouffe. 1985. *Hegemony and Socialist Strategy*. London: Verso.

Le Grand, Julian, and Saul Estrin, eds. 1989. *Market Socialism*. Oxford: Clarendon Press.

Lenin, V. I. 1943. *What is to Be Done?* New York: International Publishers.

Lenin, V. I. 1960. *Lenin on Proletarian Revolution and Proletarian Dictatorship*. Peking: Foreign Languages Press.

Lenin, V. I. 1963. *Collected Works,* vol. 21. Moscow: Progress Publishers.

Lenin, V. I. 1965. *The State and Revolution*. Peking: Foreign Languages Press.

Lenin, V. I. 1970. *Two Tactics of Social-Democracy in the Democratic Revolution*. Peking: Foreign Languages Press.

Leonhard, Wolfgang. 1971. *Three Faces of Marxism*. New York: Holt, Rinehart and Winston.

Lichtheim, George. 1965. *Marxism*. New York: Praeger.

Liebman, Arthur. 1979. *Jews and the Left*. New York: Wiley.

Lilley, Samuel. 1973. "Technological Progress in the Industrial Revolution." In Cippolla.

Lorber, Judith, Rose Coser, Alice S. Rossi, and Nancy Chodorow. 1981. "On The Reproduction of Mothering: A Methodological Debate." *Signs: A Journal of Women and Society* 6, no. 3 (Spring).

Lukács, Georg. 1971. *History and Class Consciousness*. Cambridge, Mass.: MIT Press.

Lukács, Georg. 1975. *Tactics and Ethics*. New York: Harper & Row.

Luxemburg, Rosa. 1970. *The Accumulation of Capital*. New York: Monthly Review.

Luxemburg, Rosa. 1971. *Selected Political Writings*. New York: Monthly Review Press.

McDonough, Rosin, and Rachel Harrison. 1978. "Patriarchy and the Relations of Production." In Kuhn and Wolpe 1978.

McIntosh, Mary. 1978. "The State and the Oppression of Women." In Kuhn and Wolpe 1978.

MacIntyre, Alasdair. 1984. *Marxism and Christianity*. South Bend, Ind.: University of Notre Dame Press.

McMurty, John. 1978. *The Structure of Marx's World-View*. Princeton: Princeton University Press.

Magdoff, Harry. 1969. *The Age of Imperialism*. New York: Monthly Review Press.

Mandel, Ernest. 1978. *Late Capitalism*. London: Verso.

Mandel, Ernest. 1980. *The Second Slump*. London: Verso.

Marcuse, Herbert. 1941. "Some Social Implicatons of Modern Technology." *Studies in Philosophy and Social Sciences* 9.

Marcuse, Herbert. 1958. *Soviet Marxism*. New York: Vintage.

Marcuse, Herbert. 1964. *One Dimensional Man*. Boston: Beacon Press.

Marcuse, Herbert. 1969. *An Essay on Liberation*. Boston: Beacon Press.

Marcuse, Herbert. 1972. *Counterrevolution and Revolt*. Boston: Beacon Press.

Marx. Karl. 1963. *The Poverty of Philosophy*. New York: International Publishers.

Marx, Karl. 1964. *The Economic and Philosophical Manuscripts of 1844*. New York: International Publishers.

Marx, Karl. 1967. *Capital,* vols. 1–3. New York: International Publishers.

Marx, Karl. 1968. *The Eighteenth Brumaire of Louis Bonaparte*. New York: International Publishers.

Marx, Karl. 1970. *A Contribution to the Critique of Political Economy*. New York: International Publishers.

Marx, Karl. 1971. *The Grudrisse,* edited by David McLellan. New York: Harper & Row.

Marx, Karl. 1973. *Grundrisse,* New York: Vintage.

Marx, Karl, and Frederick Engels. 1947. *The German Ideology*. New York: International Publishers.

Marx, Karl, and Frederick Engels. 1954. *The Communist Manifesto*. Chicago: Gateway.

McKibben, Bill. 1989. *The End of Nature*. New York: Anchor.

Menashe, Louis. 1973. "An Essay on Lenin." *Socialist Revolution* no. 18 (November–December).

Merchant, Carolyn. 1983. *The Death of Nature: Women, Ecology, and the Industrial Revolution*. New York: Harper & Row.

Merleau-Ponty, Maurice. 1969. *Humanism and Terror*. Boston: Beacon Press.

Miller, Richard. 1984. *Analyzing Marx*. Princeton, N.J.: Princeton University Press.

Millett, Kate. 1971. *Sexual Politics*. New York: Avon.

Mitchell, Juliet. 1972. *Women's Estate*. New York: Vintage.

Morgan, Robin, ed. 1970. *Sisterhood Is Powerful*. New York: Vintage.

Nicholson, Linda. 1986. *Gender and History*. New York: Columbia University Press.

Oakley, Ann. 1976. *Women's Work*. New York: Vintage.

O'Connor, James. 1973. *The Fiscal Crisis of the State*. New York: St. Martin's Press.

O'Connor, James. 1988. "Capitalism, Nature, Socialism: A Theoretical Introduction." *Capitalism, Nature, Socialism* 1 (Fall).

Ouchi, Z. 1981. *Theory Z*. Reading, Mass.: Addison-Wesley.

Parsons, Howard, ed. 1977. *Marx and Engels on Ecology*. Westport: Greenwood Press.

Peffer, R. G. 1990. *Marxism, Morality, and Social Justice*. Princeton, N.J.: Princeton Universtiy Press.

Piercy, Marge. 1970. "The Grand Coolie Damn." In Morgan.

Poster, Mark. 1980. *Critical Theory of the Family*. New York: Seabury.

Rader, Melvin. 1978. *Marx's Interpretation of History*. New York: Oxford University Press.

Rader, Melvin. 1982. "Marx's Three Worlds and their Interrelation." In Norman Fischer, ed. *Continuity and Change in Marxism*, New Jersey: Humanities Press.

Reich, Michael. 1980. *Racial Inequality: A Political-Economic Analysis*. Princeton, N.J.: Princeton University Press.

Reich, Wilhelm. 1946. *The Mass Psychology of Fascism*. New York: Orgone Institute Press.

Reich, Wilhelm. 1972. *Sex-Pol*. New York: Vintage.

Reich, Wilhelm. 1976. *Character Analysis*. New York: Simon & Schuster.

Rorty, Richard. 1982. *Consequences of Pragmatism*. Minneapolis: University of Minnesota Press.

Rosaldo, Michelle Zimbalist, and Louise Lamphere, eds. 1974. *Women, Culture, and Society*. Stanford, Calif.: Stanford University Press.

Ross, Robert, and Kent Trachte. 1990. *Global Capitalism: The New Leviathan*. Albany: SUNY Press.

# BIBLIOGRAPHY

Rothman, Sheila M. 1980. *Women's Proper Place: A History of Changing Ideals and Practices, 1870 to the Present.* New York: Basic Books.

Rowbotham, Sheila. 1973. *Women's Consciousness, Man's World.* New York: Penguin.

Rowbotham, Sheila. 1974. *Women, Resistance and Revolution.* New York: Vintage.

Rowbotham, Sheila, Lynne Segal, and Hilary Wainwright. 1979. *Beyond the Fragments: Feminism and the Making of Socialism.* London: Merlin Press.

Rubin, Gayle. 1975. "The Traffic in Women: Notes on the 'Political Economy' of Sex." In R. R. Reiter, ed. 1975. *Towards an Anthropology of Women.* New York: Monthly Review Press.

Ruddick, Sara. 1989. *Maternal Thinking: Toward A Politics of Peace.* Boston, Mass.: Beacon Press.

Sacks, Karen. 1974. "Engels Revisited: Women, the Organization of Production, and Private Property." In Rosaldo and Lamphere 1974.

Sartre, Jean-Paul. 1963. *Search for a Method.* New York: Vintage.

Sartre, Jean-Paul. 1965. *Anti-Semite and Jew.* New York: Schocken.

Sartre, Jean-Paul. 1976. *Critique of Dialectical Reason.* London: New Left Books.

Schmitt, Richard. 1987. *Introduction to Marx and Engels: A Critical Reconstruction.* Boulder, Colo.: Westview.

Sennett, Richard and Jonathan Cobb. 1973. *The Hidden Injuries of Class.* New York: Random House.

Shaw, William. 1978. *Marx's Theory of History.* Stanford: Stanford University Press.

Shiva, Vandana. 1989. *Staying Alive: Women, Ecology, and Development.* London: Zed Books.

Siranni, Carman. 1975. "Rereading Lenin." *Socialist Revolution,* no. 23 (April).

Sklar, Holly, ed. 1980. *Trilateralism.* Boston: South End Press.

Smith, Tony. 1987. *Thinking Like a Communist: State and Legitimacy in the Soviet Union, China, and Cuba.* New York: Norton.

Spellman, Elisabeth. 1988. *Inessential Woman.* Boston: Beacon Press.

Stone, Lawrence. 1977. *The Family, Sex, and Marriage.* New York: Harper & Row.

Sweezy, Paul. 1942. *The Theory of Capitalist Development.* New York: Monthly Review Press.

Tilly, Louise, and Joan Scott. 1978. *Women, Work, and Family.* New York: Holt, Rinehart & Winston.

Tobias, H. T. 1972. *The Jewish Bund in Russia.* Stanford: Stanford University Press.

Trotsky, Leon. 1961. *Terrorism and Communism.* Ann Arbor: University of Michigan Press.

Trotsky, Leon. 1970. *The Revolution Betrayed.* New York: Pathfinder.

Tucker, Robert V. 1972. *The Marx-Engels Reader.* New York: Norton.

Wallerstein, Immanuel. 1974a. *The Modern World-System*, vol. 1. New York: Academic Press.

Wallerstein, Immanuel. 1974b. "The Rise and Future Demise of the World Capitalist System." *Comparative Studies in Society and History* 16, no. 4.

Wallerstein, Immanuel. 1980. *The Modern World-System*. Vol. 2 *Mercantilism and the Consolidating of the European World-Economy, 1600–1750*. New York: Academic Press.

Warren, Bill. 1980. *Imperialism: Pioneer of Capitalism*. London: Verso.

Weinryb, B. D. 1970. "Anti-Semitism in Soviet Russia." In L. Kochan, ed. *The Jews in Soviet Russia*. London: Oxford University Press.

Williams, Robert G. 1981. "The Political Economy of Hub Currency Defense." *Review of Radical Political Economy* 3, no. 3 (Fall).

Wolfe, Alan. 1977. *The Limits of Legitimacy: Political Contradictions of Contemporary Capitalism*. New York: Free Press.

Wolff, Robert Paul. 1984. *Understanding Marx*. Princeton, N.J.: Princeton University Press.

Wood, Allen. 1981. *Karl Marx*. London: Routledge.

Wright, Erik Olin. 1979. *Class, Crisis, and the State*. New York: Schocken.

Young, Iris Marion. 1990. *Throwing Like A Girl and Other Essays in Feminist Philosophy and Social Theory*. Indiana: Indiana University Press.

# INDEX

Adorno, Theodor, 110, 114–16, 123, 216, 217
Alienation 19–22, 28
Anger, 207–215
Aristotle, 5, 6
Aronowitz, Stanley, 174–78
    *The Crisis in Historical Materialism*, 174–76
    and political strategy, 176
Anti-Semitism, 50, 210, 211

Baran, Paul, 152–55, 165, 166
    *Monopoly Capital*, 152–53
Bernstein, Edward, 60, 70–72, 152
Bowles, Samuel, 158–60
Buchanan, Allen, 53
Buhle, Mari Jo, 143
Buddhism, 201
Bund, 95
Business cycle, 29–31

Capital-Labor accord, 159
Capitalism 22–32, 47–8, 52, 68–71
    and contemporary politics, 176–77
    contradictions in 28–31, 122–23, 218
    and ecology, 216–18
    evolution of, 27–8, 47, 151–52, 161–4, 187–89
    and modern state, 155–57
    and mothering, 180–81

and technological change, 189–91
    and women, 134–36, 139–40, 179, 181
Castells, Manuel, 155
Character Structure, 125
Chodorow, Nancy, 178–81
Cohen, G.A., 181–91
    *Karl Marx's Theory of History: A Defence*, 181–92
    and technocratic ideology, 190–1
Class struggles, 12, 24–6, 32–33, 52–3, 72–4, 122–23, 151, 157–60, 218–19
Colletti, Lucio, 21, 68
Commodity, 21, 22–23
Commodification, 122–23
Communism xv, 77–105
    after the fall of, 104–05
    development of 96–104
    and Western Marxism, 113–14
Communist Party of America, 143–44
Compassion, 212–214

Darwin, Charles, 62
Day, Doris, 181
Democracy, 65–68, 70, 73,
Deconstruction, 192–96
    criticism of, 194–96
    and politics, 196
    and selfhood, 195
Derrida, Jacques, 192–93
Domination, 175–6

Dworkin, Andrea, 214
Dual Labor Market, 154

Economic Classes, 11–12, 22–4, 68–70, 114
Ecology, 215–219
Edwards, Richard, 154
Ego, 198–204, 205–06
  and ecology, 218
  and individualism, 200, 202–03, 205–06
Engels, Friedrich, 10, 12, 18, 31, 35, 59, 60–4, 77, 89, 111, 132, 182, 189, 192, 216, 218
Enlightenment, 115
Ethnicity, 50
Evans, Sara, 131
Existentialism, 16
Exploitation, 23–26

Falling Rate of Profit, 29
Family, 124–25, 134–36
Feldberg, Roslyn, 133
Fanon, Franz, 208
Feminism, 55–6, 207, 209, 220 (see also "socialist-feminism")
Fetishism (of commodities). 20, 21
Fiscal Crisis of the State, 157–59
Forces of Production 9–11, 27, 181–92
Forgiveness, 214–15
Foucault, Michel, 192–193
Frye, Marilyn

Genealogy, 193–4
Gandhi, Mohandas, 205, 208, 214
Giddens, Anthony, 171–75
  A Contemporary Critique of Historical Materialism, 171–73
  theory of structuration, 171–2
Gintis, Herbert, 158–160
Global Capitalism, 167–68
Gordon, David, 162, 164
Gorz, Andre, 53, 129
Gramsci, Antonio, 86, 110, 117, 123, 126, 133
Greek Philosophy 5–6
Greenspan, Miriam, 136
Griffin, Susan, 214

Habermas, Jurgen, 54, 114–15, 160–61
Hartmann, Heidi, 135
Hegel, G.W.F., 5–8, 11, 14, 15, 21, 44, 46, 114
Hegemony, 120–21
Historical Materialism 8–15, 16, 181–92
  criticism of 40–8, 171–73
  and contemporary spirituality, 219–222
Hitler, Adolph, 125
Holocaust, 211
Hooks, Bell, 142
Horkheimer, Max, 110, 112, 114–116, 123, 124, 126–26, 216, 217
Human nature 4–8, 36–7, 38

Idealism 6
Ideology, 15–19, 48–51, 118
  definition of 18–19
Imperialism, 52–3, 68–9, 71, 80
Individualism, 11, 15–16, 17, 103
Israeli-Palestinian conflict, 211

Joll, James, 72

Kant, Immanual, 5–7
Kautsky, Karl, 60–3, 65, 74, 80, 95
Kierkegaard, Soren, 16
King, Martin Luther, 205, 214
Kingston-Mann, Esther, 84
Kolakowski, L., 62
Korsch, Karl, 95, 110–11, 113–14, 117–19, 123

Labor aristocracy, 69
Legitimation Crisis, 160–61
Lenin, V.I., 52, 69, 77–83, 86–90, 92–5, 99, 102, 113, 152, 214
  State and Revolution, 86, 102
Leninism, 79–81, 86–90, 109, 121
  flaws of, 87–90
Long Waves, 161–163
Leonhard, Wolfgang, 85–6, 92
Liebman, Arthur, 144
Locke, John
Lukacs, Georg, 53, 86, 110–12, 118, 121–23, 133, 173
Luxemburg, Rosa, 60, 66, 72–77, 95, 145, 206
  and economic determinism, 75–6

"Mass Strike Party and Trade
Unions" 72
"Social Reform or Revolution" 72
Magdoff, Harry, 166
Malcolm, X, 214
Mandel, Ernest, 162, 166
Marcuse, 88–9, 96–7110, 114–15, 123,
128–29, 205, 216–17
Marx, Karl
Capital, 187
Class Struggles in France, 64
Communist Manifesto 8, 65, 188
"Contribution to a Critique of Hegel's
Philosophy of Right", 8
Critique of the Gotha Program, 34
Economic and Philosophical Manuscripts
of 1844 8
The German Ideology 8, 182, 184
Grundrisse, 186, 187
The Poverty of Philosophy 8
(see 'Marxism')
Marxism xv
basic flaws of, 39–56
concept of socialism 34–36
and contemporary capitalism, 149–69
and contemporary critics, 170–96
and deconstruction, 192–96
and ecology, 216–19
economic theory of, 22–32
and exploitation, 20–1, 184
and happiness, 19–20, 53–6
and historical development, 14–15, 17,
19, 27–30, 44–45, 47, 185–8
historical materialism 8–15, 181–92
and human freedom, 20–22
labor theory of value 24–26
and markets, 105
and morality, 53–6, 98–101
origins of, 5–8
political theory of 25, 32–6, 65–6,
174–76
positivist Marxism, 43–47, 61–5, 111
and post-modernism, 192–96
and science, 17–8, 42–46, 111–12
and selfhood, 199–202, 204–05
and spirituality, 197–222
and Stalinism, 93–104
and suffering, 207–11
theory of alienation 19–22
theory of capitalism 22–32

theory of crisis, 30–2
theory of ideology 15–19
and violence, 100–02
and women, 48–50, 132–33
Mensheviks, 82
McMurty, John, 216
Merleau-Ponty, Maurice, 100–01
Mode of Production 9–11, 17, 42–46,
50, 117
and women, 13–14, 48–9
Monopoly capitalism, 167, 152–53
Mothering theory, 178–81
and capitalism, 180–1
Mussolini, Benito, 125

New Economic Policy, 83
New Social Movements, 208–10
New Left, 144
Newton, Isaac, 42
Nietzsche, F., 16, 209

O'Connor, James, 154, 158, 217

Parsons, Howard, 216
Piercy, Marge, 131
Plato, 5–6, 114
Politics of Difference, 141–44
Post-Modernism, 192–96
criticism of, 194–96
Pre-Socratic Philosophers 4–5
Primitive accumulation, 52, 188

Race, 50–1, 174
Racism, 50, 101, 127, 142, 143, 154,
209–10, 211
Rader, Melvin, 8
Rationality, 5–8, 114–15
Rationalization, 112–13
Reich, Wilhelm, 110, 123–27, 154, 205
"What is Class Consciousness", 126–
28
Relations of Production 9–11, 181–92
Reproduction, 49–50
Revisionism, 68–71, 72, 104
Revolution, 32–4, 55, 64–6, 60, 71, 73–
5, 99–104, 119
and anger, 207–15
and socialist-feminism, 140–41
Rorty, Richard, 192
Ross, Robert, 167–68

Rowbotham, Sheila, 135, 140–41
Rubin, Gayle, 133
Russian Communist Party (Bolsheviks),
  82, 83, 94–96, 98–100, 102
Russian Revolution, 46, 77–105
  degeneration of, 97–101
  history of, 81–85

Sartre, Jean-Paul, 16, 55, 114, 123, 222
Second International, 62, 66, 97, 164
  and nationalism, 67–8
Segal, Lynn, 141
Sex-affective labor, 135–36
Sex/gender system, 133–34, 136
Sexism, 101, 136–38
Smith, Tony, 93–4, 98
Social-Democracy, 59–76
  program of, 61–65
Social-Democratic Party of Germany,
  61–65
  origins of 61–3]
  concept of revolution, 65–7
  and revisionism, 70–72
Social Structures of Accumulation, 163–
  64
Socialist Party of America, 143
Socialist-Feminism, 130–45
  and the liberation of women, 138–41
  origins of, 131–2
  theory of women's oppression, 132–
  136
Social Differentiation, 48–51
Socialism, 34–40, 63,, 128–29
Socialization, 51
Socrates, 5
Spirituality,
  definition of, 197–98

and ecology, 218–19
and the ego, 198–205
and historical materialism, 219–222
and human fulfillment, 202–04
and political life, 210–15
Stalin, Josef, 77–8, 83, 91–93, 95–6, 102
Stalinism, 91–3, 109, 192
Sweezy, Paul, 152–53, 155
  Monopoly Capital, 152–53

Thales, 4
Trachte, Kent, 167
Trotsky, Leon, 84, 89, 94–5, 98
  The Revolution Betrayed, 95–6

Underconsumption 29
Unions, 72–4

Wainwright, Hilary, 141
Wallerstein, Immanual, 165–6
Weber, Max, 66, 172
Weinryb, H., 95
Western Marxism, 76, 110–129
  and class consciousness, 119–26
  and historical materialism, 116–19
  and psychoanalysis, 124–26
  and science, 110–16
  and socialism, 126–129
  and women, 133
Williams, R, 159
Wright, E.O., 163
Women, 48–9, 55, 129
  liberation of, 138–41
  and mothering, 178–81
  and paid labor, 137–38
  also 'socialist-feminism',
World-Systems theory, 165–67